Praise for
Your Complete Guide to a
Successful and Secure Retirement

"A comprehensive guide to the emotional and financial issues involved in achieving a fulfilling and stress-free retirement. The wise advice is accessibly presented with a sensitivity that can only come from years of advising individual clients how to make some of the most important decisions of their lives."
— **Burton G. Malkiel, author of** *A Random Walk Down Wall Street*
(now in its 12th edition)

"A highly sophisticated look at smart ways of managing money in retirement, creating a 'homemade paycheck,' and securing your standard of living."
— **Jane Bryant Quinn, author of** *How to Make Your Money Last*

"What a great resource! Covers all the bases. In my opinion, it's Larry's magnus opus. Read it and reap."
— **Mel Lindauer, President of The John C. Bogle Center for Financial Literacy, and co-author of** *The Bogleheads' Guide to Investing* **and** *The Bogleheads' Guide to Retirement Planning*

"Students tell me that they crowd my 'financial strategies' course, which features Swedroe and Balaban's *Investment Mistakes Even Smart People Make*, because they like practical down-to-earth advice, illustrated with stories. This new book will serve as the capstone in the course. Now I can teach about the many dimensions of retirement: such as spending down your assets in retirement, training your kids to spend and invest right, reckoning with the possibility of losing your marbles, and how to prevent elder abuse. I will be teaching a broader course and even inducing a few students to contemplate a career as a financial advisor. I have already passed the book on to my wife and kids. What a gift!"
— **Edward Tower, Professor of Economics at Duke University**

"Larry and Kevin's new book lives up to the promise of its title. It deals with subjects rarely covered in books authored by investment advisors (like insurance, annuities and reverse mortgages) and does so in a thorough and objective way. It's a valuable planning guide for everyone concerned about a secure and dignified retirement."

— **Dan Solin, author of the *Smartest* series of investing books**

"Larry does a deep dive into all the moving parts of a holistic financial plan for retirees. The result is an essential and invaluable resource for anyone in or contemplating retirement. The scope of the material is unparalleled, making this the most comprehensive guide to retirement planning I have ever seen. Meticulously researched, and clearly presented."

— **Frank Armstrong III, President/Founder, Investor Solutions**

"Family and friends constantly share with me their concerns regarding planning for retirement, which is particularly challenging in today's market environment. Finally, I can point them to a single resource for comprehensive and thoughtful advice. Larry and Kevin's book is replete with insights and answers to the difficult questions that need to be considered to ensure a prosperous retirement. Relying upon decades of experience, they demystify the vast world of retirement by sharing their own science-based investment approach and collaborating with industry experts to provide a complete overview of complicated and commonly misunderstood topics such as Social Security, Medicare and Estate Planning. Their book is your guide to a successful and secure retirement."

— **Marat Molyboga, Chief Risk Officer, Director of Research, Efficient Capital Management**

"Investing is hard enough when saving for retirement, but coordinating all of the components of a holistic plan IN retirement is even more complex... and risky in today's era of high valuations and low yields. Fortunately, Swedroe and Grogan break down each key issue into a retirement framework that anyone can use to navigate this challenging environment!"

— **Michael Kitces, publisher of the Nerd's Eye View at Kitces.com, Director of Wealth Management for Pinnacle Advisory Group**

"Larry Swedroe and Kevin Grogan are leading a financial revolution by producing the definitive book on building a solid retirement plan. Swedroe and Grogan give you the necessary tools to navigate the daunting path of financial topics that need to be addressed for your own safety and emotional well-being in retirement. Their work will have a profound impact on your golden years."

— **Bill Schultheis, author of *The Coffeehouse Investor***

"As an endowed investments professor and member of the *Wall Street Journal's* 'The Experts' panel, I have spent my professional life addressing the more quantitative and rigorous retirement issues Swedroe and Grogan discuss, including asset allocation, asset location, and Monte Carlo simulations. They provide excellent tax-related guidance related to IRAs and other retirement plans as well as distribution strategies in retirement. As someone nearing retirement myself, I learned a lot reading about the softer retirement issues like planning beyond the financials, the discovery process, preparing heirs, and threats of elder abuse. This is, indeed, your complete guide to retirement!"

— Dr William Reichenstein, CFA, Professor Emeritus of Investments, Baylor University, Hankamer School of Business, Principal, Social Security Solutions, Inc.

"I've had the privilege of reviewing a number of Larry's books and they just get better and better. *Your Complete Guide* continues the trend. If you are contemplating retirement or are currently there do yourself a favor: read and profit from his thoughtful wisdom. Besides, it's a fun read."

— Harold Evensky, Chairman, Evensky & Katz/ Foldes Financial Wealth Management

"Successful investing often comes down to having a strong philosophy you can stick with over time. In *Your Complete Guide to a Successful and Secure Retirement*, Larry Swedroe and Kevin Grogan help investors understand how they can increase their chances for a great retirement experience."

— David Booth, Executive Chairman of Dimensional Fund Advisors

"Yet again, Larry Swedroe takes a topic that mystifies most of us, cuts through the confusion and misguided conventional wisdom, and leaves us with a clear, evidence-based strategy for success. This time, it is retirement. Swedroe and Grogan present a comprehensive guide to financial success in retirement, with compelling evidence from the academic world and their own practical experience from years of helping clients. In typical Swedroe fashion, the authors deal in facts and are not afraid to take on the asset management industry for its sins. The book begins with wise advice and empathy about the non-financial aspects of retirement – that is, *life* – that most financial advisors overlook or are afraid to talk about. From now on, when I'm asked for advice about retirement, I'll send a copy of Larry's book to clients and friends – and most importantly, my parents."

— Brendan Corcoran, CFA, Partner & Head of North America, Partners Capital Investment Group

Your Complete Guide
to a Successful and
Secure Retirement

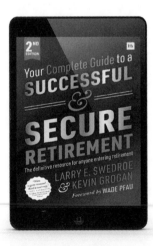

Your Complete Guide to a Successful and Secure Retirement

Second Edition

Larry E. Swedroe
&
Kevin Grogan

Hh

Harriman House

HARRIMAN HOUSE LTD
3 Viceroy Court
Bedford Road
Petersfield
Hampshire
GU32 3LJ
GREAT BRITAIN
Tel: +44 (0)1730 233870

Email: enquiries@harriman-house.com
Website: harriman.house

First published in 2019. This second edition 2021.
Copyright © Larry E. Swedroe and Kevin Grogan

The right of Larry E. Swedroe and Kevin Grogan to be identified as the Authors has been asserted in accordance with the Copyright, Design and Patents Act 1988.

Paperback ISBN: 978-0-85719-837-2
eBook ISBN: 978-0-85719-838-9

British Library Cataloguing in Publication Data
A CIP catalogue record for this book can be obtained from the British Library.

This book is dedicated to the associates of the Buckingham Group Services and the advisors at the hundreds of independent, fiduciary, registered investment advisory firms with whom we at Buckingham have strategic alliances. Each and every one of them works diligently to educate their clients on how markets really work and helps them fulfill their life and financial goals by building long-term relationships and doing the right thing.

Also by Larry E. Swedroe and Kevin Grogan

*The Only Guide You'll Ever Need for the Right Financial Plan:
Managing Your Wealth, Risk, and Investments*

*Reducing the Risk of Black Swans: Using the Science of Investing
to Capture Returns with Less Volatility*

Also by Larry E. Swedroe

*The Only Guide to a Winning Investment Strategy You'll Ever Need:
The Way Smart Money Invests Today*

*Rational Investing in Irrational Times: How to Avoid the Costly
Mistakes Even Smart People Make Today*

*What Wall Street Doesn't Want You to Know: How You Can Build
Real Wealth Investing in Index Funds*

*The Successful Investor Today: 14 Simple Truths You Must Know
When You Invest*

*Wise Investing Made Simple: Larry Swedroe's Tales
to Enrich Your Future*

*The Only Guide to Alternative Investments You'll Ever Need:
The Good, the Flawed, the Bad, and the Ugly*

Wise Investing Made Simpler: Larry Swedroe's Tales to Enrich Your Future

*Think, Act, and Invest Like Warren Buffett: The Winning Strategy
to Help You Achieve Your Financial and Life Goals*

Investment Mistakes Even Smart Investors Make and How to Avoid Them

The Quest for Alpha: The Holy Grail of Investing

*The Incredible Shrinking Alpha:
How to be a successful investor without picking winners*

*Your Complete Guide to Factor-Based Investing:
The Way Smart Money Invests Today*

Contents

Appendices

Acknowledgments

Books are seldom the work of one person, or in this case two people. Ours represents the collective wisdom of the investment professionals at the Buckingham Group.

Too many of our colleagues and friends contributed to list them all. However, several of the chapters and appendices are mainly the work of the following people:

- Bert Schweizer: Financial Discovery, with assistance from Tim Maurer.
- Alan Spector: Retirement Planning Beyond the Financials with assistance from Tim Maurer. We highly recommend Spector's book, *Your Retirement Quest: 10 Secrets for Creating and Living a Fulfilling Retirement.*
- Steve Weiss, with assistance from Jim Cornfeld and Bethany Ketron, Social Security, and Health Savings Accounts, with assistance from Anna Beasley.
- Scot Colgrove: Medicare.
- Jim Cornfeld, with assistance from Connie Brezik, Ernest Clark, Elliot Dole, and Aaron Grey: Spend Down Strategies.
- Aaron Vickar, assisted by Chris Brauner, Director of Risk Management, First Element Insurance Planners and Brant Steck, Vice President of BUI: The Role of Insurance.
- Eric Ess, a partner at Husch Blackwell LLP: Estate Planning.
- Katie Keary and Manisha Thakor: Women's Unique Retirement Issues.
- Carolyn Rosenblatt, RN and Elder law attorney: The Threat of Elder Financial Abuse. We highly recommend her book, *Hidden Truths About Retirement & Long Term Care.*

Each of them has our deep appreciation for their efforts. And while they wrote the first drafts of their section, the usual caveat of any errors being our own certainly applies.

We also thank Vivian Dye, Reverse Mortgage Specialist at GuardHill Financial Corp., Wade Pfau, and Kevin Conlon, Executive Vice President of Mason-McDuffie Mortgage, for their assistance with the chapter on reverse mortgages.

We also thank William Reichenstein for his editorial suggestions as well as his insights on Social Security. We recommend his book, co-authored by William Meyer, *Social Security Strategies: How To Optimize Retirement Benefits*.

And we thank Bill Bender, Jean-Luc Bourdon, Craig Pearce at Harriman House, and especially Leslie Garrison for the many helpful editing suggestions. And finally, we thank the management team at Buckingham, especially Adam Birenbaum and David Levin, for providing the support that made this work possible.

Larry thanks his wife, Mona, the love of his life, for her tremendous encouragement and understanding during the lost weekends and many nights he sat at the computer well into the early morning hours. She has always provided whatever support was needed—and then some. Walking through life with her has truly been a gracious experience.

Kevin thanks his wife, Julie, who makes every day a joy, for her love and patience. He also thanks his son, Ryan, who makes every day unpredictable and fun. He also thanks his parents, brother and sister-in-law, who have always supported him and had his best interests in mind.

Preface

I have been the director of research for Buckingham Strategic Wealth for almost 25 years. During that period, I have authored, or co-authored, 17 other books on investing. Each of them was based on what we call the "science of investing"—evidence from peer-reviewed academic journals. I have also authored more than 3,000 articles/blog posts and had two papers published in peer-reviewed journals.

Prior to joining Buckingham, I was Vice-Chairman of one of the country's largest residential mortgage companies, Prudential Home Mortgage, where I was in charge of the management of the company's financial risks: interest rate, credit, and liquidity. And in case the Great Financial Crisis, which was fueled by losses on residential mortgages, has you wondering, I am proud to say that to my knowledge, no one who invested in our investment-grade bonds ever lost a penny. Before that I was Western Region Treasurer for Citicorp's investment bank, responsible for advising some of the largest companies in the world on interest rate and foreign exchange risks. I also ran one the bank's larger FX trading rooms and was responsible for funding an offshore bank.

This book is based on the collective wisdom of all of my experiences. While it covers many topics covered in my prior books, the breadth and scope of this book doesn't allow for as deep discussions as was the case in more narrowly focused books. Where that is the case, references are provided so you can dig deeper into the topic in which you are interested. As one example, in this book there is a brief introduction to alternative investments we have recently introduced into our client portfolios. For those interested in much greater detail, we refer you to the 2018 edition of *Reducing the Risk of Black Swans*.

And finally, this work is the third book I have co-authored with Kevin Grogan. It has been a pleasure and privilege to work with him.

Larry E. Swedroe
January 2021

Foreword by Wade D. Pfau

P LANNING FOR LIFE post-retirement is complicated because it is a completely different life experience from what comes before. Prior to retirement, we work and save and invest with the intention of accumulating a nest-egg to support us through our retirement years. Then, once we retire, we have to make this nest-egg last. But for how long? Longevity risk is the first complexity; we don't know how long our savings need to last. Also, once we stop working and start taking distributions from our assets, we must deal with amplifications to traditional investment volatility created by sequence-of-returns risk. We also must be prepared to deal with spending shocks, which are significant expenses that fall outside of our retirement budget, for things like long-term care or helping other family members. We must do this planning in the face of cognitive decline, with the knowledge that as we age it will become increasingly difficult to manage the complexities of a financial plan. Retirement income is about much more than just managing an investment portfolio.

This is why Larry Swedroe and Kevin Grogan's new book, *Your Complete Guide to a Successful and Secure Retirement*, is such an important and refreshing contribution. They know investing inside and out and have written numerous books on investment-related topics. But as a part of a comprehensive financial planning firm, Buckingham Strategic Wealth, they also understand that so much more than investment management goes into a retirement income plan.

I'm honored to write a foreword for this important book. I've known Larry for some years, as we have both been contributors to the Bogleheads Forum, an online message board for individuals to discuss investing and financial planning topics. As well, I serve as chief financial planning strategist for inStream Solutions, the Monte Carlo-based financial planning software program used by advisors at Buckingham and referred to throughout the book. As a professor of retirement income at The American College for Financial Services, I'm also glad to see that their advice is grounded within and vetted by the academic research. Many still base their advice on intuition or outdated rules of thumb. We are very much aligned in terms of how we think about retirement topics.

As you read this guide, you will find a number of issues where Larry and Kevin provide insightful commentary to demonstrate their appreciation for the complexities of retirement income planning in ways that go well beyond what those who tend to think investment management can be a solution for all of retirement's problems are able to appreciate. The issue with investments is that the low-interest-rate environment combined with high stock-market valuations and increasing longevity make it increasingly expensive and complex to try to fund retirement by thinking only in terms of an investment portfolio. The authors repeatedly emphasize that it is important to have a team of professionals aligned toward managing the complexities related to financial planning, tax planning, estate planning, long-term care support, and protecting the plan in the face of cognitive decline. The financial planner can serve as a quarterback to coordinate the activities of these professionals as they work toward the common goal of creating a successful and efficient retirement approach. And beyond finances, one must also find life satisfaction and ways to spend time in a meaningful way to replace all of the hours previously spent at work.

Here are some of the matters discussed in the book that I hope readers will really appreciate:

- You need a vision for your life in retirement beyond just ensuring that your nest-egg is large enough.
- You need to plan ahead for efficient lifetime tax strategies in terms of what types of accounts to hold assets in and how to draw from different accounts over time, while also managing required minimum distributions from qualified retirement accounts and taxes on Social Security benefits.
- You need a strategy for claiming Social Security benefits that seeks to provide the best financial outcome rather than relying on the easy, but potentially costly, solution of claiming as soon as possible.
- You need to understand Medicare and decide among the numerous options it provides for basic and supplemental coverage and prescription drugs.
- You need to consider whether lifetime income guarantees through annuity products may improve plan success through their ability to help manage longevity and sequence-of-returns risk in retirement.
- You need a plan for managing potentially large long-term care expenses, whether that be through self-funding, long-term care insurance, or spending down assets and relying on Medicaid.
- You need to decide on the best way to incorporate home equity into the retirement plan, and whether a reverse mortgage opened earlier in retirement may be a valuable option to manage different retirement risks.
- You need a risk-management strategy using different types of insurance, which may include term or permanent life insurance, disability insurance, homeowners insurance, an umbrella policy, and so on.
- You need an estate plan, including documents such as powers of attorney, wills, and consolidated information to help those who may need to manage the household finances in the event you cannot.

- You need to educate your heirs on how they can continue with financial and life success over multiple generations.
- You need to plan ahead for protecting yourself from elder financial abuse.
- And finally, you do need an investment management strategy based on low-costs, diversification, proper exposure to the different risk factors, and that is shown through Monte Carlo software to provide the best risk/return tradeoffs to maximize the probability of plan success as well as to minimize the harm of failure.

I encourage you to read this book and appreciate its broad scope and many lessons for developing a successful retirement income plan.

Wade D. Pfau, Ph.D., CFA
The American College of Financial Services
McLean Asset Management
inStream Solutions

Introduction

RETIREMENT CREATES MANY challenges. Unfortunately, while about 10,000 Americans retire daily, the sad truth is that most people seem to spend less time planning for retirement than they do for a vacation. The result is that a 2016 survey by GoBankingRates found that 56 percent of Americans have less than $10,000 saved for retirement. And a 2017 study, "Do Households Have a Good Sense of Their Retirement Preparedness?" by the Center for Retirement Research at Boston College, found that even if households work to age 65 and annuitize all their financial assets, including the receipts from reverse mortgages on their homes, 52 percent will be at risk of being unable to maintain their standard of living in retirement.

Anxiety regarding our futures is a common ailment, especially among the millions of Americans rapidly approaching the end of their working years. And there are good reasons for that anxiety:

- Retiring can be as stressful as getting married, losing your job or having a close family member become ill.
- The highest suicide rate in the United States for any segment of the population is men over 70. That's 50 percent higher than the suicide rate among teenagers. The speculation is that these men have lost their life's purpose and their zest for living.
- Only 35 percent of retirees have a written plan for their future finances. This is unfortunate because successful retirement is no different than successful investing: Those who fail to plan, plan to fail.

From an investment standpoint, retirement generates a number of financial challenges. First, your ability to take risk has been reduced because your investment horizon is now shorter. In addition, you no longer have labor capital that can be used to earn income to help offset investment losses. Second, once you enter the withdrawal stage of the investment lifecycle, the negative implication of losses increases because spent assets cannot benefit from future market recoveries. Third, it's likely that your willingness to take risk will fall, and thus your stomach's ability to absorb the acid created by bear markets will be reduced. And that can lead to panic selling and the abandonment of even a well-thought-out plan.

As the chief research officer for Buckingham Strategic Wealth and Buckingham Strategic Partners, I've learned that the very act of retirement creates another problem, one that impacts not only quality of life but the quality of investment decisions as well. One-third of all men over 65 become depressed within one year of retirement. The generally accepted reason is that work had been their primary source of meaning and the biggest occupier of their daytime hours. Replacing that time with activities both mentally challenging and/or emotionally fulfilling doesn't happen automatically. Additionally, for married couples, the shift in daily household routine to one where both spouses are at home at the same time can also lead to marital stress.

Combine the challenge of finding a replacement for work with the increased investment risks discussed previously and retirees often begin obsessing about their portfolios. The time they used to spend at work is now spent watching CNBC, reading financial publications and browsing financial sites online. And despite Warren Buffett's advice to ignore all market forecasts because they tell you nothing about the market (although they do tell you much about the forecaster), the increased attention retirees give to the markets can lead them to become more worried about the latest predictions of gloom and doom from "gurus" who are nothing more than the financial equivalent of a soothsayer.

Retirees also become more susceptible to the dreaded twin diseases of recency (pursuit of the latest hot asset classes and funds) and tracking error regret (panic when a globally diversified portfolio underperforms some common index, like the S&P 500). While this is not an exclusively male problem, both my own experience and the research show that women make better investors because they tend to be less active, adhering to their plans to a greater degree.

Not only does all of this activity create increased anxiety, but it often leads investors to abandon even well-thought-out plans. The result is that those well-thought-out plans end up in the "trash heap of emotions." The evidence shows that the actions most investors take are usually the wrong ones. In fact, studies have shown that investors actually underperform the very mutual funds in which they invest. They tend to buy after periods of good performance and sell after periods of poor performance.

Instead of focusing on the latest economic report or the latest presidential poll (political biases can also cause us to make investment mistakes), you should be focusing on what have been called the "big rocks" in life—be it spending time with family and friends, doing community service, working on your hobbies, or whatever brings you fulfillment. These are the things that we can actually control and bring us joy, instead of angst.

Believe it or not, it will also make you a better investor. The research shows that the more time we spend on our investments, and the more frequently we check the value of our portfolios, the worse our investment outcomes. Again, that's because inaction (other than rebalancing and tax managing the portfolio) is more likely to be the right strategy.

Compounding the problem of a failure to plan is that even a well-thought-out investment plan is only a necessary condition for success, not a sufficient one. The reason is that even the "perfect" investment plan can fail for reasons that have nothing to do with investment results. Examples of how plans can fail for non-investment reasons include premature death of the main income earner combined with insufficient life insurance, forced early retirement, lack of sufficient personal liability insurance (such as an umbrella policy), poor estate planning (such as not keeping beneficiary designations updated), lack of appropriate medical care insurance (such as long-term care), and even living longer than expected. This is why the right plan is to have a fully integrated estate, tax, and risk management (insurance of all kinds) plan.

However, even that is not sufficient. The reason is that life happens and the best laid plans often go awry. For that reason, a common theme throughout this book is that plans, be it life plans, investment plans, estate plans, or insurance plans, must be revisited on a regular basis—especially when any of the plan's underlying assumptions have changed. This book is about building that integrated plan and maintaining its relevance throughout your life. Before diving in, we want to make you aware of several hurdles that must be addressed whether planning for retirement, or already in the withdrawal phase. These are hurdles our predecessors didn't have to deal with. What follows is not meant to scare you. Instead, it is to help emphasize the need to plan, because if these hurdles are not planned for, the odds of being alive without sufficient assets to maintain a desired, let alone a minimally acceptable standard of living, can be greatly increased.

The Four Horsemen of the Retirement Apocalypse

In the Book of Revelation, the last book in the New Testament of the Bible, the Four Horsemen of the Apocalypse are a quartet of immensely powerful entities that personified the four prime concepts that drive the Apocalypse. They are respectively known as: War, Famine, Pestilence, and Death. The equivalent of those four horsemen to your retirement plan are: historically high equity valuations, historically low bond yields, increasing longevity, and the resulting increasing need for what can be very expensive long-term care.

1. Historically High Equity Valuations

From 1926 through 2019, the S&P 500 provided an annualized (compound) rate of return of 10.2 percent. Unfortunately, many make the naïve assumption of extrapolating historical returns when estimating future returns. In this case, it's a bad mistake because some of the return to stocks in this period was a result of a declining equity risk premium, resulting in higher valuations. Those higher valuations forecasted lower future returns. The best metric we have for estimating future returns is the Shiller CAPE (Cyclically Adjusted Price-to-Earnings Ratio) 10. The inverse of that metric is an earnings yield (E/P). It is used to forecast real returns.

As we entered 2020, the Shiller CAPE 10 stood at 30.3. The best predictor we have of the real future returns to equities is the inverse of that ratio, or the earnings yield (E/P), producing a forecasted real return of just 3.3 percent. To get an estimate of nominal returns we can add the difference between the yield on the 10-year nominal Treasury bond (which stood at about 1.9 percent) and the 10-year TIPS (which stood at about 0.1), or about 1.8 percent. That gives us an expected nominal return to stocks of just 5.1 percent, or about half the historical level.

Before moving on to looking at bonds, it's important to note that the forecasts for international returns were better, though, again, well below historical returns. The Shiller CAPE 10 earnings yield for non-U.S. developed markets and emerging markets at year end 2019 were 5.2 percent and 6.7 percent, respectively. Again, if forecasting nominal returns you should add 1.8 percent for expected inflation. Thus, if you have an allocation to international markets your forecast for returns should be somewhat higher than for a U.S.-only portfolio.

Unfortunately, the story on the bond side is not any better.

2. Historically Low Bond Yields

From 1926 through 2019, the five-year Treasury bond returned 5.1 percent, and the long-term (20-year) Treasury bond returned about 5.7 percent. The yields at the end of 2019 on those two Treasury securities were about 1.7 percent and 1.9 percent, respectively. Clearly, those relying on historical returns are likely to be disappointed as the best estimate we have of future returns is from the current yield curve.

Now let's combine stocks and bonds in a traditional 60/40 portfolio.

Traditional 60/40 Portfolio

Over the last 38 years, from 1982 through 2019, a 60 percent S&P 500/40 percent Five-Year Treasury portfolio returned 10.3 percent, with volatility of

10.3 percent. Note that the 10.3 percent return was 1.6 percent a year higher than the portfolio's return over the full 93-year period from 1926 through 2019, which was 8.7 percent, with a volatility of 12 percent.

Those building plans based on that 10.3 percent return over the last 38 years, or even the 8.7 percent return figure covering the last 93 years, are running great risks as the expected returns are now much lower.

The lesson here is that when designing a plan, you should be sure to use current estimates of returns, especially if there have been major changes in stock valuations and bond yields since you last reviewed your plan. A good example of the importance of this lesson was provided by the financial crisis caused by the coronavirus. While that crisis led to a sharp drop in equity prices, it also raised future expected returns as valuations fell. The earnings yield on the Shiller CAPE 10 had risen from 3.1 percent to 4 percent by the end of March, raising the expected real U.S. equity return by 0.9 percent. However, the sharp fall in Treasury bond yields that occurred lowered the yields on the five- and 20-year Treasury bonds to 0.4 percent and 1.0 percent, respectively. While lower valuations on stocks helped, lower yields on bonds hurt.

3. Increasing Longevity

When Larry was growing up (he is 69), there were very few people who lived to collect Social Security for more than a few years. Today, that story is very different. Consider the following:

The average remaining life expectancy for those surviving to age 65 is now about 13/15 years for the male/female 1940 cohort, and about 15/20 years for the male/female 1990 cohort. However, these are just averages. When thinking about longevity risk you should also consider that today a healthy male (female) at age 65 has a 50 percent change of living beyond the age of 85 (88) and a 25 percent chance of living beyond the age of 92 (94). For a healthy couple, both 65, there is a 50 percent chance one will live beyond the age of 92 and a 25 percent chance one will live beyond the age of 97. This means that an investment portfolio should have a planning horizon greater than 30 years, assuming the individual is in their mid-60s.

And that is what we know today. It seems likely that medical science will continue to advance and extend life expectancy even further. Does your plan account for this type of longevity risk? We provide recommendations on how to address this issue in the chapters on Social Security and annuities.

We now turn to the fourth "horseman" facing retirees: The longer we live, the greater the risk that we will need expensive medical care.

4. The Risks of Long-Term Care

Today, nearly one of six Americans is 65 or older. The scary truth is that the likelihood of developing Alzheimer's doubles about every five years after 65. After age 85 it increases even faster, with one in three people 85 and older being diagnosed with the disease—with some estimates as high as 50 percent.

Sadly, the all-too-common unwillingness of the elderly to even discuss the possibility of losing their independence, and the awkwardness of the subject for other family members, leads to the lack of planning for the financial burdens that long-term care can impose.

If these "four horsemen" didn't present enough of a problem, there's a fifth that should be considered when designing your retirement plan.

A Fifth Horseman?

The other threat lurking is the failure of government to fully fund the Social Security and Medicare programs. Because of sharply declining birth rates (from three to two children per woman), the Social Security Board of Trustees projects the cost of providing Social Security benefits to rise by 2035 so that taxes will be enough to pay for only 79 percent of scheduled benefits. Thus, there is at least the risk that benefits will be cut. And for those remaining in the workforce, this deficit could lead to greater taxes on earned income.

The situation is similar regarding Medicare. The 2019 report of Medicare's trustees finds that Medicare's Hospital Insurance (HI) trust fund will only be able to pay 100 percent of the costs of the hospital insurance coverage that Medicare provides through 2025, four years sooner than the 2017 report projected. When the HI trust fund is projected to be depleted, incoming payroll taxes and other revenue will still be sufficient to pay only about 89 percent of expenditures starting in 2026. However, that is projected to decline to as low as 78 percent in 2043, before bouncing back into the 80s by the end of the 75-year period covered by the report. The shortfalls will need to be closed through raising revenues, slowing the growth in costs, or most likely both. Each of the five issues have important implications and should be considered when designing your plan.

These are not the only hurdles that need to be overcome though. The lack of planning can also lead to making mistakes that could otherwise have been avoided. The following is a list of nine common mistakes we have seen made when planning for retirement—each of which we address.

You can use this as a checklist to ensure you do not make them.

Nine Planning Errors to Avoid

1. Sequence Risk: Failing to Consider that the Order of Returns Matters

Unfortunately, returns are not constant, and systematic withdrawals during bear markets exacerbate their effects, causing portfolio values to fall to levels from which they may never recover. Consider the following example:

Over the 26-year period from 1973 through 1999, the S&P 500 provided a nominal return of 13.9 percent a year and a real return of 8.2 percent a year. With hindsight, you might think that given the 8.2 percent real return, it would have been safe to only withdraw 7 percent a year in real terms (taking 7 percent of the portfolio's starting value and increasing the withdrawal by the inflation rate each year). Unfortunately, had you retired at the end of 1972, and followed that strategy, you would have run out of funds within 10 years, by the end of 1982! This is because the S&P 500 Index lost almost 40 percent in the 1973–1974 bear market.

For simplicity purposes, the table below assumes that the amount needed to fund that year's expenditures was withdrawn at the start of the year and did not earn any interest. Offsetting that is the assumption that no taxes were due on investment returns, the sale of assets needed to provide the funding, or on funds withdrawn from a tax-deferred account.

	Beginning Portfolio	Return of S&P 500 (%)	Ending Portfolio	Inflation (CPI) (%)	Funding Requirement for Following Year
1973	930,000	−14.7	793,000	8.8	76,160
1974	716,840	−26.5	526,877	12.2	85,451
1975	441,426	37.2	605,637	7.0	91,432
1976	514,205	23.8	636,585	4.8	95,821
1977	540,764	−7.2	501,830	6.8	102,337
1978	399,493	6.6	425,859	9.0	111,547
1979	314,312	18.4	372,146	13.3	126,383
1980	245,763	32.4	325,390	12.4	142,054
1981	183,336	−4.9	174,352	8.9	154,697
1982	19,655	21.4	23,861	3.9	160,730

Systematic withdrawals work like a dollar-cost averaging program in reverse, and market declines are accentuated. This can cause principal loss from which the portfolio may never recover. As the above table demonstrates, the combination of the bear market and relatively high inflation caused the portfolio to shrink by almost 56 percent in just two years. In order for the portfolio to be restored to its original $1,000,000 level, the S&P Index would have had to have returned 127 percent in 1975. And because of the inflation experienced, the amount needed to be withdrawn had increased from $70,000 to over $90,000. In cases such as this one, if adjustments are not made to the plan (such as increased savings, delaying retirement, or reducing the spending goal), the odds of outliving your assets greatly increase.

Since 1975, we have had three similar drops in market values—during the 2000 through 2002 bear market, during the Great Financial Crisis, and the most recent one being the result of the coronavirus. Clearly such risks should be incorporated into a withdrawal strategy. Historically, a safe harbor withdrawal rate for a 65-year-old couple has only been about 4 percent of the portfolio's initial value (adjusted each year for inflation). As we have discussed, given today's lower bond yields, lower expected stock returns, greater longevity, and greater need to save for medical expenses, that figure may be too aggressive for many.

2. Underestimating Needs

The average person will need to replace 80 percent to 90 percent of their pre-retirement income.

3. Overestimating Ability to Continue Working

People frequently retire early, often for good reasons. Unfortunately, there are also negative reasons (such as having to leave the workforce due to health reasons, loss of job, or having to take full-time care of a spouse or elderly parent). A good retirement plan considers contingencies, including the need for disability insurance.

4. Becoming Too Conservative

Unfortunately, too much of a "safe" thing may not be safe because of the risk of inflation, especially for those with pensions without inflation adjustments. While the return on bonds can be eroded by inflation, equities provide better long-term protection against the risk of unexpected inflation.

5. Underestimating Tax Rate

People often assume that their tax rate will be lower than actually proves to be the case.

6. Failing to Provide for a Spouse

Couples should take into account that upon the first death, Social Security benefits will be reduced. While living expenses may be reduced, the reduction in income should also be considered. And employees working for companies with defined benefit plans often fail to consider the surviving spouse when deciding on payment options.

7. Taking Withdrawals from the Wrong Location

The rule-of-thumb approach for the most efficient order is to first draw down the taxable accounts, then the tax-deferred accounts (such as traditional IRAs and 401(k)s), and finally the non-taxable accounts (Roths). As with any rule-of-thumb, this may not be applicable to your specific circumstances. We discuss tax-efficient withdrawals in Chapter 11.

8. Underestimating the Importance and Need for Diversification

When approaching or entering retirement we often make the mistake of believing that our horizons are too short to diversify our stock holdings to such asset classes as small-cap stocks, international stocks, and emerging market stocks. However, diversification across non-highly correlating asset classes is the winning strategy no matter what the investment horizon. Diversification across equity asset classes is actually more important as the investment horizon shortens. This is because any asset class can underperform by a very large amount over even fairly long horizons, let alone over relatively short ones. For example, most investors would be surprised to learn that there have been three periods of at least 13 years over which the S&P 500 Index underperformed totally riskless one-month Treasury bills: the 13-year period 2000 through 2012, the 15-year period 1929 through 1943, and the 17-year period 1966 through 1982. Diversification reduces the risk of any single asset dragging down the portfolio.

9. Underestimating the Risks of Inflation

The impact of inflation can be devastating. Historically, the rate of increases in wages has exceeded the inflation rate. Thus, while employed, the risk of rising inflation is not that great. However, once we enter retirement, the risks of inflation increase. One reason is that Social Security benefits are indexed to inflation, not to the cost of living of seniors, which tends to increase faster. For example, the cost of medical care has historically risen at a faster rate than overall inflation.

Your Journey

You are about to embark on a journey that will lead the way to the development of your retirement plan, one that includes not only an integrated approach to financial security, but also a rich and diverse portfolio of meaningful activities. As always, the place to begin any journey is at the beginning—which Plato called the most important part of the work. Unfortunately, it is our experience that even those who do plan for retirement focus solely on financial issues—ignoring a plan for living a fulfilling life in retirement.

As we noted earlier, the failure to plan is to plan to fail. While so many of us have carefully planned our education, career choices, and family responsibilities, we tend to fail to prepare a written retirement life plan that considers, among other things, our passions, financial security, charitable endeavors, relationships, intellectual stimulation, and having fun. The result of lack of planning for a fulfilling life after work is why research shows that the majority of retirees say they do not enjoy their first year in retirement. As one example, couples are challenged by living together under new life circumstances.

To help you plan for a fulfilling life in retirement, we asked an expert in the field, Alan Spector, to help with the writing of the first chapter. Because there is no way to write an effective plan without first establishing your goals and objectives, the chapter is about helping you change the focus from retiring *from* something to retiring *to* something, providing you with the information and tools you need to develop a plan that will enable you to have a fulfilling life in retirement.

Before setting off on your journey with us we want to provide you with the following advice to keep in mind as you read each chapter. Having a well-thought-out plan is important. However, planning is not a one-and-done event. To be effective, plans must be living things that must be revisited whenever any of the assumptions upon which the plan was based have changed. That's the only way a plan can maintain its relevance and provide the greatest utility. Planning for retirement at 40, or even 50, is smart. But, ideas and circumstances change for many reasons. Being willing to review your plan whenever there are significant changes in retirement thinking or circumstance will make the journey more valuable. Remember, sticking to a plan in the face of new circumstances is the folly of fools.

We hope you enjoy the journey.

CHAPTER I

Retirement Planning
Beyond the Financials

R ETIREMENT IS ONE of life's significant transitions. Virtually everything changes. During your career, you merely need to show up each day to be exposed to many of the things that make up a fulfilling life. Your work gives you a sense of purpose. You are nurtured by the relationships you have with colleagues. You are energized by the self-esteem you achieve because you are good at what you do and others recognize it. You attain a level of financial security from a regular paycheck. You are comforted by the predictable structure of your days, weeks, and years. You are intellectually stimulated by ever-changing circumstances.

One day, all of that is yours. Then, because of a decision by your boss, or "the organization", or by personal choice, you retire. The day after your retirement party, all that your career provided is gone. You must find your life's meaning and basis of self-esteem elsewhere. You realize few collegial relationships are really lasting friendships. The security of a regular paycheck must come from other sources. You need to find a way to rebuild a daily, weekly, and yearly structure and to replace the intellectual stimulation that so readily came from your work. Despite being excited about your new phase of life, if you are like most others, you also approach retirement with a healthy dose of anxiety. You may be unaware of the challenges you may face, and you may not be prepared to identify and take advantage of the opportunities that will come your way.

Unless you replace what your career provided, understand and address the challenges, and recognize the opportunities, you and those close to you may not live the retirement you have worked so hard to deserve. Fewer than half of retirees enjoy their first year. Many experience symptoms of depression. The segment of society with the fastest growing divorce rate is couples over 55, reflecting the difficulty of having to live together in new life circumstances.

It is not the intent of sharing all of this to suggest that your retirement will be a disaster. In fact, your retirement can be, and should be, fulfilling, satisfying, and successful. Rather, the intent of making you aware of what you could be facing is to begin a conversation about what you can be doing, starting now, to make your retirement what you want it to be.

As is the case with most endeavors, the best way to prepare for the transition, stave off the challenges, and identify and take advantage of the opportunities, is to develop a written retirement life plan before you retire, practice that plan while you are still working, and have the relevant crucial retirement planning conversations with those closest to you. We will address practicing retirement and crucial conversations later in the chapter. For now, let's get started on your retirement life planning.

As mentioned in the Introduction, a failure to plan is a plan to fail. And despite most people having extensive planning experience at work (such as business strategies, lesson plans, and customer meetings) and at home (such as vacations, home improvements, and entertaining), most tend not to plan for retirement. Of those who do plan, most focus solely on the financial aspects. While doing so is critical—and we will spend the bulk of this book helping you create your financial plan—it is far from sufficient. In this chapter, we will build a framework upon which you can develop your retirement life plan—beyond the financials.

Importantly, doing so will also enable you to create an even more meaningful financial plan. Your financial advisor will tell you that he or she would prefer you to say, "Here is what I plan to do in retirement. Let's work together to build a financial plan that supports my life plan." A less-preferred statement goes something like, "I'm planning to retire. Make sure I do not run out of money." The reasons, therefore, to have a written retirement life plan are to have a smooth and quick transition into retirement by replacing those important life components that your career provides, to increase the odds you live the retirement you deserve, to have a more robust financial plan, and to enable you to practice retirement while still working.

Why should it be a written plan? If you write your plan, you increase the odds that it will be well thought through and that you will actually live the plan. In addition, you will create something you can show to others, like family and friends, and your advisor, so that they can align it with your financial plan.

A Retirement Vision

You have worked hard to earn a fulfilling retirement, and your investment of time and energy to develop your written plan will enable you to make the rest of your life the best of your life. Consider this vision of retirement.

Envision a time in your life when you have the freedom to choose what to do, when to do it, and with whom you want to do it. It is a time in your life when you are full of energy and contented at the same time. Your life is full of close relationships with family and friends; you are contributing your time and resources to helping others; your days, weeks, months, and years are filled with activities that you love, that help you grow, and that are just plain fun. You awaken each day with a sense of purpose and a positive attitude. You have the resources and general well-being to live the life that makes you happy and can foresee living it well into your future. You take advantage of new-found opportunities and you deal well with life's inevitable setbacks, because you are resilient and have a plan that helps guide you through them.

Is that the retirement you would like to create and live?

Your Retirement Life Plan

In their book, *Your Retirement Quest*, which we highly recommend, Alan Spector and Keith Lawrence identify what they refer to as the "10 key elements of a fulfilling retirement." These components are the building blocks of your retirement life plan. We will review each key element, and as we do, consider two things:

1. How are you positioned to transition into retirement for each key element? Candidly assess which of these statements apply:

   • I have never thought about this key element before, or I have considered it but haven't really done anything about it.
   • I have positive aspects of this key element in my life, but I certainly have room for improvement.
   • This key element is already a fulfilling part of my life.

2. What would you need to begin doing, or perhaps stop doing, to make each key element a more fulfilling part of your life, especially as you transition into and through retirement?

Once we've reviewed all of the key elements, we will discuss some simple tools you can use to develop your written plan.

Key Element—Life Purpose

Many of us characterize our identity by the role we play: teacher, executive, doctor, engineer, pastor… When you retire and that role ends, how do you establish your new identity? What is your purpose in life?

There are a number of online approaches to help you craft your life purpose or life mission statement. And you can be guided by your answers to the following questions: 1) Envision a time when your 15-year-old grandchild asks you, "What has your life been about?" You could answer, "I was an attorney," but, I am not one any longer. What would you answer that grandchild in language he or she would understand? 2) If you had complete freedom and were told you had a year to live, what would you do with your remaining time and, importantly, why? Create a purpose statement that is meaningful to you and then align your activities to be consistent with that purpose. We discuss this further in the next chapter in the Life Discovery section.

Key Element—Passions

Just as it is important to identify your life purpose and align your activities to it, it is important to identify your passions and pursue them. What are your passions?

What do you love to do? What excites you to look forward to, learn more about, tell others about? What are you doing that makes you lose track of time? What makes you want to jump out of bed in the morning and get started? What are you good at?

If you are still struggling to identify your passions, try asking yourself the question, "What did I love to do when I was 10 years old?" When you were 10, you were old enough to make choices about what you enjoy doing, but at that age, other aspects of life had not yet gotten in the way of pursuing them. Many retirees find that those 10-year-old's passions trigger something for them—fulfilling childhood dreams without parental supervision.

Key Element—Attitude

The research consistently shows that having a positive attitude makes a difference in both quality of life and longevity, as much as a seven-year difference.

Many believe that attitude is hardwired into their personalities. This is not the case. You can positively affect this key element. As examples, work on gratitude—begin and end your day by expressing appreciation for all that is right in your life. Sincerely say "thank you" more frequently. Surround yourself with people who have a positive attitude. Look for or, better yet, create opportunities for random acts of kindness. Act like Tigger instead of Eeyore.

To learn more about how you can positively impact this key element, we recommend reading *The Happiness Advantage* by Shawn Achor.

Key Element—Financial Security

Financial security is but one of the 10 key elements of a fulfilling retirement, but it is critical for two reasons. It is important in its own right. And if done well, it will enable you to focus your time and energy on the meaningful non-financial aspects of your retirement. Consider these three facets of what it takes to achieve financial security: 1) Matching your lifestyle (budget) to your available resources. It's not about the size of your nest egg, but about managing spending. 2) Developing a support team with the necessary expertise and coordinated by your financial advisor. 3) Ensuring you and those closest to you (such as your spouse, partner, and adult children) are understanding of, and in alignment with, your financial plan.

Key Element—Giving Back

Why should helping others be an integral part of a fulfilling retirement? Certainly, if you apply your time, talent, and treasure to help individuals and organizations, it's good for your community. But let's be selfish for a while—what's in it for you? Research has shown time and again that the person giving back actually gets more from the experience than the person on the receiving end. For instance, retired volunteers greatly benefit from lower mortality rates, higher functional ability later in life, lower stress, and better morale. Essentially, volunteering can add years to your life and life to your years. That sounds like a win-win situation, and it is.

When asked if they plan to volunteer in retirement, 70 percent of baby boomers answer "Yes." Yet, less than 30 percent actually do. Those who do not are missing an opportunity for a more satisfying retirement.

Key Element—Healthy Relationships

Research has shown that low social interaction—not having healthy relationships—has the equivalent effects of smoking 15 cigarettes per day or being an alcoholic, is more harmful than being inactive, and is twice as harmful as obesity.

But what is a healthy relationship? It is spending real face-to-face personal time with friends and family. It is being a part of networks of people with common interests. And it is having many, some say as many as 10, two-o'clock-in-the-morning-friends. These are the people in your life, family or friends, who you would have no qualms calling in the middle of the night to ask for help and know without hesitation or question that your friend would be on the way, and vice versa.

Key Element—Growth

Many retirees struggle to replace the intellectual stimulation that came naturally in the workplace. Keeping mentally active is critical as we transition into and age through retirement. We are inundated with information about the value of keeping the mind active, and unfortunately, most of us know someone who is dealing with, or has dealt with, dementia, either personally or as a caregiver.

"Use it or lose it" is but one of the reasons growth is key to a successful retirement. It is all too easy to find ourselves settling into a small comfort zone. Yet, what if instead of limiting your activities to what you are comfortable with, you use your new-found freedom to stretch yourself? What if instead of passively sitting in front of television or social media, you engaged in new, exciting activities?

There is nothing wrong with watching television or engaging in social media, unless they dominate your time. The things you can do to stimulate your brain and get you fully engaged in life can be big things, like taking a class at a local community college, getting involved in a new volunteer project, learning a new language, or traveling to a place you've never been before. Or they can be small things. The next time you drive to the grocery store, take a different route. Brush your teeth with the opposite hand (seriously, try it). Eat dessert first. Read different genres. Expand your comfort zone. Keep your mind active and sharp. Enjoy new and different opportunities. Use it or lose it.

Key Element—Fun

Your career may be something you love to do, and it can be fun… at times. But, regardless of whether you view your career as fun or not, as you look forward, do you know how to build fun into your retirement? And will you?

It is non-controversial that fun and the more frequent laughter that derives from it has health benefits. It improves the body's immune system, helps stave off the physical and emotional characteristics of stress, has a positive effect on blood pressure and heart function, and decreases pain. It strengthens relationships, helps reduce conflict, and promotes group bonding. "Laughter (and fun) is the best medicine."

You can plan fun into your life, or you can take advantage of being spontaneous. In either case, will you have activities in your retirement life that are just plain fun to do?

Key Element—Well-Being

A holistic approach to thinking about well-being is to follow the daily habits that create the personal energy you need to do what you want to do now, and that will sustain your energy into your future. Energy derives from four components: physical energy, emotional energy, mental energy, and the energy of purpose. Sound familiar? Attitude, healthy relationships, growth, purpose, and the other key elements can and should be your sources of energy. Add in the right daily habits of nutrition, exercise, and sleep, and the right attention to your medical health, and you have a formula to create and sustain energy.

Key Element—Retirement Life Plan

You would not expect to be successful in your career without a plan. The same applies in your retirement life. To be successful, the plan should be "holistic," in that it includes all of the key elements. As we will discuss, one of the tenets of a robust financial plan is to ensure you have a diverse portfolio of investments. To be holistic, your life plan should also have a diverse portfolio of meaningful activities. The tools we will cover shortly will help you create that holistic plan.

Crucial Conversations

Crucial conversations about retirement life planning are intended to make your plan even better and ensure that those closest to you have been involved in its development. This is not only about discussions with a spouse or partner. Consider who else in your life will significantly affect your retirement and who your retirement will significantly affect. It might be aging parents, adult children, other relatives, or close friends.

The objective is to have these sometimes-difficult conversations upfront to avoid surprises later. Some possible subjects to discuss are whether your plans, both life and financial, are mutually understood and agreed to, when is the right time to retire, where will you live, who else should you be involving in the retirement life planning discussions, what financial and caregiving commitments will you make to parents, children, and grandchildren.

Practicing Retirement

When you have your life plan developed, it will include those activities you are looking forward to doing in retirement. The concept of practicing retirement is to bring those activities into your life while you are still working, even if in a small way.

There are a number of reasons to do this. You may find that something you thought would excite you does not have that effect, enabling you to change your plan prior to your retirement transition. Your life plan informs your financial plan. Practicing retirement can help you confirm what you want your finances to support and work with your advisor on that basis.

The most compelling reason to practice retirement is that if you've identified those things you are excited about doing in retirement, why not bring as much of that as possible into your life now? Why wait? The best time to begin is now.

Retirement Life Planning Tools

There are a number of simple, yet useful, tools you can use to develop your retirement life plan. As you consider each one, keep in mind the key elements and your assessment of how you are positioned to transition into retirement for each element. Recognize that in doing your assessment, you actually completed the first step of the planning process, to determine where you stand now. The second step, which we will address as we review the tools, is to develop your plan for how you want to improve from where you are. The third step is to actually live your plan. And the final step is to review and renew your plan periodically, and when circumstances warrant.

Retirement Life Planning Tool—Bucket List

There is a more uplifting approach to this planning tool than was presented in the 2007 movie, *The Bucket List*. Think about your bucket list as those things you are excited about looking forward to doing, about planning to do, about actually doing, about relating to others, about reminiscing afterwards, and about deciding whether you'd like to do them again.

Most people think about bucket list items as the big dreams, like traveling to Australia/New Zealand, writing that novel, or hiking the Appalachian Trail. The big dreams are great and should be included, but the items can be smaller as well. Go to that new neighborhood restaurant; see a live performance of *Porgy and Bess*; teach your granddaughter to play gin; visit each of the county parks in your area.

Sit down with a pen and paper or at your computer, and without making any judgment about whether you will actually be able to pull them off, just begin writing items on your list. You will find that just creating the list is energizing and that once you have it, you will be adding to it as you come across new ideas. When you complete an item, physically check it off. It just feels good to do so. The bucket list can be a good way to get the planning juices flowing, so you may want to consider using this tool first. Remember, no judgment. Just write!

Retirement Life Planning Tool—Start/Stop/Continue

The next tool is based specifically on the key elements. Create a chart with two columns—label the first "Key Elements," and list them down the column. Label the second column "Start/Stop/Continue."

To begin, select one or two of the key elements you assessed as needing a lot of improvement. Eventually, you'll address each of the key elements—remember, you want your plan to be holistic.

For the first one or two key elements you choose to work on, think about two things: 1) Are there things missing from your life that if you began to do them, they would enhance that key element? These are your potential "Start" items. An example for Well-Being would be, "Start taking a one-mile walk at least five days each week, increasing the length and intensity over time." 2) Are there things in your life that are getting in the way of enhancing that key element? These are your potential "Stop" items. Another Well-Being example would be, "Stop drinking soda and eating M&Ms."

Once you've brainstormed a list of possible Starts and Stops, select one or two for each key element that you think will make a difference. Keep the others on a separate list—you may choose to get to them later as you renew your plan.

Once you get some practice by working on your first key element or two, move on to the others. You will find that it will not take an inordinate amount of time to get to a doable and meaningful plan. You will also find that a Start or Stop in one key element will also positively affect others.

A final point before moving on to discuss the "Continue" part of the plan—keep your Starts and Stops specific. For example, you may be addressing Well-Being, because you haven't spent much time over the past years (or decades) exercising. If you write a Start item that reads, "Get fit," it is too broad to act upon. Rather, write something actionable like, "Take a daily walk" or "Join the local gym and engage a personal trainer."

If you have assessed yourself for a key element as, "This key element is already a fulfilling part of my life," there may not be any Starts or Stops to capture. Instead, there are likely things you are doing in your life that are making that key element go well. Write down the key things you would want to "Continue." Doing so acknowledges what's working for you, and if sometime later that key element needs a boost, you may find that you had failed to continue what was working, and you will know what to re-Start. An example would be, "Continue having the immediate family over for dinner every other Sunday."

Retirement Life Planning Tool—Find the Magic

One way to think about choosing what you may want in your life's diverse portfolio of meaningful activities is to "find the magic" using this tool. Envision three overlapping circles. One is labeled "Passions," another "Strengths," and the third "Needs." Where the three overlap is a smaller, but powerful, circle labeled "Magic."

To use this tool, write down answers to the following questions: 1) What are you passionate about? There will likely be more than one. 2) What are your strengths? What are those things you are great at and have experience with? These may have derived from your career or other activities you've been involved in. 3) What does your community need?

Said another way, where can you passionately apply your strengths to make a difference in something that matters? Magic!

Retirement Life Planning Tool—Ideal Day

This tool helps you create the retirement you want by helping you figure out how to spend your most valuable resource: your time. And in doing so, it helps you address the loss of the structure that your career provided.

As you've become accustomed, it's time to write it down—create a two-column table, labeling the first "Time" and the second "Activity." In the first column, list times in half-hour increments, starting with when you would like to wake up for your ideal day and ending when you would like to go to sleep.

The Activity column is where you enter how you would prefer to ideally spend those half-hour time slots. You can adjust timing by combining rows in the table. For example, if your ideal day includes a workout from 8:30 to 9:30, combine two half-hour rows to give you that one hour.

The ideal day exercise gives you a benchmark to compare to how you are actually spending your time. Making the comparison can help you strive to move your life toward your ideal.

When to Retire

Although retirement timing is sometimes dictated by your organization, one of the choices you may have as you develop your retirement life plan is deciding when to retire. To do so, ask yourself the following four questions. When the answer to all four is "yes," it's time to retire.

1. Do I have enough? This is the question of whether you have a sufficient level of financial security.
2. Have I had enough? Despite having a successful career, it may no longer light your fire.
3. Will I have enough to do? Another way to ask this question is "Do I have a written, holistic retirement life plan that promises to be fulfilling?"

4. Does my spouse/partner or someone else close to me want me home 24/7? This is an assessment of whether you have had sufficient retirement life planning crucial conversations to be aligned to your plan.

There is no right or wrong about if and when to retire. However, developing and living your retirement life plan will increase the odds that, when you do retire, you'll be prepared to make the rest of your life the best of your life. To help you answer the four retirement timing questions, we recommend that you also consider the findings from the 2020 study "Working Longer Solves (Almost) Everything: The Correlation Between Employment, Social Engagement and Longevity."

The authors, Tim Driver and Amanda Henshon, began by noting: "Working longer provides additional lifetime earnings and the opportunity for incremental saving, augments the size of eventual pension and social security benefits and also reduces the number of years of retirement during which these augmented assets will be consumed. Even without considering any health benefit, deferred retirement results in greater resources amassed to support fewer years of retirement." This helps address the problems posed by the "four horsemen of the retirement apocalypse."

Driver and Henshon then noted that continued participation in the workforce provides a means for older adults to remain engaged in their communities. In addition to reaping economic benefits from employment, those remaining in the workforce will be "healthier, less isolated, and happier. Objective social isolation has repeatedly been found to be a risk factor for poor mental and physical health, including higher prevalence of disease and increased risk of mortality." In addition, they note: "Work provides opportunities for learning, reasoning, and social engagement, all of which help stave off the adverse effects aging can have on the brain." They cited a long-term study in England that "assessed memory in more than 3,000 civil servants over a 30-year period covering the final part of their careers, as well as the early years of their retirement. Results showed that verbal memory, which declines naturally with age, deteriorated 38 percent faster after retirement." They noted that other research has suggested that cognitive declines nearly double post-retirement. They also noted that research has found that "mortality rates decreased among those who worked past age 65."

Driver and Henshon went on to note that those who continued to work into their older years had a 25 percent increase in the size of their social networks, while people who retired saw their social networks shrink. Given that social isolation has been identified as a health determinant equal to smoking 15 cigarettes per day, the reduced social networks resulting from retirement are cause for significant concern. They also noted: "Older adults who have a 'retirement job' also often volunteer. It is quite possible then that social interaction can be maintained if older adults choose to volunteer rather than work. Research on the benefits of volunteering by older adults is more extensive and has been going on for longer than for older employees. Although not conclusive, there is a correlation between volunteering and improved health outcomes, including larger social networks." Driver and Henshon added: "In addition to the benefits derived from increased social interactions, for many people, life derives some meaning, purpose, affiliation, and structure from the fact that they are working. Maintaining a satisfying career can help older people sustain their sense of worth and contribute to their happiness."

Driver and Henshon concluded: "There is a strong positive correlation between employment, social engagement, and longevity. Facilitating continued or new employment of older workers not only adds more years to those individuals' lives, but also adds more 'life' to their later years".

You can learn more about the retirement life planning concepts and tools described in this chapter in Alan Spector's book *Your Retirement Quest*, and at www.YourRetirementQuest.com.

The retirement Key Elements and Retirement Life Planning tools also feed well into our next chapter, which provides you with an additional approach to moving from hopes and dreams to plans and next actions. We will cover both the Life Discovery Process and the Financial Discovery process and then integrate them into an achievable One-Year Plan. The authors were Bert Schweizer, one of the founders and ex-chairman of the Buckingham Group, and Tim Maurer. Bert was beloved and respected by employees and clients alike. He was also a great and willing teacher. And although he is no longer working full-time, he continues as a consultant, helping to train a new generation of advisors in the processes we use to help clients achieve their life and financial goals. Tim is the Director of Advisor Development for Buckingham Wealth Partners.

CHAPTER 2

Discovery: Life and Financial

A s WE APPROACH retirement, most people fail to think about what we need or want to do when work becomes an option, or we are no longer able to work. We fail to put forth any meaningful thought about planning for what lies ahead after retirement, both personally and financially. So that you don't fail we will walk you through the two discovery processes we use at Buckingham Strategic Wealth—Life Discovery and Financial Discovery.

Discovery

The Discovery process, while designed to be conducted with a wealth management professional, can successfully be completed with a spouse, partner, or trusted friend. Doing it on your own will take some planning as well as requiring the other party to have skills at reflective listening and probing for more answers to their questions. They should never provide the answer to the question they are asking—even if it is your partner or spouse. A recording device can be helpful to professionals and non-professionals alike as it enables the questioner to focus on your answers and think about the next question without having to write down each response.

There are never wrong answers to Discovery questions. And it is perfectly alright for spouses or partners to disagree with answers. Another helpful practice is to recognize that one spouse or partner may be more engaged than the other. The questioner should be alert to this situation and be sure to direct questions so that each participant contributes responses to the questions.

Life Discovery

There are four steps in the Life Discovery process:

1. Explore life areas.
2. Identify vision and values.
3. Articulate and prioritize goals.
4. Address and overcome concerns.

Explore Life Areas

There are four broad areas of life that are worthy of exploration at any phase of life, and especially in, or preceding, retirement:

- Family and Relationships.
- Work and Career.
- Health and Wellness.
- Interests and Causes.

There is no particular order of priority implied in this list, as each individual and household will go through phases of life where various elements will take center stage. The simple but powerful question to ask yourself in this life area audit is: What is important to me about [life area]?

Family is one area of life that is often all consuming for us as parents of minor children. A contributing factor is that relationships beyond our children are often driven by our children's academic, athletic, and extracurricular activities. Even marriages can easily become less romantic and more utilitarian—that is if they survive this challenging time of life. Therefore, retirement for many is a time to work on reestablishing your life partnership and recreate relationships unbound by the connection to PTA meetings and lacrosse games. And for those who are parents of adult children, retirement is an excellent time to consider and articulate what is important about how we would like our vital role as parent, and perhaps grandparent, to look, even as our children are, hopefully, exercising their independence.

You may wonder why Work and Career is listed at all as we are considering the notion of retirement, presumably from work. The reason is that, as we have mentioned, the dissatisfaction many face early in retirement is often due, at least in part, to the loss of that sense of purpose inherent in one's occupation or vocation. Therefore, while the need for income-producing work may be diminished in retirement, having purposeful work to which you can apply yourself throughout retirement helps instill a sense of purpose. It may even be that a second or third career creates a substantive bridge into a fulfilling retirement experience. If income from that work is also a byproduct, this helps lessen the stress and strain inherent in the retirement transition.

Health and Wellness begins for many in retirement as a celebration of freedom to be even more active, as less time is devoted to a job and/or parenting. This is a freedom worthy of exploration that often fuels the early years of retirement. However, it is important to recognize that our physical vitality recedes in the later years of retirement as we age. However unpleasant acknowledging this might be, we must address it. For example, while not every retiree needs long-term care insurance, every retiree needs a long-term health care plan, a topic addressed in Chapter 15.

Lastly, Interests and Causes is how you envision retirement—spending the time you did not have prior to retirement taking longer, more meaningful trips and excursions, and dedicating more time to hobbies, pursuits, and charitable initiatives that have long held our interest. Many retirees have even found their interests and causes surprisingly squeezed out of a busy retirement calendar they expected to be empty. Therefore, it is important to prioritize, and even calendarize, those interests and causes that are truly important to you.

So, what is important to you in each of these four life areas? Consider jotting some bullets or journaling your response to each. Remember, writing a formal plan increases the odds that you will follow it.

Identify Vision and Values

When looking at the output from your exploration of the four life areas, what jumps out to you? What themes do you find repeating themselves across multiple life areas? What three or four elements would you be inclined to underscore with a highlighter?

While all good companies deliberate on what is most important to them and articulate it in the form of a vision and mission statements, only great companies keep that vision and mission foremost in their plans and processes. Unfortunately, few individuals and households apply this notion. Discerning and articulating your Vision and Values can become the true north of your retirement planning compass, providing both meaning and momentum to your plans. To help you think about your values, in his book, *The Seven Stages of Money*, George Kinder, considered by many to be the "father of life planning" suggests asking the following questions:

1. Imagine that you are financially secure, that you have enough money to take care of your needs, now and in the future. How would you live your life? What would you do with the money? Would you change anything? Let yourself go. Do not hold back your dreams. Describe a life that is complete, that is richly yours.

2. You visit your doctor who tells you that you have five to 10 years left to live. The good part is that you won't ever feel sick. The bad news is that you will have no notice of the moment of your death. What will you do in the time you have remaining to live? Will you change your life, and how will you do it?

3. Your doctor shocks you with the news that you have only one day left to live. Notice what feelings arise as you confront your very real mortality. Ask yourself: What dreams will be left unfulfilled? What do I wish I had finished or had been? What do I wish I had done? What did I miss?

Answering these questions will help you discover what makes you unique, what you long for, and what should be reflected in your planning.

Vision and Values Statement

What does a Vision and Values statement look like? Ultimately whatever you choose, but we suggest three possibilities:

1. Bullet points: Are you a bullet point person who loves concise lists? Then consider drawing out a few themes that you'd like to see as your statement of Vision and Values. Try to be as specific as possible so that these points are uniquely you. Less like "travel" and "family" and more like:

   • Rediscover marriage through intention.
   • Craft legacy through travel with kids and grandkids.
   • Maintain health through regular, fun exercise.

2. Prose: Or maybe you are more of a verbal processor who benefits from a prose statement, like:

   "We plan to be frugal in many areas of life so that we can be extravagant in others, such as crafting memorable travel experiences with our family that demonstrate a living legacy. We can provide no better example for our children's families than through a loving marriage rekindled by intention. And one of those intentions is to enjoy our dormant love of athletics as a couple, fueling our health through something that is fun for both of us."

3. Pictures: It may be that your Vision and Values statement does not have any words at all. Instead a few pictures may say more to you.

Regardless of the form it takes, your Vision and Values statement should demonstrate: that which is most important to you; that which you don't want to compromise; and that which would fill you with a sense of meaning and purpose in retirement.

Articulate and Prioritize Goals

The themes highlighted in your Vision and Values statement should not be specific goals in and of themselves. Instead, they should be the inspiration for your goals that you will craft. For example, a handful of goals that could correspond with the vision above might be:

- Start playing in a mixed-doubles tennis league.
- Kick off rotating dinner club with four couples.
- Host family meeting to discuss legacy plans.
- Plan, and fund, a big family trip.
- Teach English as a second language classes at the community college.
- Take trip to Costa Rica as a couple.

You do not need to worry about how you will accomplish your goals at the time you do Discovery. That will be developed as you, or your professional wealth advisor, create your plan.

You will note that this list of goals does not yet meet the helpful criteria of being entirely specific, measurable, and attainable. That is perfectly fine. You will get there as you work from idea to action. At this point, do not restrict your thinking based on time or money. However, because none of us has enough time or money to do everything we want to do at the same time, we must prioritize goals. You can do this by asking the following question: Is that goal a *need*, a *want*, or a *wish*?

Armed with greater clarity in the form of your prioritized goals, you are ready to address the biggest hurdle to accomplishing our plans for life or retirement—yourself.

Address and Overcome Concerns

As we move from intention to action, what often stops us is the silent killer of hopes and dreams—our own worries or concerns, spoken and often unspoken:

- "I cannot afford that."
- "It is too late to learn [fill-in-the-blank]."
- "Everyone won't want to go along with that."
- "But I am not good in front of people."
- "I don't know how to [fill-in-the-blank]."

While you might not be able to afford to have a second home closer to your adult children, what if you downsized to a city nearby and used that new adventure as part of the bonding process in your marriage and a platform for building new relationships? While you might have picked up a racket in the past 10 years, you might not be able to return to the club circuit in the A-league— but the mixed-doubles B-league could be even more fun. You get the idea.

For each of your needs, wants, and wishes, ask yourself a two-part question: What concerns do I have about reaching that goal? And what solutions could reduce or eliminate those concerns?

If you write these questions and the corresponding answers down, you'll be surprised how often simply asking and answering them will bring you to your own solution. But what if you get to a dead-end? If you cannot find a solution, that is where asking your spouse, inviting a wise friend to breakfast, or talking through your concerns with your financial advisor can help lead the way.

The LifeMap

Once you and your spouse or partner have completed the answers to all of the Discovery questions, you should prepare an organized list of your observations and conclusions. Buckingham Strategic Wealth creates a one-page LifeMap that summarizes the information collected above. See the example in Appendix A.

The LifeMap will enable you to capture all that you learn throughout Discovery, review the content, and easily update it as your life and finances change. It should become a living, breathing document. It is also an essential tool to use when working with your professionals in creating and maintaining a financial plan, doing income tax and estate planning, considering risk-protection strategies and developing charitable-giving strategies.

While in the midst of Life Discovery, we do not want you to restrict your thinking only to that which appears to be financially feasible. Before we get to Financial Discovery, we would like to take you one step further in your life planning exercise by specifically addressing the elements of life that are unique to the transition into and through retirement.

Once a regular work day and paycheck ceases, we face many new opportunities and challenges. We have spent a lifetime accumulating wealth. Now, we face the remainder of our life spending it. Suddenly, we are faced with challenges that were not so important before retirement. The challenges might include:

- What is my source of cash to pay the bills?
- When do I take Social Security?
- How do I tax-efficiently drawdown from taxable, tax-deferred, and tax-free accounts?

- Can I afford to maintain my pre-retirement lifestyle?
- What happens if I have an extended need for long-term health care?
- Do I want to help family members during their lives?
- Are my children going to be financially independent?
- How much can I donate to charities and causes I would like to support?
- What is this RMD I hear so much about?
- Do I still have the need for life insurance, and if so, how much should I have?
- Do I have the right legal documents such as durable powers of attorney for both financial and health matters, trusts, wills, living wills, DNRs, and so on?
- Who is there to help the survivor, especially if the survivor is not well informed about the above concerns?
- Do our children understand and are they capable of carrying forth our family values? Do they know where all the important documents are and who our trusted advisors are?
- Is my investment portfolio structured to assure we have the highest probability of meeting our financial goals during our lifetime, or post-mortem if appropriate?

As Bill Bachrach says in his book, *Values Based Financial Planning*: "In the grand scheme of things, money's not that important. It's significant only to the extent that it allows you to enjoy what is important to you. And not worrying about your finances is critical to having a life that excites you, nurtures those you love, and fulfills your highest aspirations."

That is why you have done the important work to identify these aspirations through a version of Life Discovery specifically geared toward the retirement phase of life. Now you are ready to couple that work with the no-less-important Financial Discovery. We will conclude this chapter by combining Life and Financial Discovery through a practical exercise called a One-Year Plan.

Whether you choose to work with a financial professional or do it yourself, this process will provide you with a systematic way to develop a well-thought-out plan that incorporates your LifeMap, affording the greatest likelihood of achieving your goals, rather than a hodge-podge of investments, insurance policies, and often useless documents.

Financial Discovery

Having explored the qualitative through Life Discovery, we turn our focus to the more quantitative elements of your retirement plan:

1. Financial assets and liabilities.
2. Income.

3. Advisors.
4. Process.

1. Financial Assets and Liabilities

Financial assets are the dollar values of your assets and your liabilities, including your expected Social Security and other pension benefits. You should prepare a personal financial statement or engage the services of a wealth advisor or CPA to help you prepare this important document. This is necessary for you to determine where you are today in relation to your being able to live a lifetime in the lifestyle that you wish, with a very low probability of outliving your assets. You should gather documents such as:

- Income tax returns.
- Brokerage statements.
- Mortgage statements.
- 401(k) plan statements.
- Insurance policy contracts for life, health, disability, property and casualty, and long-term care.
- Bank account statements.
- Estate documents such as wills, trusts, powers of attorney and health-care directives.
- Business documents such as buy-sell contracts.

In addition, ask the following:
- What assets do you own?
- What assets does your spouse own?
- What assets are jointly owned?
- What assets are held in trusts?

Describe your retirement plan:
- What life insurance do you have? Describe its type, face value, cash value, and ownership structure.
- What property—including real estate, art and jewelry—do you have?
- What new assets do you expect to receive (such as stock options or proceeds from sale of business)?

2. Income

Now that you have addressed what you own and what you owe, we turn to examining one of the most important questions for every retiree: What is your income going to be?

To answer this, you must answer the following:

- What is your current income?
- What is its source?
- How stable is your income?
- Are you still saving? How do you save or set aside money to invest? How is that likely to change in the next three years?
- When would you like to retire (if you haven't already)?
- What income do you need in retirement to fund the lifestyle you want?
- Where would you like to be when you are 50, 60, 70, 80, 90?
- What would you like your investments to achieve?
- Are you interested in leaving an estate? If so, to whom and how much?
- What do you want to do for your children, parents, siblings, other relatives, friends, and society?

3. Advisors

It is important to think about the advisors that are currently in your life. Typically, they would include your CPA, your private client attorney, and insurance professional. Identify what you currently like and value about working with each of these professionals. Next, think about what shortcomings may exist. What would the ideal advisor look like to you?

Specific questions include:

- Do you have an investment advisor or financial planner? How do you feel about the relationship?
- Do you have an attorney? How do you feel about the relationship?
- Do you have a tax professional? How do you feel about the relationship?
- Do you have a life insurance agent? How do you feel about the relationship?

4. Process

When you think about process, you want to focus primarily on how you will regularly update your own planning, or how involved you will want to be if you choose to work with a wealth management professional. How often will you want to meet or be updated on your plan? Do you prefer to be contacted by email or phone? Do you prefer meetings in person or through technology such as Skype or GoToMeeting? Are there any concerns about your other advisors?

More specifically you might focus on the following questions:

- How involved do you like to be in the investing process?
- What is the best way to contact you?
- How often would you prefer to meet with an advisor? Are there any specific issues an advisor should be sensitive to related to your financial confidentiality?

The One-Year Plan

How do we bring it together? First, either you or a financial advisor must test the veracity of your prioritized goals—your needs, wants, and wishes—against what you learned throughout Financial Discovery.

What if you've concluded that a goal is not feasible, the financial realities considered? You have two options:

1. Wait. As mentioned before, no one has sufficient time or money to do everything their heart desires in a single moment. Therefore, one must determine if all that is necessary is the passage of time (which often makes more money available).
2. Shift your plans. Maybe you determine you're not quite ready for the round-the-world sailing excursion, financially or personally, but you can reasonably take that Rhine River cruise. And we use the word shift quite purposefully, because the shift need not always appear in the form of an apparent downgrade to your plans. One of the best ways to consider the appropriate shift is to focus less on the specific goal and more on your vision. What is a similar goal that helps satisfy that vision or value that requires a different level of financial—or personal—sacrifice, but without sacrificing the vision or value?

Then, with a finalized list of personally and financially achievable goals, we recommend limiting your scope—because often the best way to achieve more goals is to have fewer of them—and arranging your goals in the form of a One-Year Plan. Here is an example:

Goal	Task	Concerns	Solutions	Next Actions
Start playing in mixed-doubles tennis league	Join Pleasant Valley Racket Club	Haven't played tennis in a long time	Sign up for refresher lessons	Set appt with PVRC membership
				Sign up for lessons
				Buy 2 new rackets
Plan and fund a big family trip for 2022	Determine the optimal location for trip	How to make everyone happy?	Work with a vacation consultant	Set meeting for consult
				Prepare 3 options
				Schedule family dinner to explore
Teach English as a second language	Explore options for teaching at community college	Does this opportunity even exist, or could it?	Schedule coffee with friend who teaches full-time at CC	Schedule coffee
				Explore non-credit course offerings

Please notice a few things about this simple instrument:

- There's a difference between a goal and a task. Often times a goal is comprised of many different tasks.
- There's a further difference between a task and a next action. Next actions should be as specific, measurable, and attainable as possible. It's literally the next thing you need to do, even if it appears obvious.
- We keep our concerns and their respective solutions in view to help ensure our momentum is maintained. When we arrive at a new concern, it should also be mentioned and solved.
- Like the LifeMap, the One-Year Plan is a living, breathing document that grows and changes along with you and your overall retirement life plan.

Summary

The Discovery process facilitates the crucial conversations that are necessary to develop an actionable and meaningful retirement life plan. Upon completion of the initial Discovery process, you will be well positioned to develop both your investment plan and strategies that ensure your plan is enhanced through customized income tax minimization, the prudent transfer of wealth to family members or charity, and protection from creditors and predators.

With that said, Discovery should not be thought of as being a one-and-done event. Instead, it should be considered a lifelong process. The reason is that the assumptions on which we build plans—our vision, values, goals and important relationships—often change. Thus, Discovery should be thought of as an ongoing process so that we make sure that the answers to the key questions have not changed in a way that would lead to altering plans.

Remember, having a successful life in retirement is more than about just financial issues. It is into those issues that we now dive as the next chapter moves on to addressing the investment issues you will face. Doing so will help ensure the effective funding of your retirement life plan, beginning with the all-important asset allocation decision.

CHAPTER 3

Asset Allocation

W E BEGIN THIS chapter on asset allocation with an important discussion on the difference between risk and uncertainty. Investing deals with both risk and uncertainty. In 1921, University of Chicago professor Frank Knight wrote the classic book, *Risk, Uncertainty, and Profit*. Knight defined risk and uncertainty as follows: "Risk is present when future events occur with measurable probability. Uncertainty is present when the likelihood of future events is indefinite or incalculable."

In some cases, we know the odds of an event occurring with certainty. The classic example is that we can calculate the odds of rolling any particular number with a pair of dice. Because of demographic data, we can make a good estimate of the odds a 65-year-old couple will have at least one spouse live beyond age 90. We cannot know the odds precisely because there may be future advances in medical science extending life expectancy. Conversely, new diseases may arise, shortening it. Other examples of uncertainty are: the odds of an oil embargo (1973), the odds of an event such as the attacks of September 11, 2001, or the odds of North Korea launching a nuclear missile. That concept is uncertainty.

It is critical to understand the important difference between these two concepts, risk and uncertainty. Consider the following example. An insurance company might be willing to accept a certain amount of hurricane risk in Dade and Broward Counties in Florida. They would price insuring this risk based on perhaps 100 years of data that includes the likelihood of hurricanes occurring and the extent of their damage. But only a foolish insurer would place a bet large enough to bankrupt the company if more or worse hurricanes occurred than in the past. That would be ignoring the uncertainty about the odds of hurricanes occurring—the future might not look like the past. (A number of insurers made this bad bet, incurring massive losses when Hurricane Andrew swept through Florida in 1991.)

Just as there are foolish insurance companies, there are foolish investors. The mistake many make is to think that equities have risk with odds that can be precisely calculated. This tendency appears with great regularity when economic conditions are good. Their "ability" to estimate the odds gives a false sense of confidence, leading them to decide on an equity allocation exceeding their ability, willingness, and need to take risk.

During crises the perception about equity investing shifts from risk to uncertainty. We often hear commentators use phrases like "there is a lack of clarity or visibility." Since we prefer risky bets (where we can calculate the odds) to uncertain bets (where the odds cannot be calculated), when we see markets as uncertain, the risk premium demanded rises. It is the rise in the risk premium that causes severe markets.

The historical evidence is clear that dramatic falls in prices lead to panicked selling as investors eventually reach their "GMO" point. The stomach screams, "Do Not Just Sit There. Do Something: Get Me Out!" Investors have demonstrated the unfortunate tendency to sell well after market declines have already occurred and buy well after rallies have long begun. The result is they dramatically underperform the very mutual funds in which they invest. That is why it is so important to understand that investing is always about uncertainty and you should never choose an asset allocation that exceeds your risk tolerance. Avoiding that mistake provides the greatest chance of letting our heads, not our stomachs, make investment decisions. Stomachs rarely make good decisions.

With this understanding of the difference between risk and uncertainty, we turn to discussing the role of the traditional assets of stocks and bonds in a portfolio.

From 1926 through 2019, the S&P 500 returned 10.2 percent per year, outperforming five-year Treasury bonds, which returned 5.1 percent per year, by 5.1 percent, and one-month Treasury bills (considered the riskless investment), which returned 3.3 percent per year, by 6.9 percent. Those higher returns were not a free lunch as they were accompanied by much greater volatility. The annual standard deviation of the S&P 500 was almost 20 percent, 3.5 times as great as that of five-year Treasuries, and more than six times that of one-month Treasuries. In other words, investors in stocks earned an equity risk premium for taking on much greater risk.

That leads us to understanding the role of stocks and bonds in a portfolio. Basically, because of the equity risk premium, the role of equities is to provide growth of the portfolio. The role of bonds then is to have an amount that is sufficient to dampen the risk of the overall portfolio to an acceptable level. With that understanding, we will look at the decision-making process you should use.

In their book, *Investments*, Zvi Bodie, Alex Kane and Alan Marcus define asset allocation as "the distribution of risky investments across broad asset classes." Taking a broader view, asset allocation can be defined as the process of investing assets in a manner reflecting one's unique ability, willingness and need to take risk. Consider these as three different tests.

The Three Tests

1. The Ability to Take Risk

An investor's ability to take risk is determined by four factors:

1. Investment horizon.
2. Stability of earned income.
3. Need for liquidity.
4. Options that can be exercised should there be a need for "Plan B."

We begin with the issue of the investment horizon. The longer the horizon, the greater the ability to wait out the virtually inevitable bear markets. In addition, the longer the investment horizon, the more likely equities will provide higher returns than fixed-income investments.

The following table provides a *guideline*, a starting point, for this part of the ability to take risk. For those who have read our prior books, while this is more conservative than prior tables, it is based on the outcomes from Monte Carlo simulations and minimum estimated odds of success of 90 percent. If you require a higher estimated success rate, you should be more conservative. Further, the maturity of the fixed income portion of your portfolio should not be longer than your time horizon. The reason is that the main role of fixed income in the portfolio should be safety, not return. Owning bonds whose maturity is beyond your investment horizon takes on risk that is inappropriate.

Ability to Take Risk

Investment Horizon (Years)	Maximum Equity Allocation (%)
0–3	0
4	10
5	20
6	30
7	40
8–9	50
10	60
11	70
12–15	80
16–19	90
20+	100

However, the investment horizon is not the only consideration: Labor (human) capital must also be considered. This asset is often overlooked because it does not appear on any traditional balance sheet.

An investor's ability to take risk is impacted by the stability of their labor (human) capital. We can define labor capital as the total value of an individual's labor. It is a unique asset because it varies by age, health, education, occupation, industry and experience, among other variables, and is non-tradeable and difficult to insure/hedge. The greater the stability of labor (earned income), the greater the ability to assume the risks of owning stocks. For example, tenured professors, doctors, or government employees have a greater ability to take risk than either a worker in a highly cyclical industry where layoffs are common, or an entrepreneur who owns a business with cyclical earnings. The reason is that the first group's earned income has bond-like characteristics. All other things being equal, it has a greater ability to hold stocks. The entrepreneur's earned income has equity-like characteristics, so should hold more bonds. In other words, investors should ask themselves, "Am I a stock or a bond?"

For some, particularly high-net-worth investors and those approaching retirement, labor capital may be a very small part of their overall wealth. For such investors, labor capital considerations should have less impact on the asset allocation decision. For others, labor capital is the dominant asset and should play a major role in the asset allocation decision.

A third factor impacting the ability to take risk is the need for liquidity, which is determined by the amount of near-term cash requirements as well as the potential for unanticipated calls on capital. The liquidity test begins by determining the amount of cash reserve one requires to meet unanticipated needs for cash such as medical bills, car and home repair, or job loss. Financial planners generally recommend a cash reserve of about six months of ordinary expenses.

The fourth factor impacting the ability to take risk is the presence (or absence) of options (a Plan B) one can exercise should a severe bear market create the risk the investment plan will fail. Options include delaying retirement, taking a part-time job, downsizing the current home, selling a second home, lowering consumption, or moving to a region with a lower cost of living. The more options one has and is willing to exercise, the more risk one can take.

2. The Willingness to Take Risk

The willingness to take risk is determined by what can be called the "stomach acid" test. Ask yourself these questions: Do I have the fortitude and discipline to stick with my predetermined investment strategy when the going gets tough? Will I be able to enjoy life and not lose sleep worrying about my portfolio? The answers to these questions help define your willingness to accept risk and play an important role in determining the percentage of equity assets allocated to a portfolio.

To a large degree, successful investment management depends on the investor's abilities to withstand periods of stress and overcome the severe emotional hurdles present during bear markets like the ones experienced in 1973–1974, 2000–2002 and 2008–2009.

The following table provides a guideline for investors to test their willingness to take risk.

Willingness to Take Risk

Maximum Tolerable Loss (%)	Maximum Equity Exposure (%)
10	10
15	20
20	30
25	40
30	50
40	60
45	70
50	80
55	90
60	100

3. The Need to Take Risk

The need to take risk is determined by the rate of return required to achieve the investor's financial objectives. The greater the rate of return needed to achieve one's financial objective, the more equity (and/or small and value) risk one needs to take. A critical part of the process is differentiating between real needs and desires. These are very personal decisions, with no right answers. However, the further one is from being able to provide for what they identify as their needs, the more risk one will need to take.

Therefore, in considering the financial objective, carefully consider what economists call the marginal utility of wealth—how much any potential incremental wealth is worth relative to the risk that must be accepted in order to achieve a greater *expected* return. While more money is always better than less, at some point most people achieve a lifestyle with which they are very comfortable. At that point, taking on incremental risk to achieve a higher net worth no longer makes sense: The potential damage of an unexpected negative outcome far exceeds any benefit gained from incremental wealth. Put another way, to most people, the possibility of going from rich to poor is unthinkable. And staying rich requires an entirely different approach to getting rich. One gets rich by working hard (or being lucky to inherit wealth) and taking risks (often big ones). However, one stays rich by limiting risk and not spending too much.

Each investor needs to decide at what level of wealth their unique utility of wealth curve starts flattening out and begins bending sharply to the right. Beyond this point there is little reason to take incremental risk to achieve a higher expected return. Many wealthy investors have experienced devastating losses that could easily have been avoided if they had the wisdom to know what author Joseph Heller knew. Kurt Vonnegut told this story about Heller:

> "Heller and I were at a party given by a billionaire on Shelter Island. I said, 'Joe, how does it make you feel to know that our host only yesterday may have made more money than your novel *Catch-22* has earned in its entire history?' Joe said, 'I've got something he can never have.' And I said, 'What on earth could that be, Joe?' And Joe said, 'The knowledge that I've got *enough*.'"

The lesson about knowing when enough is enough can be learned from the following incident. In March of 2003, Larry was in Rochester, Minnesota for a seminar based on his book, *Rational Investing in Irrational Times, How to Avoid the Costly Mistakes Even Smart People Make*. During his visit, he met with a 71-year-old couple with financial assets of $3 million. Three years earlier their portfolio was worth $13 million. The only way they could have experienced that kind of loss was if they had held a portfolio that was almost all equities and heavily concentrated in U.S. large-cap growth stocks, especially technology stocks. They confirmed this. They told Larry that they had been working with a financial advisor during this period—demonstrating that while good advice does not have to be expensive, bad advice almost always costs you dearly.

Larry asked the couple if, instead of their portfolio falling almost 80 percent, it doubled to $26 million, would it have led to any meaningful change in the quality of their lives? The response was a definitive no. Larry told them the experience of watching $13 million shrink to $3 million must have been very painful. In addition, they probably had spent many sleepless nights. They agreed. He then asked why they had taken the risks they did, knowing the potential benefit was not going to change their lives very much, but a negative outcome like the one they experienced would be so painful. The wife turned to the husband and punched him, exclaiming, "I told you so!"

Some risks are not worth taking. Prudent investors do not take more risk than they have the ability, willingness or need to take. Think about it this way: If you've already won the game, why still play?

When Conflicts Arise

When the analysis of your ability, willingness and need to take risk leads to the same conclusion, the asset allocation decision is easy. However, there are often conflicts. For example, one can have a high ability and willingness to take risk, but little need. In that case, the answer is simple: because the marginal utility of wealth is likely low, the need to take risk should dominate the decision. Sometimes the choices are more difficult. Consider the following situation with which Larry dealt.

Philip was an extremely nervous investor. His willingness to take risk would probably produce an equity allocation approaching zero. He knows, however, that a very low equity allocation is apt to produce very little, if any, growth in the real value of his portfolio. This directly conflicts with his personal objective to retire within 10 to 15 years. To attain this objective, Philip knows he must take more risk—he would have to choose an equity allocation of 80 percent. The lower the equity allocation, the longer he would have to continue in the workforce. His willingness to take risk proved to be in direct conflict with his personal goals. Larry told Philip there was no correct answer to this conundrum. He would have to choose which of his objectives would have greater priority— the need to sleep well or the desire for early retirement. Ultimately, Philip decided his early retirement objective should take priority. He realized this decision was apt to produce those sleepless nights and that his ability and willingness to stay the course might be sorely tested.

Choosing the higher equity allocation (taking more risk) was the right choice for Philip. However, it will not be the right choice for everyone. In general, we recommend choosing the lowest equity allocation derived from the three tests and then altering your goals. For example, if you find you have a higher need to take risk than your ability or willingness suggests, your plan should use the lower equity allocation recommended by the ability and willingness to take risks. Otherwise, if the risks show up—in the form of bear markets or negative events such as divorce or job loss—the plan will fail and you may not be able to successfully adapt to the change in circumstances. The alternative is to lower your goal, save more now and/or plan on working longer. As discussed earlier, the more options one has, the more risk one can take. Having said that, before taking a higher level of risk, make sure you are truly willing to exercise those options. While it may be possible to move to a lower cost of living area, if your spouse does not want to leave family or friends, it is not likely to be an option you can actually exercise.

The tables provided in this chapter are useful tools, good starting points for deliberations on the asset allocation decision, but many other factors influence that decision. The following sections provide examples to help you make the appropriate recommendation. With that said, the use of a Monte Carlo simulator (see Chapter 5) is also highly recommended for determining your asset allocation. In fact, in most cases, we do not know how you can make an informed decision without utilizing a Monte Carlo simulator—while there are various rules of thumb, they may not apply to your specific situation.

Asset Allocation Decisions

Equities versus Fixed Income

This is the most important asset allocation decision and the primary determinant of the expected return and risk of a portfolio. We will now examine reasons why an investor should consider having a higher or lower equity allocation.

Reasons to Increase Equity Exposure

- **Longer time horizon.** Younger investors have more human capital (more future labor income) to offset investment risk. In addition, investors with longer horizons have the ability to "wait out" a bear market without being forced to sell in order to meet cash flow needs. This is especially true for investors who are still working. The longer your time horizon, the less likely equities will underperform fixed income investments.
- **High level of job stability.** This is particularly true for individuals with income from jobs having little or no correlation to the economic risks of equity investing and the economy in general. A doctor or a tenured professor has income with bond-like characteristics. A business owner whose income is affected by the performance of the stock market, or does poorly when the economy is doing poorly, has income with more equity-like characteristics.
- **High tolerance for risk.** These individuals may have a full understanding and faith that in the long run they will likely be compensated with higher returns for the increased risk. Or, they may simply not watch their accounts closely. Most importantly, they are willing to accept the consequences if returns are well below those of safe fixed income investments.
- **Need for higher returns to reach financial goals.** In these cases, the willingness and ability to take risk should be carefully evaluated against the need to take risk to ensure the investor fully understands the implications. An alternative to taking extra risk would be to either cut current consumption (providing more investment capital), or to revise goals to ones less financially demanding.
- **Retirees with multiple streams of stable income (such as pensions and Social Security) that are relatively high compared to needs.** We

can view these streams of income as quasi-fixed income exposure. High-net-worth investors may also have other streams of income affecting the allocation process.

- **High marginal utility of wealth.** Those whose next dollar earned provides a high marginal utility will have a high willingness and perhaps high need to take risk.

- **Ability to adjust the "supply" of human capital.** Consider the following: You develop a financial plan allowing you to retire at age 65. However, the market's return falls below the expected return. Or you do not save as much as you expected. You need to work longer. To evaluate the situation, you need to answer questions such as: Will you have the ability to continue in the labor force? What level of income will you be able to generate? Will the market allow you to sell your skills, and at what price? Younger workers typically have more ability to adjust their supply of human capital. Those with a variety of skill sets also have a greater ability to adjust their supply to economic conditions. Those with more ability to adjust their supply of human capital can take more equity risk.

- **The presence of options one can exercise should a severe bear market create the risk the investment plan will fail.** The more options one has, the more risk one can take. It is critical to only include options one is actually prepared to exercise.

Reasons to Reduce Equity Exposure

The reasons to reduce equity exposure are the opposite of those above, with one additional issue to consider: Human capital should have less impact on appropriate allocations for retirees or high-net-worth investors, who typically have no earned income or minimal earned income relative to their net worth.

U.S. Equity versus International Equity

Investing in international stocks provides the benefit of diversifying the economic and geopolitical risks of domestic investing. There have been long periods when stocks performed relatively poorly compared to international stocks. And the reverse has also been true. Today, the U.S. market makes up about 50 percent of the global equity market. Developed markets account for about three-eighths of the global market capitalization, with emerging markets accounting the remaining one-eighth. Since the evidence suggests that there is no reason to believe that you can allocate capital more efficiently than the collective wisdom of the market, an allocation of 50 percent U.S., 37.5 percent international developed markets, and 12.5 percent emerging markets is a good starting point. Having said that, there is a reason for having at least some home country bias—international investing is a bit more expensive.

First, fund expense ratios are a bit higher. Second, trading costs in the form of bid/offer spreads and commissions tend to be higher. Third, other costs such as custodial fees and stamp taxes are greater outside the U.S.

The logic of diversifying economic and political risks is why investors should consider allocating at least 30 percent, and as much as 50 percent, of their equity holdings to international equities. This is especially important for those employed in the United States, as their labor capital is likely more correlated with domestic risks. Unfortunately, due to what is called home country bias (confusing familiarity with safety), most investors have less than a 20 percent allocation to international equities. Note that this is not just a U.S. phenomenon.

To obtain the greatest diversification benefit, the exposure to international equities should be unhedged. The reason is that while hedging the currency risk dampens the volatility of the equity portfolio, it increases the correlation of returns of international stocks to U.S. equities.

Reasons to Increase International Equity Exposure

- **Investor has non-U.S. dollar expenses.** An investor may live part of the year overseas, or frequently travel overseas. The investor should consider tailoring the portfolio to gain specific exposure to the currency in which the expenses are incurred. This could also be accomplished by making fixed income investments in the local currency.

Reasons to Decrease International Equity Exposure

- **Tracking error.** Tracking error is defined as underperformance versus a benchmark. Some investors may not be able to stomach the tracking error associated with a portfolio with 40 percent or 50 percent of equity invested internationally.

Emerging Markets

Emerging markets comprise those nations whose economies are considered developing or emerging from underdevelopment, including almost all of Africa, Eastern Europe, Latin America, Russia, the Middle East and much of Asia, excluding Japan, Hong Kong and Singapore. Many investors shy away from emerging markets, viewing them as either highly risky investments or pure speculations. The fact that emerging markets are risky should not preclude investors from allocating some portion of their portfolio to them because sometimes we can add risky assets and actually reduce the risk of the overall portfolio—when the correlation of returns is low.

Another reason to consider investing in emerging markets is that because it is a risky asset class, an efficient market will appropriately price that risk. The result is higher expected returns. They also have low correlations to both domestic and developed international markets, providing diversification benefits.

Reasons to Increase Emerging Markets Equity Exposure

- **Increased expected return.** The primary reason to increase one's allocation to emerging markets is to increase the expected return of the portfolio. Investors who need to increase their expected return to meet their financial goals can use an allocation to emerging markets to help meet this objective.

Reasons to Decrease Emerging Markets Equity Exposure

- **Tracking error.** Emerging markets equity has a relatively low correlation with both the overall U.S. markets and international developed markets. Therefore, emerging markets' returns may be below their average when the U.S. and/or other developed markets are producing above average returns. Some investors may not be able to tolerate this tracking error. Also, the correlation of emerging markets equity could be high enough in some periods that inclusion of a large allocation to emerging markets could actually increase the volatility of the overall portfolio to an unacceptable level.

It is also important to understand that the correlation of emerging markets to other equity asset classes typically rises during periods of financial turmoil. Thus, when the low correlation is most needed, the correlation is likely to increase. Investors who are either highly sensitive to tracking error risk or highly risk averse should consider limiting their exposure to emerging markets.

There are two other major asset classes we need to discuss.

The Three-Factor Model

In their June 1992 *Journal of Finance* article, "The Cross-Section of Expected Stock Returns," professors Eugene F. Fama and Kenneth R. French revolutionized the way we think about investing. Prior to the publication of this study, the prevailing theory (known as the "capital asset pricing model" or CAPM) was that the risk and return of a portfolio was largely determined by one factor: market beta. Market beta is a measure of equity-type risk of a stock, mutual fund or portfolio, relative to the risk of the overall U.S. stock market. An asset with a beta greater than one has more equity-type risk than the overall market; one with a beta less than one has less equity-type risk than the overall market.

Fama and French demonstrated that we actually live in a three-factor world—the risk and return of a portfolio is also explained by its exposure to two other risk factors: size and price. Fama and French hypothesized that while small-cap and value stocks (stocks with low prices relative to metrics such as earnings, book value, and cash flow) have higher beta—more equity-type risk—they also have additional risk unrelated to beta. Thus, small-cap and value stocks are riskier than large-cap and growth stocks, explaining their higher historical returns and implying such stocks should have higher expected returns in the future. Studies have confirmed the three-factor model explains more than 90 percent of the returns of diversified equity portfolios.

Using the Fama-French data series for the period from 1927 through 2019, the average annual returns to these three risks factors were:

1. Market Factor (the return of the all-equity universe minus the return on one-month Treasury bills): 8.6 percent.
2. Size Factor (the return of small-cap stocks minus the return of large-cap stocks): 3.1 percent.
3. Price Factor (the return of high book-to-market [value] stocks minus the return of low book-to-market [growth] stocks): 4.5 percent.

Independent Risk Factors

Size and price are independent (unique) risk factors in that they provide investors with exposure to different risks than those provided by exposure to market risks. Evidence of this independence can be seen when we examine the historical correlations of the size and price factors to the market factor. High correlations would mean the risk factors would be relatively good substitutes for each other. If that were the case, while investors could increase the expected return (and risk) of the portfolio by increasing their exposure to these risk factors, there would be no real diversification benefit. If the correlations are low, investors could both increase expected returns for a given level of risk and gain a diversification benefit.

For the period from 1927 through 2019, the correlation of the market risk factor to the size risk factor was a low 0.32 and its correlation to the price risk factor was a very low 0.24. The correlation of the size risk factor to the price risk factor was also very low at 0.13. In other words, one can effectively diversify equity risks by diversifying across the three independent risk factors, and each risk factor has the potential for increasing investment returns. Thus, investors should at least consider having more exposure to these factors (or asset classes) than does the market portfolio.

Value versus Growth

When thinking about the guidelines below, remember that the market portfolio is completely neutral with respect to value and growth exposure. It is neither value nor growth-tilted. Most investors with value-tilted portfolios choose to do so for one of two reasons. They believe either:

1. **Value stocks are riskier than growth stocks.** Therefore, value stocks should provide a risk premium in the same way that equities should provide a risk premium over the return of safer fixed income investments. This is the traditional finance point of view.
2. **Value stocks are not riskier than growth stocks.** They believe investors systematically overprice growth stocks and underprice value stocks. The value premium is a free lunch, not a risk premium. They argue that value stocks provide superior risk-adjusted returns than growth stocks. This is the behavioral finance point of view. Behavioralists use the internet and technology bubble of the late 1990s to bolster their argument.

Our view is that the issue is neither black nor white, with both traditionalists and behavioralists being partially right: value stocks are riskier than growth stocks, but the risk premium has been too large to be explained totally by the excess risk. In other words, while it may not be a free lunch, it just might be a free stop at the dessert tray.

For discussion purposes, we will assume the traditional financial view of the value premium being a risk story, but it is helpful to be aware of all viewpoints.

Reasons to Increase Value Exposure

- **Increased expected return with increased risk.** From a traditional finance point of view, investors should tilt toward value if they need to increase the expected return of their portfolios to meet their goals—but only if they are willing and able to accept the incremental risk of value stocks.
- **Diversification of sources of risk.** Consider an investor needing a certain rate of return to achieve his goals. That rate of return can be achieved with a certain exposure to beta (total stock market) risk. The appropriate allocation to the total market (which has no value exposure) might be 60 percent. Another way to achieve the same goal is to lower the exposure to beta (50 percent), but add sufficient value exposure so the two portfolios have the same expected return. Historically, the value-tilted portfolio with a lower exposure to beta has exhibited less volatility. The reasons are that the value premium has been less volatile than the equity premium and has had low correlation to the equity risk premium. We discuss this further in the next chapter.

Reasons to Decrease Value Exposure (or Maintain a "Market" Exposure)

- **Reduced risk.** Those taking the traditional finance point of view should favor tilting towards growth stocks to reduce portfolio risk. Investors exposed to value risk factors in ways other than their investments should use this strategy. This includes owners of distressed businesses and employees and top-level managers of value companies. For this type of investor, a neutral exposure to value or even a growth tilt (compared to the market) may be more appropriate.
- **Tracking error.** Portfolios tilted toward value will not move in lockstep with the overall market. Investors with value-tilted portfolios must be able to stomach the tracking error occurring during the inevitable periods of value underperformance. Depending on the investor, a more neutral exposure to value might make sense.
- **An owner or employee of a value company should probably not tilt as heavily toward value stocks as a tenured professor.** Other individuals who should consider not tilting to value stocks (or limiting their tilt) are construction workers, automobile workers, or any employee or owner of a highly cyclical business. For these investors, a neutral exposure to value, or even a growth tilt (compared to the market), might be more appropriate.

Small-Cap versus Large-Cap

Considerations on how much to invest in small-cap stocks versus large-cap stocks are basically the same as for the value versus growth decision. Small-cap stock risk tends to appear during periods of economic distress, which is when value stocks also tend to perform poorly. Large-cap stocks tend to perform better during these periods because large companies have more diverse sources of capital, are less likely to be cut off from those sources, and are less prone to bankruptcy.

Reasons to Increase Small-Cap Exposure

- **Increased expected return with increased risk.** Investors should tilt toward small-cap stocks if they need to increase the expected return from their portfolios to meet their goals—but only if they are willing and able to accept the incremental risk of small-cap stocks.
- **Stable human capital.** Investors not particularly exposed to economic cycle risk might consider tilting their portfolios toward small-cap stocks. Doctors, tenured professors, and retirees with defined benefits generally fit this description. Advertising company executives, construction workers,

and most commissioned salespeople are more exposed to this type of economic cycle risk.

- **Diversification of sources of risk.** As was discussed in the value section, tilting more to small-cap stocks while lowering the exposure to market beta maintains the expected return of the portfolio while reducing the potential dispersion of returns. The diversification benefit arises from the low correlation of the size risk factor to both the market risk and value risk factors.

Reasons to Decrease Small-Cap Exposure

- **Less stable human capital.** Tilting toward large-cap stocks might be a valid strategy for investors vulnerable to periods of economic distress. Investors whose business, employment or income might be negatively affected by a poor economy might want to tilt toward larger, safer stocks.
- **Lower risk.** Tilting toward large-cap stocks reduces the volatility of a portfolio. Risk averse investors and those with a low marginal utility of wealth may prefer to focus on reducing volatility as opposed to maximizing returns.
- **You are a small business owner whose company tends to do poorly when the overall economy does poorly.** With inherent exposure to small-cap risk, you might want to tilt toward large-cap stocks.

New Factors Uncovered

Advances in our understanding of asset prices and returns did not end with the introduction of the Fama-French three-factor model. Since then, three other unique factors have been identified that have provided premiums that have been persistent across time and economic regimes, pervasive across the globe and asset classes, are robust to various definitions, are implementable (survive transaction costs), and have intuitive risk- or behavioral-based explanations for why we should expect them to continue.

The three factors are momentum (stocks with positive momentum outperform those with negative momentum), profitability (more profitable companies outperform less profitable ones), and quality (high-quality companies outperform low-quality companies). Quality stocks have the following characteristics: low earnings volatility, high margins, high asset turnover (indicating efficient use of assets), low financial leverage (low debt-to-equity ratio), low operating leverage (indicating a strong balance sheet and low macroeconomic risk), and low stock-specific risk (volatility that is unexplained by macroeconomic activity).

From 1927 through 2019, the momentum premium was 9.1 percent. From 1964 through 2019, the profitability premium was 3.3 percent. And from 1958 through 2019, the quality premium was 4.6 percent.

In addition, these three factors would have provided important diversification benefits, as from 1964 through 2019: the momentum factor was negatively correlated with market beta (-0.2), size (-0.1) and value (-0.2); the profitability premium was negatively correlated with market beta (-0.3) and size (-0.2), and had very low correlation with value (0.1); and the quality premium was negatively correlated with market beta (-0.6), size (-0.5), and was uncorrelated with value (0.0).

Note that the profitability and quality factors could be considered "kissing cousins." They are related because one of the traits of quality companies is that they are profitable (have high margins). This explains why they were highly correlated over the period (0.7). The implications are that investors who have exposures to market beta, size, and value should consider adding exposure to momentum, profitability and/or quality.

There is one other asset we need to cover—gold.

Gold

Investor interest in gold tends to arise from three beliefs. The primary one is the belief that gold is a great hedge against inflation. This is a particularly important issue for retirees whose assets include non-inflation-adjusted pensions and payout annuities that do not include an inflation adjustment. The second belief is that gold provides a hedge against currency risk. The third belief is that gold can act as a haven of safety in bad times. Are these valid reasons?

We begin by addressing the issue, "is gold a good inflation hedge?" The following example should provide the answer. On January 21, 1980, the price of gold reached a then record high of $850. On March 19, 2002, gold was trading at $293, well below where it was 20 years earlier. Note that the inflation rate for the period from 1980 through 2001 was 3.9 percent. Thus, gold's loss in real purchasing power was about 85 percent. How can gold be an inflation hedge when over the course of 22 years it loses 85 percent in real terms?

As additional evidence of gold's inflation hedging abilities, Goldman Sach's "2013 Outlook" contained the following finding: During the post-World War II era, in 60 percent of episodes when inflation surprised to the upside, gold underperformed inflation. That said, gold has been a good hedge of inflation over the very long run.

In their study "The Golden Dilemma," published in the July/August issue of the *Financial Analysts Journal*, Clause Erb and Campbell Harvey presented evidence that led them to conclude that there is little relation between the nominal price of gold and inflation when measured over even 10-year periods.

However, they also presented two pieces of evidence suggesting that gold does hold its value over the very long run. Their first example was that the wage of a Roman centurion (in gold) was approximately the same as the pay earned by a U.S. Army captain today. They also showed that the price of bread (again in gold) thousands of years ago was about the same as we would pay today at an upscale bakery. Unfortunately, that is a much longer investment horizon than that of most investors. It is also a very long time to go without earning any real return! In terms of being a currency hedge, Erb and Harvey found that the change in the real price of gold was largely independent of the change in currency values. In other words, gold is not a good hedge of currency risk.

As for gold serving as a safe haven, meaning that it is stable during bear markets in stocks, Erb and Harvey found gold was not quite the excellent hedge some might think. It turns out that 17 percent of monthly stock returns fall into the category where the price of gold was falling at the same time stocks posted negative returns. If gold acts as a true safe haven, then we would expect very few, if any, such observations. Still, 83 percent of the time on the right side is not a bad record.

The conclusion we draw is that despite having some value in terms of being a safe haven in bear markets, gold's lack of value as an inflation hedge over any reasonable time horizon, its lack of value as a currency hedge, and the fact that it has provided no real return for centuries, means there are far better alternatives for you to consider including in your portfolio.

We next discuss how to view assets that do not appear on most investors' balance sheets: their home and their Social Security benefit.

Your Home

A home is very different from financial assets. You cannot perform the normal portfolio maintenance tasks such as rebalancing and tax management. While clearly an asset with value that should appear on the balance sheet and be considered a possible source to fund future cash flow needs (through a reverse mortgage, rental, or sale), a home should be excluded from consideration when thinking about asset allocation.

Social Security

The Social Security benefit should be treated as an income stream that reduces the need to take the risks required to achieve your financial goal. By reducing the need to take risk (by the amount of the benefit), the allocation to less risky fixed income assets can be increased, and required allocation to riskier equity asset classes reduced. All pensions from stable sources can be treated in the same way.

As we have mentioned, investment plans should include contingency plans (Plan Bs) that can be implemented if the unexpected occurs.

The Need for Plan B

Investment plans should consider both the expected returns on equities and bonds, and the possibility returns could be well below those expectations. For example, it is likely that in January 1990, few Japanese investors expected Japanese large-cap stocks to produce no return (even before considering inflation) over the next 29 years (through 2018). Another example: The S&P 500 Index produced negative real returns over the 14-year period from 1969 through 1982, losing 0.8 percent per year in real terms.

Since we know severe bear markets are likely to occur from time to time, but cannot know how long they will last, a critical part of the financial planning process is developing a contingency plan (Plan B)—a plan of action implemented if a "black swan" (a major unexpected event) appears. The plan should detail what actions should be taken if financial assets fall to such a degree the investor runs an unacceptably high level of risk of failure. For example, their portfolio may run out of assets if Plan A is not adapted to the existing reality. Or, it may be an investor has an important bequeathment goal they do not want put at risk, such as a special needs child.

Plan B should list the actions to be taken if financial assets drop below a predetermined level. Those actions might include remaining in, or returning to, the workforce, reducing current spending, reducing the financial goal, and selling a home and/or moving to a location with a lower cost of living. Consider the following example.

Mr. and Mrs. Smith

It is 1993, and Mr. and Mrs. Smith are each 40. Mrs. Smith is a successful dentist and Mr. Smith is a CPA. They both plan to retire at 65. Working with their advisor, they decide their risk tolerance means holding a portfolio with a "worst case" cumulative loss of 25 percent. Thus, they decide to set their equity allocation at 40 percent. Based on historical evidence, the Smiths know there is a reasonably high probability their portfolio will not experience a cumulative loss of more than 25 percent. However, they also know it is possible a greater loss could occur. A Monte Carlo simulation (see Chapter 5) shows their plan has a 93 percent chance of success.

The mistake many investors make is to focus solely on the high odds of success and ignore the odds of failure. That is the same mistake as not buying life insurance because the odds of dying in the near future are so low. The

Smiths do not make that mistake. They recognize the possibility of failure exists, but do not plan on that scenario as the "base case."

The Worst Case Should Not Be the Base Case

Using the worst case as the base case means that ability to take risk is low, so returns are going to be low. Therefore, investors making the worst case their base case will reduce risk. However, they will have significantly less to spend in retirement than if they had not done so and the worst never happened.

The Smiths had worked hard, saved well, and wanted to enjoy the rewards of their efforts. But they did not ignore the risk of the possibility of "failure." They agreed with their advisor that if a bear market occurred, resulting in a new Monte Carlo simulation producing odds of success of less than 85 percent, they would consider taking some or all of the following steps, depending on the size of their losses:

- Sell their second home.
- Reduce their daily spending requirements by 10 percent.
- Reduce their travel budget by 50 percent.
- Continue working until at least age 65.
- Move to a region with a lower cost of living.

While the Smiths hoped they would never have to execute any of these steps, they did recognize the risk that it could be necessary, and were prepared to do so. They had their Plan B in place.

Returning to our example, for the next several years the Smiths lived well and enjoyed their lifestyle. In fact, returns were well above their expectations. Eventually their Monte Carlo simulation showed that they could reduce their equity exposure to 50 percent without lowering their odds of success. And when the 2000 bear market arrived they not only were well prepared for it, but having lowered their equity allocation they experienced smaller losses than they would have otherwise.

If we took the same situation and moved the start date to 2005, when the financial crisis of 2008 hit, the Smiths would have been well prepared to take the steps needed to prevent their plan from failing.

As you can see, there are many issues that need to be considered before you can develop a formal investment plan in the form of an investment policy statement and the regular care and maintenance of your investment plan, which is where we are going next.

CHAPTER 4

The Investment Policy Statement and the Care and Maintenance of the Portfolio

A FORMAL INVESTMENT policy statement (IPS) is the foundation of the investment plan, serving as a guidepost that helps provide the discipline needed to adhere to your strategy over time. Using the information contained in Chapter 3, the IPS should clearly state:

- The objectives/goals you have for your financial assets, such as preservation of capital or growth of capital.
- The planning horizon—how long is the portfolio expected to last?
- Your ability, willingness, and need to take risk—are you a conservative or aggressive investor?
- The maximum loss expected in a 12-month period and the maximum drawdown.
- Your need for liquidity—assets held in reserve to meet emergency needs.
- Your investment philosophy—active management or passive management (discussed in Chapter 6).
- The rate of return required to achieve your goals.
- Who is responsible for monitoring and managing the portfolio (a family member or a financial advisor), what regular actions will be taken, and a timetable for those actions (monthly, quarterly, annually, and so on)?
- Who has authority to take actions or delegate the authority to act to others?
- How often performance reports will be generated—tracking performance against the plan and its goals so that appropriate adjustments can be made along the way.
- How assets are to be allocated across different investments—we provide a sample IPS table later in the chapter.

- How assets are to be located across taxable, tax-advantaged, and tax-free accounts.
- The credit quality requirements for fixed income assets, as well as their maturity.
- Your willingness to accept tracking error risk.
- Your cash flow requirements.

A Living Document

It is important to understand that writing an IPS is not a "set it and forget it" endeavor. It must be viewed as a living document. Whenever any of the Plan's underlying assumptions change, the IPS should be altered to adapt to the change. Life-altering events (a death in the family, divorce, a large inheritance, or loss of job) can impact the asset allocation decision in dramatic ways. Thus, the IPS, and resulting asset allocation decisions, should be reviewed whenever a major life event occurs.

Even market movements can lead to a change in the assumptions behind the IPS and the portfolio's asset allocations. For example, a major bull market, like the one we experienced in the 1990s, lowered the need to take risk for those investors who began the decade with a significant accumulation of capital. At the same time, the rise in prices lowered future expected returns, having the opposite effect on those with minimal amounts of capital (perhaps just beginning their investment careers). The lowering of expected returns to equities meant that to achieve the same expected return investors would have to allocate more capital to equities than would have been the case had returns been lower in the past. The reverse is true of bear markets. A bear market raises the need to take risk for those with significant capital accumulation while lowering it for those with little. A good policy is to review the IPS and its assumptions at least annually.

The Care and Maintenance of the Portfolio

Think of your portfolio like a garden: To keep it producing the desired results, it needs disciplined care, weeding, and nourishing. Your investment portfolio also requires regular maintenance to control the most important determinant of its risk—the portfolio's asset allocation. The way to maintain control is through rebalancing—the ongoing process of restoring a portfolio to its original asset allocations and risk profile. The reason that rebalancing is an ongoing process is that each investment within the portfolio is likely to change in value by a different percentage over time, altering the risk of the portfolio.

The Rebalancing Process

There are two ways to rebalance. The first is to sell one or more funds to raise sufficient cash to purchase the appropriate amount of one or more other funds. The other way is to use money being added or withdrawn from the portfolio to adjust asset classes to their targeted levels. A combination of the two strategies can be used. Utilizing cash being added is preferred, as it reduces transactions costs and for taxable accounts reduces/eliminates the generation of capital gains. Whenever new cash is available for investment purposes, it should be used to rebalance the portfolio.

One strategy that can be employed is having distributions paid in cash rather than automatically reinvested, using that cash to rebalance. When making this decision, consider the size of the portfolio and size of the transactions costs. For small accounts, where transactions costs are present, this might not be a good strategy. Here are some other recommendations on the rebalancing process:

- As previously discussed, whenever new cash is available it should be used to rebalance the portfolio. This may limit the number of trades required and also minimize the need to realize taxable gains.
- If rebalancing is required, consider if incremental funds will become available in the near future—a tax refund, a bonus, or proceeds from a sale. If capital gains taxes will be generated by rebalancing, it might be beneficial to wait until the new cash is available.
- Consider delaying rebalancing if it generates significant short-term capital gains. The size of the gain should be a major consideration: The larger the gain, the greater will be the benefit of waiting until long-term gains treatment can be obtained. Another consideration: How long before additional funds can be generated to rebalance?
- If capital gains taxes are generated, when possible use tax-advantaged accounts.
- In general, for taxable accounts do not rebalance if it results in the realization of short-term capital gains. Wait until either long-term gains can be realized, or until new cash becomes available. The exception would be if there were losses that could be used to offset the gains.
- When rebalancing requires the realization of gains, we suggest that rebalancing be performed only to the minimum/maximum ranges set (see sample rebalancing table on page 59), rather than to the target allocation.
- The exception to the guidance on minimizing the realization of gains when performing rebalancing is when there are long-term gains that can be realized from the sale of taxable fixed income investments. Here the "conventional wisdom" gets spun on its head. If there is a long-term gain that could be realized (whether for rebalancing purposes or not), investors in all but the lowest tax bracket should take it. The reason is that doing so

converts future interest income that would have been taxed at the ordinary income tax rate (e.g., 35 percent) into a long-term capital gain that is taxed at a much lower rate. Of course, the loss of the present value of having to pay taxes early and the costs of the transaction should be considered.

• Rebalancing should be considered in tax-deferred accounts first, if doing so avoids realizing capital gains. However, if capital losses are available, the rebalancing should be done in the taxable accounts. It is important to note that the belief, "if I have all asset classes represented in tax-deferred accounts, that will allow me to tax-efficiently rebalance in the future," is not correct. The reason is that the tax inefficiencies deriving from the wrong location are greater than any benefit when rebalancing is needed.

Reinvest Dividends and Capital Gains Distributions or Not?

For taxable accounts, the general recommendation is to not reinvest dividends and distributions. The reason is that the cash generated can be used to rebalance by buying what has performed relatively poorly. That either avoids, or at least minimizes, the need to sell what has performed relatively well (and having to realize capital gains). And it may minimize transactions costs as you are only buying, instead of buying and selling. In addition, if distributions are needed to meet cash flow needs, taking them as cash minimizes or avoids the need to sell assets (and the taxes that may be associated with that transaction).

There are some myths about rebalancing that we need to address.

Rebalancing Myths

The first myth about rebalancing is that it is a "reversion to the mean" strategy. This is false: Consider a portfolio with an asset allocation of 50 percent stocks/50 percent bonds. Stocks have returned 10 percent and are expected to return 10 percent, while bonds have returned 6 percent and are expected to return 6 percent. The first year stocks return 9 percent and bonds 7 percent. A strategy based on reversion to the mean of returns would sell bonds (since they produced above average returns) to buy stocks (since they produced below average returns). However, since the portfolio would then have an asset allocation of greater than 50 percent for stocks, rebalancing would require stocks be sold to buy more bonds, or buying sufficient bonds to increase the bond allocation to 50 percent.

The second myth about rebalancing is that it increases returns. That will not be the case most of the time. Most of the time rebalancing will require investors sell some of the higher expected returning asset class to purchase more of the lower expected returning asset class. For example, we would usually expect to have to sell stocks to buy fixed income assets. Similarly, we should expect we will mostly have to sell value stocks to buy growth stocks, small stocks to buy large stocks, and/or emerging market stocks to buy developed market stocks.

While achieving the objective of restoring the portfolio's risk profile, in each of these cases rebalancing lowers the expected return of the portfolio. This will not always be true. When bonds outperform stocks, rebalancing will increase the expected return of the portfolio, as you reduce the allocation of the lower expected returning asset class to increase the allocation of the higher expected returning asset class.

The Rebalancing Table

Your investment policy statement should include both an asset allocation table and rebalancing table. The table should include both the target levels for each asset class and the minimum and maximum levels to which the allocations will be allowed to drift. Some drift should be allowed to occur because rebalancing generally involves costs, including transactions fees and taxes in taxable accounts. We suggest using a 5/25 percent rule in an asset class's allocation before considering rebalancing. In other words, consider rebalancing if the change in an asset class's allocation is greater than either an absolute 5 percent or 25 percent of the original percentage allocation. The actual percentages used are not as important as having a specific plan and the discipline to adhere to the plan. In your own situation, a 4/20 rule might be as appropriate as a 5/25 rule.

Application of 5/25 Rule

Assume an asset class was given an allocation of 10 percent. Applying the 5 percent rule, one would rebalance only when that asset class's allocation had either risen to 15 percent (10 percent + 5 percent) or fallen to 5 percent (10 percent – 5 percent). Using the 25 percent rule, however, one would reallocate if the asset class had risen or fallen by just 2.5 percent (10 percent × 25 percent) to either 12.5 percent (10 percent + 2.5 percent) or 7.5 percent (10 percent – 2.5 percent). In this case the 25 percent figure is the governing factor.

If one had a 50 percent asset class allocation, the 5/25 percent rule would make the 5 percent figure the governing factor, since an absolute 5 percent is less than 25 percent of 50 percent (12.5 percent). So, one rebalances if either the 5 percent or 25 percent test indicates such a need.

The need for rebalancing should be checked at three levels.

1. The broad level of equities and fixed income.
2. The level of domestic and international asset classes.

3. The more narrowly defined individual asset class level, such as emerging markets, real estate, small-cap and value. In addition, if alternative strategies are included in the portfolio, they should be part of the table.

The following is an example of a rebalancing table using the recommended 5/25 rule.

Sample Rebalancing Table

Asset Class	Minimum Allocation (%)	Target Allocation (%)	Maximum Allocation (%)
U.S. Equity			
U.S. large	3.75	5	6.25
U.S. large value	3.75	5	6.25
U.S. small	3.75	5	6.25
U.S. small value	3.75	5	6.25
Real Estate	3.75	5	6.25
Total U.S.	**20**	**25**	**30**
International Equity			
International large	3.75	5	6.25
International large value	3.75	5	6.25
International small	3.75	5	6.25
International small value	3.75	5	6.25
Emerging markets	3.75	5	6.25
Total International	**20**	**25**	**30**
Total Equity	**45**	**50**	**55**
Alternative Investments			
Reinsurance	3.75	5	6.25
Alternative Lending	3.75	5	6.25
Total Alternatives	**7.5**	**10**	**12.5**
Nominal Bonds	15	20	25
TIPS	15	20	25
Total Fixed Income	**35**	**40**	**45**

We now turn to addressing tax management strategies.

Tax Management Strategies

In managing the portfolio for tax efficiency, the most important decisions are at the beginning—making sure asset location decisions are made correctly and utilizing the most tax-efficient vehicles such as core and tax-managed funds. However, there are other important strategies.

Tax Loss Harvesting

Tax management is a year-round job. Far too many investors wait until calendar year end to check for opportunities to harvest losses. They should be checked throughout the year.

A loss should be harvested whenever the value of tax deduction significantly exceeds the transaction cost of the trades required to harvest the loss, immediately reinvesting the proceeds in a manner avoiding the wash sale rule. Waiting until the end of the year is a mistake: Losses that might exist early in the year may no longer exist. In addition, it can be important to realize any short-term losses before they become long term. Short-term losses are first deducted against short-term gains that would otherwise be taxed at the higher ordinary income tax rates. Long-term losses are first deducted against long-term gains that would otherwise be taxed at the lower capital gains rate.

For example, before any loss harvesting, imagine a taxpayer has *realized* short- and long-term gains and *unrealized* short-term losses. These losses can be harvested, reducing the short-term gain that would have otherwise been taxed at higher ordinary tax rates. If not harvested until they became long-term losses, they would reduce long-term gains that would have been taxed at the lower long-term capital gains rate.

The Mechanics of Harvesting

Investors who tax-loss harvest reset their cost basis to a new lower level. The tax-rate differential then provides the opportunity to arbitrage the tax system. Here's how such arbitrage might work.

On January 1, 2019, you invest $10,000 in a fund. On March 1, 2019, the value of the fund has shrunk to $7,000. You sell the fund. Since the fund was held for less than one year, the loss is characterized as short term. Assuming a 35 percent ordinary federal income tax rate, you will have a $1,050 tax saving, leaving a net economic loss of $1,950.

Note that the deduction of capital losses in excess of capital gains is limited to a deduction against $3,000 of other income, though losses can be carried forward indefinitely during a taxpayer's lifetime. If there are net long-term gains in a given year, any net short-term losses not already used to offset short-term gains must be applied against those long-term gains, reducing the value of the deduction to that of the lower long-term capital gains rate.

Since you do not wish to be out of the market for 30 days—the time needed to avoid the "wash sale" rule—you use the $7,000 of sale proceeds to immediately purchase a similar fund. For example, if you had sold a Total Stock Market Fund you might purchase a Russell 1000 Fund. Since they would be similar in their exposures to the major determinants of equity risk, they have similar expected returns.

Continuing the example, jump forward to March 2, 2020 (one year and a day). Both the fund you sold and the one you purchased have each risen to $10,000. If you had simply held the first fund, you'd have had neither gain nor loss, and no tax benefit in the prior year. If, however, you harvested the loss, replaced the original fund with the similar fund and then sold it on March 2, 2020 (to repurchase the preferred holding), you would have a gain of $3,000 on which you would pay taxes at the long-term capital gains rate. Assume it is 20 percent. You owe taxes of $600 and have a net gain of $2,400. You picked up a $450 arbitrage of the tax system (by receiving a $1,050 tax savings in March 2019 and incurring only $600 more in March 2020), and gained the time value of the tax savings for a full year. Note you did not have to sell the fund in March 2020. If you'd continued to hold it, the tax on any unrealized gain would be deferred until the fund was sold. State taxes, if applicable, should also be considered.

Swapping Back

After the wash-sale time period has expired, you will likely want to swap back into the original holding. That can create further tax problems. If there is a further loss, there is no problem, as you simply harvest it. However, if there is a gain, it could be short term and taxed at ordinary income tax rates. Generally, you much prefer to pay taxes at the long-term capital gains rate. Harvesting the prior losses has mitigated part of the problem. You may be able to use the loss to offset gains. However, you should not assume that the losses generated will be available to offset the realized short-term gain, especially if the loss was long term in nature. It is important to be aware of gains realized in other areas of your portfolio. By selling only when a reasonably large loss is being harvested (see below), you can maximize the likelihood the harvest ends up being an overall benefit.

Here are some guidelines to help:

- We suggest taking only significant losses. You should establish a minimum percentage loss of the invested assets and a minimum absolute dollar. A loss is large enough to consider harvesting when it exceeds a predetermined hurdle. For example, you might set a hurdle of $5,000 for bonds and 2 percent of the value. For equities, hurdles of $5,000 and 5 percent might be set. However, for highly volatile asset classes like emerging markets, the hurdles might be $5,000 and 7.5 percent. The better the fit in terms of asset class exposure and greater the tax efficiency of the fund you are swapping into (while avoiding investments "substantially identical" to the original holding), the lower the hurdles can be.
- Switch back to the original fund if the following conditions are met:
  - You do not, and will not, have realized capital gains in other areas that will fully offset the long-term loss that was harvested.
  - The 31-day gain in the replacement investment is smaller than 1 percent.
- If the 31-day gain in the replacement investment is greater than 1 percent, we recommend staying in the replacement investment.
- Once the gain has matured to long-term capital gains treatment, we recommend switching back to the original fund if the gain is less than 2 percent.

When Does Similar Become Too Similar?

There are several mutual funds and ETFs that make good substitutes for one another. To avoid the wash sale rule, the investor cannot sell and buy two investments considered "substantially identical" in nature; the IRS would likely disallow the deduction. For example, selling one S&P 500 Index Fund and using the proceeds to buy another S&P 500 Index Fund is not recommended. Instead, an investor might purchase a Russell 1000 Fund. Its risk and expected return is substantially similar, but not substantially identical, thereby avoiding the wash rule. The sale of a tax-managed fund and purchase of a non-tax-managed fund in the same asset class would not constitute a wash sale. Always consult with a qualified tax advisor.

For individual bonds, the replacement bond must be "materially different" from the one sold. Although this term appears in the tax code and numerous IRS rulings, no specific rules define what makes one bond materially different from another. Also note that when swapping individual bonds for loss harvesting purposes, there is no need to reverse the swap after 31 days.

What if Capital Gains Taxes Rise in the Coming Years?

An increase in tax rates, including capital gains tax rates, may have a substantial impact on a portfolio, so should be considered when harvesting losses. For investors who may need to take withdrawals from their taxable accounts in the near future (to buy a house or support children in college), harvesting tax losses will reset the cost basis lower and may hurt more than help. A tax-loss harvest may save an investor 20 percent in capital gains taxes, but could cause the investor to pay an increased rate in the future on an even lower cost basis. This issue will have less effect on investors who do not expect to need withdrawals from their taxable accounts for many years.

There is one other point to consider: If you (1) have gains; (2) will need the money within a few years; and (3) believe tax rates will rise or your own tax bracket will be higher, you may want to harvest gains now to minimize total taxes.

Avoiding the Wash Sale Rule

The IRS prohibits claiming a loss on the sale of an investment if that same or substantially similar investment was purchased within 30 days before or after the sale date. The investor has a choice: Stay out of the market for 30 days after a tax loss harvesting transaction or immediately purchase a similar, but not substantially identical, investment.

Since a large percentage of the return over any long period typically comes in short bursts, we recommend immediately reinvesting the proceeds. If you're out of the market, you can miss out on those returns. For example, from 1926 through 2019, 189 out of 1,128 months (16.8 percent) produced returns to the total market in excess of 5 percent. Twenty-seven months had returns in excess of 10 percent, five in excess of 20 percent, and three in excess of 30 percent. Being out of the market for a month also meant you had a 10.2 percent chance (115 months out of 1,128) of avoiding a loss of at least 5 percent. So historically there has been a 70 percent greater likelihood you would "miss" a large gain instead of a large loss.

Given this evidence, the strategy should be to immediately reinvest the proceeds from any loss harvesting sales in similar funds. If there is another loss after 31 days the investor can swap back and receive yet another deduction, and again reset the cost basis. The evidence suggests there is about a one-in-six chance of having a gain in excess of 5 percent within the wash sale window. It is important to choose a substitute fund you would be willing to hold for a full year (in order to obtain long-term capital-gains treatment) or longer. Any choice should be low cost and tax efficient.

Other Tax Management Strategies

In general, never intentionally realize significant short-term gains. Do not sell any shares until the holding period is sufficient to qualify for the lower long-term capital gain rate. If your equity allocation is well above target, you may wish to override this suggestion, weighing the risks of an "excessive" allocation to equities versus the potential tax savings.

If a fund has been held for more than a year, always check to see what estimated distributions the fund plans to make during the year. Specifically focus on amounts that will be ordinary income, short-term capital gains and long-term capital gains. Most funds make distributions once a year, usually near the end of the year. Some make them more frequently, and sometimes they make special distributions. Check to see if there are going to be large distributions that will be treated as either ordinary income or short-term gains. If this is true, you might benefit from selling the fund before the record date. By doing so the increase in the net asset value will be treated as long-term capital gains, and taxes will be at the lower long-term rate. If the fund making the large payout is selling for less than your tax basis, consider selling the fund prior to the distribution. Otherwise you will have to pay taxes on the distribution, despite having an unrealized loss on the fund. Also consider the potential distribution from the replacement fund so you do not exacerbate the problem. Investors should coordinate any tax-planning activities with their CPA or tax attorney to ensure all activity is beneficial to their overall situation, not just when viewed in isolation.

Final Considerations

The following are some additional considerations to be addressed prior to implementing tax-loss harvesting:

- Any associated trading costs should be evaluated to ensure they do not exceed the value of the tax benefit.
- Be careful with reinvested dividends: They could trigger a wash sale if it occurs within 30 days.
- An investor might consider immediately repurchasing the sold security inside the investor's tax-advantaged account. This will not work—the IRS considers this a wash sale.

We now turn to the use of a critical planning tool, a Monte Carlo simulator.

CHAPTER 5

Monte Carlo Simulations

ONCE AN INVESTOR has exited the labor force, financial planning takes on greater significance than ever. The reason is that it is much more difficult, if not impossible, to recover from major mistakes. When investors are still gainfully employed they may be able to recover from even major planning mistakes. During your working life, a few bad years in terms of negative investment returns can be overcome, and wages generally at least keep pace with inflation. Being employed also provides other options, such as increasing savings or working longer to make up for any portfolio shortfall. In retirement, however, money is being withdrawn both in good and bad years. Thus, some options available while employed may no longer be available, viable, or desirable once you have left the workforce. These issues heighten the importance of having a well-thought-out retirement plan.

In "traditional" retirement planning, annual investment returns are assumed to be a constant number, such as 6 percent per year. Retirement planners arrive at this number based on a portfolio's asset allocation and on assumptions about the returns of various investments. Outcomes using this computation typically are presented as expected wealth values over the anticipated period of retirement.

The problem with this approach is that investment returns are not deterministic. While investing is about risk, retirement calculators that present single scenarios treat outcomes either as a certainty or, at best, a 50/50 proposition (for instance, the odds are 50/50 that you will do better or worse than the expected result). Investing is not a science in the same way physics is. No one knows with precision, beforehand, what the return of different investments will be over any given number of years. Investment returns are random variables, characterized by expected values (averages), standard deviations and, more generally, probability distributions. For this reason, projections of an investment program's possible results should also be expressed in terms of probabilities. For example, an expected outcome should be presented in terms such as:

- There is a 95 percent chance you will not run out of money in retirement.
- There is a 50 percent probability you will accumulate at least $3.1 million.
- There is a 25 percent chance you will accumulate $5.2 million or more. But, there is also a 10 percent chance you will accumulate only $400,000 or less.

To arrive at this type of conclusion, it is necessary to use a tool known as a Monte Carlo (MC) simulation.

MC simulations require a set of assumptions regarding time horizon, initial investment, asset allocation, withdrawals, savings, retirement income, rate of inflation, correlation among different asset classes and—very importantly—the return distributions of the portfolio.

In MC simulation programs, the growth of an investment portfolio is determined by two important inputs: portfolio average expected return and portfolio volatility, represented by the standard deviation measure. Based on these two inputs, the MC simulation program generates a sequence of random returns from which one return is applied in each incremental period (typically one year) of the simulation. This process is repeated thousands of times to calculate the likelihood of possible outcomes and their potential distributions.

MC simulations also provide another important benefit: They allow investors to view the outcomes of various strategies and how marginal adjustments in asset allocation change the odds of these outcomes. We will examine the results for a hypothetical investor who begins with a $1 million portfolio. An initial withdrawal is made equal to the specified withdrawal rate multiplied by the $1 million starting value. The remaining assets then grow or shrink per the asset returns in the replication for that year. At the end of the year, the portfolio is rebalanced back to the investor's target allocation. In subsequent years, the withdrawal is the prior year's withdrawal plus inflation for that year. Withdrawals are made at the start of each year. It is assumed that taxes are included in the withdrawal amount.

The table overleaf shows the real return capital market assumptions used in the MC simulations that follow (they are the assumptions we were using in 2017). It is important to note that the results from any MC simulation will be based on its inputs. If we were to use different capital markets assumptions, the results in the tables that follow would be very different. We build capital market assumptions using current valuations and yields, so these assumptions will change over time.

This last point about changing assumptions is a critical one. Bull and bear markets in stocks and bonds can lead to dramatic changes in return assumptions, and, thus, the odds of a plan's success. Therefore, as we discussed in the introduction of this book, it is critical that current valuations be used.

An equally important point is to understand that while MC simulations provide us with the important benefit of considering a wide dispersion of potential outcomes, as time passes potential outcomes become realized ones. In other words, some of the uncertainties become certainties. For example, if you retired in December 2019, by the end of March 2020 you knew global equity markets had crashed and bond yields had fallen sharply. What was once perhaps in the 5 percent left tail of the potential distribution was now a certainty. At that point a new MC simulation should be run, with new assumptions, and plans may need to be adapted to meet the new reality.

Capital Market Assumptions

	Arithmetic Mean Real Return (%)	Annual Standard Deviation (%)
Total Stock Market Equity	4.5	17.3
Tilted Equity Portfolio*	6.3	20.0
Fixed Income	0.3	4.3
Inflation	1.8	—

This section will look at portfolios with various hypothetical allocations. The success rate is defined as the probability that the portfolio has at least one dollar at the end of the planning horizon. Of course, if an investor has a 95 percent success rate, this also means they have a 5 percent chance of failure (or of having to make adjustments such as implementing the rules set for Plan B discussed earlier). Outcomes are calculated over a 30-year horizon. We will review the results using three different initial withdrawal rates: 3 percent, 4 percent and 5 percent. A 4 percent withdrawal rate on a $1 million starting portfolio indicates that $40,000 is withdrawn in the first year, and then adjusted for inflation thereafter.

- Portfolio A: 60 percent total stock market/40 percent fixed income.
- Portfolio B: 60 percent equity tilted to small-cap and value/40 percent fixed income.
- Portfolio C: 40 percent equity tilted to small-cap and value/60 percent fixed income.

* The equity portion of the portfolios tilted to small-cap and value stocks have loadings of (exposure to) 0.5 on the size factor and 0.2 on the value factor.

Odds of Success (%)

	3% Withdrawal Rate	4% Withdrawal Rate	5% Withdrawal Rate
Portfolio A	93	70	40
Portfolio B	96	81	58
Portfolio C	98	80	43

At a relatively low 3 percent withdrawal rate, changes in asset allocation do not have a significant effect on success rates. However, by making such a change, an investor could slightly improve the odds of success while reducing the portfolio's equity allocation. At a 4 percent withdrawal rate, we see significant improvement in success rates by tilting the equity portion of the portfolio to small-cap and value stocks. At a relatively high 5 percent withdrawal rate, no amount of changes in the asset allocation will get the investor to an acceptable success rate. This investor should reduce their spending, plan on working longer, lower their goal or find other sources of income.

Benefits of MC Simulations

MC simulations allow investors to view the outcomes of various strategies and how marginal changes in asset allocations, savings rates and withdrawal rates change the odds of these outcomes.

For example, after examining the output an investor might decide they are taking more risk than needed to achieve their goals. It is a relatively easy fix—lowering the equity allocation and/or lowering the exposure to risky asset classes. If they are not taking enough risk to provide acceptable odds of success, the decisions get more difficult. They must (1) take more risk than they would otherwise like to take; (2) lower the goal; (3) save more (lowering their current lifestyle); or (4) accept and live with the estimated risk of needing to make unwelcome adjustments to the plan in the future, such as using Plan B discussed earlier.

The benefits of using a MC simulation are seen in this example. Assume the input results in an 80 percent chance of success (not running out of money while still alive, or turning to Plan B). The simulation shows the impact on those odds of increasing (or decreasing) savings by $X a month. If that change increased the odds of success to 85 percent, the investor might decide that it was worthwhile to reduce current consumption to improve the odds of success by that amount. If it only raised the odds of success to 81 percent, the investor might draw a different conclusion.

The output can also be analyzed to see how changes in the asset allocation impact the odds of success. If increasing the equity allocation from 70 percent to 80 percent improved the odds of success from 80 percent to 90 percent, an investor might decide it was worth the extra risk of more equity ownership (and the extra stomach acid it was likely to produce along the way). If it only increased the odds of success to 81 percent, there might be a different decision. Changes in withdrawal rates that impact future lifestyle can be analyzed. For example, if a 4 percent withdrawal rate produced a 95 percent chance of success and a 5 percent withdrawal rate lowered the odds of success to 90 percent, an investor might choose to raise the withdrawal rate, accepting a somewhat lower likelihood of success in return for greater consumption. If that decision is made and the risks do materialize, the investor must be prepared to accept an even lower lifestyle in the future.

The simulation program can be used to look at how delaying retirement by X years impacts various issues, such as the need to save, the withdrawal rate, or the required equity allocation. The same analysis can be done for earlier retirement. Investors can determine if an extra year of working is worth the greater lifestyle now and/or in the future, or how that extra year of work impacts the need to take risk. For example, each extra year of work might allow for a reduced need to save $X per year; a Y percent increase in the withdrawal rate; or a reduction in the equity allocation of Z percent.

The right answers are unique to the individual and their ability, willingness and need to take risk. For some people an 85 percent chance of running out of money or having to make perhaps difficult adjustments will be perfectly acceptable. For others, anything short of 99 percent might be unacceptable. This will depend on how acceptable the actions required in Plan B are. Ultimately, the decisions are all preferences driven by personal choice. Here are some guidelines:

- The more risk averse the investor, or lower the marginal utility of wealth, the more emphasis should be placed on the odds of making the portfolio safe instead of large.
- Lower odds of success can be tolerated the more options an investor is both able and willing to exercise if the risks do "show up."

In the following four examples applying the above principles, we will consider two investors, identical with one exception:

- The exception—one investor owns a second home. This investor has the ability to sell that home should the "left tail" (worst case result) of the potential distribution of returns show up, so he can accept greater odds of having to implement Plan B than the other investor. However, if the investor is unwilling to exercise that option—the grandkids live in that area and a high value is placed on owning the property—the option doesn't matter. Only options investors are both able and willing to exercise should be considered.

- The exception—one investor is both willing and able to lower their need for cash flow from the portfolio should the "left tail" of the potential distribution of returns show up. That investor can accept greater odds of using Plan B than one either without a Plan B or who finds a Plan B unacceptable.
- The exception—one investor is both willing and able to extend his planned time in the workforce. The other places a higher value on the ability to retire. The investor who is both willing and able to continue to work longer can accept more risk, but should consider the need for disability insurance should health prevent them from exercising the option to work longer.
- The exception—one investor has a long-term care policy. This investor can accept more investment risks than the one without a policy.

Refining the Failure Rate

While the failure rate has become an essential tool when evaluating withdrawal, as Javier Estrada, author of the October 2016 paper "Refining the Failure Rate," points out: "This variable is silent about how long into the retirement period a strategy failed." He continues: "Two strategies that sustained withdrawals for 10 and 25 years of a 30-year retirement period have both failed, but a retiree would be far from indifferent between them."

Estrada's study, which covers 21 countries over the 115-year period from 1900 through 2014, showed that two strategies with the same failure rates may have failed at very different points along the retirement horizon, with one supporting a retiree's withdrawals for a longer period.

For example, Estrada shows that over the 86 30-year retirement periods he considered, a 4 percent withdrawal strategy from a global 60/40 portfolio would have failed 20 times, or in 23 percent of the periods. However, those 20 failures looked very different. In some cases, the plan failed with only two years remaining; in others, it failed with 14 years remaining. Those are two very different outcomes, with very different consequences. Yet they both count the same way in informing the failure rate. In addition, consider two different investment (asset allocation and withdrawal) strategies A and B. Assume a Monte Carlo simulation for A fails in just 1 percent of the simulations, but when it fails, it is depleted in year 15 of the 30-year planning period. The simulation for B shows it fails in 10 percent of the simulations (10 times as likely to fail as strategy A), but when it fails it fails in year 29. Clearly, these two scenarios present very different risks. Considering both failure rate and years left allows for a more informed decision.

Because of the problem that Estrada describes in his research, the Monte Carlo software we use (MoneyGuideElite) at Buckingham Strategic Wealth not only reports the success/failure rate, but it also shows the median age at which the plan fails, and the median amount by which it fails. Thus, investors can not only determine the estimated odds of failure, but can also understand in such cases how long into retirement their portfolio was able to maintain their desired lifestyle, and how long a period was remaining. They can also determine how big an adjustment would have been required to prevent failure. This enables them to design effective Plan Bs—a contingency plan that lists the actions that would be taken if financial assets were to drop below a predetermined level.

We have one more important issue to discuss. Typically, one of the assumptions made in Monte Carlo simulations is that the spending requirement in real terms remains unchanged. While each situation is unique, based on our experience you should at least consider breaking up your retirement into three stages.

1. **Active stage (through age 75).** For many people, these are the peak spending years during retirement because we are more physically active and able to travel.
2. **Transition stage (age 75 through age 85).** Retirees gradually become less active as health declines and interest in travel wanes. While maintenance spending remains stable in real terms, discretionary expenses may start to decline.
3. **Passive stage (beyond age 85).** While there may remain many years still ahead, depending on how large a percentage discretionary items are of the total budget, expenses in real terms may experience a steep decline as discretionary spending falls.

Of course, this only addresses the expenses we control. It does not take into account medical or long-term care expenses. Unfortunately, they can increase dramatically as we age, highlighting the need for addressing them in your financial plan.

We next look at what to do if you do not have access to a MC simulator.

If You Do Not Have Access to a MC Simulator

If you do not have access to a Monte Carlo simulator, are recently retired, or near retirement, we recommend that at age 65 you consider withdrawing just 3 percent a year from your portfolio, adjusting that each year by the inflation rate. You could increase that to 4 percent if you have options that you would be willing and able to exercise that would cut expenses should the portfolio be severely damaged by a bear market. If you are older than 65, the safe withdrawal rate increases as the portfolio does not have to support as many years of spending. At age 70, you can increase the safe withdrawal rate to 3.5 percent, at age 75 to 4.5 percent, and at age 80 to 6 percent.

If you are more than 10 years from retirement, we offer the following table, created by Professor Wade Pfau and based on his paper, "Getting on Track for a Sustainable Retirement: A Reality Check on Savings and Work." It provides guidance on how much you need to save for retirement. It looks at a worst-case scenario using historical data back to 1871. The rows of this table are your current age while the columns are how much you have saved for retirement. The percentages show the pre-tax income you should save annually. The assumptions behind this chart are a 50 percent replacement rate, a retirement age of 65, a 30-year retirement and a 60/40 portfolio. As an example, if you are 35 years old and you have saved one times your annual salary (as indicated by the shaded box in the table), you would need to save 10 percent per year going forward.

Age	No Savings	½ Annual Salary	1× Annual Salary	2× Annual Salary	3× Annual Salary	4× Annual Salary
25	8%	6%	4%	–	–	–
30	12%	9%	7%	2%	–	–
35	17%	13%	10%	5%	1%	–
40	23%	20%	16%	9%	3%	–
45	35%	31%	26%	19%	12%	5%
50	55%	51%	46%	36%	27%	17%
55	95%	88%	82%	69%	57%	45%

Summary

The traditional way to think about the risk of a portfolio is in terms of its volatility—as measured by its standard deviation. The use of a Monte Carlo simulation shifts the thinking to a goals-based approach—viewing the risk not just in terms of volatility, but also in terms of the odds of achieving your financial goals. We believe the goals-based approach to wealth management to be superior, because while a low volatility portfolio might be the right choice based solely on your willingness to take risk, it might also leave you with little to no chance of achieving your goals. The reverse can also be true—while you might have a high appetite for risk taking, a portfolio based solely on that criteria, while providing the greatest chance of leaving a large estate, might also have unacceptably high odds of outliving your assets.

The use of a Monte Carlo simulation allows you to find the right balance between risk taking and achieving goals. For example, you might decide that you are unwilling to have the estimated odds of failure of meeting your basic spending needs at less than 95 percent. On the other hand, you might be willing to accept the estimated odds of having your "dream" desires met (such as having funds for extensive travel or leaving a large estate) being at least 50 percent. And sometimes, difficult choices will have to be made.

We now turn to implementing the investment plan.

CHAPTER 6

Investment Strategy Part I: Implementing the Investment Plan

E BEGIN OUR discussion on investment strategy by addressing the issue of whether you should adopt an active management or passive management strategy when implementing your plan.

Active versus Passive Management

There are two theories about investing. The conventional wisdom is that markets are inefficient—smart people, through diligent efforts, can uncover which stocks the market has under or overvalued. This is called the art of stock selection. Smart people can also time the market, getting in ahead of the bull emerging into the arena, and out ahead of the bear emerging from hibernation. This is called the art of market timing. Together they make up the art of active management.

The other theory is that markets are efficient, that the price of a security is the best estimate of the correct price—otherwise the market would clear at a different price. If markets are efficient, and accounting for the expenses of the effort, attempts to outperform (generate risk-adjusted alpha) are highly unlikely to prove productive.

The Evidence

If the markets are inefficient, we should see evidence of the persistent ability to outperform appropriate risk-adjusted benchmarks. And that persistence should be greater than randomly expected. Put simply, the evidence is overwhelming that active management is what Charles Ellis called "a loser's game." By that he meant that while it is possible to win, the odds of doing so are so poor that, just

74

like at the slot machines in the casinos in Las Vegas, the prudent, or winning, strategy is to not play. Ellis came to that conclusion in his 1998 book, *Winning the Loser's Game*. At that time, 20 percent of active managers were outperforming appropriate risk-adjusted benchmarks with statistical significance. And that is on a pre-tax basis. Since taxes are often the highest cost of active management, for taxable investors the odds of success were much lower.

Larry's 2015 book, co-authored by Andrew Berkin, *The Incredible Shrinking Alpha*, presented evidence showing that figure had fallen to just 2 percent—again, that is on a pre-tax basis. The book also provides the reasons for the sharp decline. The following is a short summary.

First, while markets are not perfectly efficient, as there are many well-known anomalies, they are highly efficient. And, importantly, they have become more efficient over time as academic research has been converting what once were sources of alpha, which active managers could exploit, into beta (exposure to, or loading on, a common factor, or characteristic). For example, in the CAPM single factor world, active managers were able to generate alpha and claim outperformance simply by investing in small stocks and value stocks. But, since 1992, that has no longer been the case, because the publication of the aforementioned study "The Cross-Section of Expected Returns" by Fama and French showed that small and value stocks outperform large and growth stocks and investors can access these investment factors through low-cost, passively managed vehicles. Thus, there is no need to pay the higher fees of actively managed funds which act as drags on their performance.

Second, to generate alpha, which even before expenses is a zero-sum game, active managers must have victims to exploit. And the supply of victims (retail investors) has been shrinking persistently since World War II. The evidence shows that the stocks retail investors buy go on to underperform and the ones they sell go on to outperform. In other words, institutional investors are exploiting "dumb" retail investors, allowing them to generate alpha (outperform). But the percentage of individuals now directly owning individual stocks has collapsed, shrinking the supply of victims. Seventy years ago, about 90 percent of stocks were held directly by individual investors. Today, that figure is less than 20 percent. In addition, 90 percent or more of trading is done by institutional investors. Thus, the competition is getting tougher as the supply of sheep that can be regularly sheared shrinks.

Third, the competition is much more highly skilled today. As Charles Ellis explained, "over the past 50 years, increasing numbers of highly talented young investment professionals have entered the competition. ... They have more-advanced training than their predecessors, better analytical tools, and faster access to more information."

Fourth, there's been a huge increase in the pool of assets chasing alpha. Consider that 60 years ago there were only about 100 mutual funds. Today there are about 10,000. And just 20 years ago, hedge fund assets were about $300 billion. Today, they are in excess of $3 trillion. Thus, you have many more dollars attempting to exploit a shrinking pool of alpha at the same time that the competition has gotten much tougher. Not exactly a likely prescription for success.

We can see the effects of these changes by examining the Standard & Poor's annual Indices Versus Active (SPIVA) Scorecards, which compare the performance of actively managed equity funds to their appropriate index benchmarks. It also puts out a pair of scorecards each year that focus on persistence of performance. This is an important issue because if persistence isn't significantly greater than should be randomly expected, investors cannot separate skill-based performance (which might be able to persist) from luck-based performance (which eventually runs out). The following are some of the highlights from the December 2019 persistence scorecard, with data through September 2019:

- Irrespective of asset class or style focus, few fund managers consistently outperformed their peers.
- An inverse relationship exists between the length of the time horizon and the ability of top-performing funds to maintain their success. Less than 1% of equity funds maintained their top-quartile status at the end of the five-year measurement period. And no large-cap fund was able to consistently deliver top-quartile performance by the end of the fifth year.
- Over long horizons, most fixed income categories showed no persistence: Of the 13 fixed income categories, seven showed no managers remaining in the top quartile over the five-year horizon.
- Of 545 domestic equity funds that were in the top quartile as of September 2017, 8.1% managed to stay in the top quartile through September 2018 and again through September 2019, slightly more than the 6.3% we would randomly expect to do so.
- Over the two non-overlapping five-year periods, it was almost as likely for a bottom-quartile large-cap fund to rise to a top-quartile performer (9.6%) as it was for a top-quartile performer to remain a top-quartile performer (10.6%). The results were similar for small-cap funds, with 18.8% of top-quartile performers becoming bottom-quartile performers while 16.1% of bottom-quartile performers became top-quartile performers. The results were better for mid-cap and multi-cap funds.

The bottom line is that, basically, there was no evidence of persistence in performance greater than randomly expected among active equity managers. The one area in which the report found evidence of persistence was that funds in the worst-performing quartile were much more likely to be liquidated or merged out of existence, highlighting the importance of making sure survivorship bias isn't in the data. And the results for fixed income funds were only marginally better.

In his 2011 book, *The Quest for Alpha*, Larry Swedroe showed that the results were similar for hedge funds, pension plans, and private equity—they were all loser's games.

The bottom line is that while active management might provide excitement and have entertainment value, the winner's game is to use passively managed investment vehicles.

Implementing a Passive Strategy

Indexing is a wonderful strategy. As you have seen, there is an overwhelming body of evidence demonstrating that the majority of investors would be better off if they adopted indexed investment strategies. The benefits of indexing relative to active management are clear:

- Low expense ratio.
- Low turnover, resulting in relatively high tax efficiency and relatively low transaction costs.
- Avoids the risk of style drift.
- Minimal cash drag.
- Total transparency.

While indexing provides all of the above benefits, it does come with some negatives. The negatives result from the fact that the sole goal of index funds is to replicate the indices they are tracking, minimizing tracking error (avoiding having a different result than the index itself). Fortunately, for investors who want to implement their strategy using passively managed funds, there is an alternative to indexing—structured portfolios. Structured portfolios incorporate the benefits of indexing, while at the same time minimizing its negatives. Let's begin with an explanation of what is meant by structured asset class investing.

Index funds and structured asset class funds are similar in the way that rectangles and squares are similar. All squares are rectangles, but not all rectangles are squares. Similarly, while all index funds are passively managed, not all structured portfolios attempt to replicate the returns of popular retail indexes like the S&P 500 or the Russell 2000. Instead, they tend to use academic definitions of asset classes and factors and design portfolios in ways that minimize the weaknesses of indexing. We will examine nine such weaknesses:

1. **Sensitivity to risk factors varies over time.** Because indexes typically reconstitute annually, they lose exposure to their asset class (or factors, such as beta, size, value, momentum, profitability) over time as stocks migrate across asset classes during the course of a year. Structured portfolios typically reconstitute monthly, allowing them to maintain more consistent exposure to their asset class/factor. That allows them to capture a greater percentage of the risk premiums in the asset classes/factors in which they invest. For example, after the annual reconstitution of the Russell 2000 in June, on average over 96 percent of its holdings are in the bottom 10 percent of stocks ranked by market capitalization. Eleven months later that figure is down to around 88 percent. In contrast, the Dimensional Fund Advisors (hereafter referred to as Dimensional) Small Cap Fund averages 96 percent for both months.

2. **Forced transactions result in higher trading costs.** Historically, this was the case for the Russell 2000 index. Imagine the following scenario for a Russell 2000 Index fund which buys and holds the stocks ranked 1,001–3,000 by market capitalization in the Russell 3000 Index. A stock is ranked 1,001 in June. When the index is reconstituted towards the end of June, based on data at the end of May, the stock is ranked 999. The fund now must sell the stock. One year later it is again ranked 1,001. The fund must again buy the stock. In order to reduce this costly, non-productive turnover, a structured fund might instead buy only the stocks with a ranking of higher than 1,000 and also create a hold range for stocks with a ranking just below that figure. For example, they might continue to hold stocks (but not buy any more) as long as they were ranked between 800 and 1,000. If a stock's ranking moved to a figure of less than 800, then it would be sold. Similarly, stocks can easily move from value to growth and back again. Not only do buy-and-hold ranges reduce costly turnover, but they also improve tax efficiency. The good news here is that both Russell and MSCI have mitigated this weakness to a great degree by implementing no-trade bands around the index breakpoints, helping to reduce unnecessary turnover.

3. **Risk of exploitation through front-running.** Active managers can exploit the knowledge that index funds must trade on certain dates. Structured portfolios avoid this risk by not trading in a manner that simply replicates the return of the index. An example of the cost of front-running is the Russell 2000 which reconstitutes its index each June. And most of the changes are well known ahead of the actual reconstitution when index funds would trade.

Aware of these problems, Russell has made some changes to attempt to mitigate these negatives:

- 2002: Share changes exceeding 5 percent of the index are made on a monthly basis.
- 2004: IPOs are included once per quarter.
- 2007: There is a transitional index over the month of June so not all trading happens on one day.
- 2007: Buffer zones are instituted around market capitalization ranges to reduce turnover.

Unfortunately, as the evidence in the table below shows, while there has been some improvement in relative returns—compared to indices from the Center for Research in Securities Pricing (CRSP) at the University of Chicago—the gap in performance is still wide.

Period	Russell 2000 Annualized Return (%)	CRSP 6–8 Annualized Return (%)	CRSP 6–10 Annualized Return (%)
1979–2001	13.7	15.7	15.2
2002–2007	8.9	10.7	10.9
2008–2019	8.2	9.0	8.9

A small-cap index fund tied to the Russell 2000 Index would have dramatically underperformed a small-cap fund tied to the similar CRSP indices, either the CRSP 6–8, or the CRSP 6–10 (which includes micro caps). Clearly, the choice of an index matters. Vanguard recognized this problem and abandoned the Russell 2000 as its benchmark index in May 2003, and now uses the CRSP Small Cap Index.

4. **Inclusion of all stocks in the index.** Research has found that very low priced ("penny") stocks (note that the Russell does exclude all stocks priced under $1), stocks in bankruptcy, IPOs, and small-cap growth stocks with high investment and low profitability all have poor risk-adjusted returns. A structured portfolio could exclude such stocks using a simple filter to screen them all out.

5. **Limited ability to pursue tax-saving strategies.** Tax management strategies include avoiding intentionally taking any short-term gains and offsetting capital gains with capital losses.

6. **Ability to preserve qualified dividends.** A fund must own the stock that earns the dividends for more than 60 days of a prescribed 121-day period. That period begins 60 days prior to the ex-dividend date. (As a side note, the

same creation/redemption process that helps ETFs minimize the realization of capital gains reduces the ability to preserve qualified dividends.)

7. **Limit securities lending revenue to the expense ratio.** When lending securities otherwise, qualified dividends become non-qualified, losing their preferential tax treatment. However, from a tax perspective securities lending revenue can be first used to offset the expense ratio of the fund.

8. **Inability to incorporate an additional screen for additional factors such as momentum.** Companies such as AQR, Bridgeway, and Dimensional have successfully been using momentum screens, incorporating them into their fund construction strategies, allowing them to avoid buying stocks that fall into their buy range, but are exhibiting negative momentum. They will wait until the negative momentum ceases before purchasing a stock. At the same time, hold ranges allow the funds to benefit from positive momentum. Similarly, exposure to the profitability and quality factors can be increased.

9. **Accepting the risk of tracking error.** Not being concerned about tracking error allows structured funds to engage in patient block trading activity that can provide opportunities to "sell liquidity" and earn a premium by purchasing stock at a discount. The opportunities arise (specifically in small- and especially micro-cap stocks) from the desire of active investors to quickly sell more stock than the market can absorb at the current bid. This can be a large benefit during periods of crisis as long as the fund itself is not subject to investors fleeing the fund in a panic.

The bottom line is that a well-designed, structured portfolio maximizes the benefits of indexing, while minimizing, or even eliminating, the negatives. And there is yet another advantage that structured funds can bring—in return for accepting tracking error risk they can gain greater exposure to the factors that have been shown to carry premiums. For example, a small value fund could be structured to own smaller and more "valuey" stocks than a small-cap index fund might have. (See Appendix G for an in-depth discussion on this subject.)

We now turn our attention to another way in which structured portfolios can add value over index funds—by creating "core funds."

Core Portfolios

Core portfolios combine multiple asset classes into one fund. The following provides a good example of why a core approach is superior to a component approach and is the most efficient way to hold multiple asset classes.

The Russell 3000 can be broken down into four components. The stocks that make up the Russell 1000 Growth Index, the stocks that make up the Russell 1000 Value Index, the stocks that make up the Russell 2000 Growth

Index, and the stocks in the Russell 2000 Value Index. At Buckingham Strategic Wealth, we have seen an institution that held all four components in exactly the same market cap weighting that the Russell 3000 holds them. In other words, they owned the same stocks, in the very same proportions, as did the Russell 3000, only in four funds instead of one. This makes no sense because when the indexes reconstitute each June, each of the four component index funds will have to sell the stocks that leave its index and buy the stocks that enter its index. That incurs transactions costs, which can be particularly large when the entire market knows you have to trade, and especially large for smaller stocks. The required trades also have tax implications for taxable investors. The benefits of owning the single (core) Russell 3000 fund are obvious.

Another example of a core fund is the Vanguard Total International Fund which combines holdings in developed and emerging markets. This is a significant improvement for investors who previously had to hold the two components separately. A single fund will avoid having to sell and buy the stocks from a country that migrates from emerging to developed markets as Israel recently did, and as South Korea is expected to do. This not only minimizes transactions costs in markets where they can be quite high, but it also avoids, or at least minimizes, the realization of capital gains.

Now consider an investor who owns four component U.S. index funds: a large company fund, a small company fund, a large value fund, and a small value fund. If there existed a single fund that held the same stocks, in the same proportions, that would be a more efficient approach. Dimensional has created a family of core funds with various degrees of "tilts" (more than market-cap weightings) to small-cap and value stocks. The major benefits of the core approach are:

- They minimize turnover created by the "migration" of stocks between large and small and value and growth, reducing transactions costs and improving tax efficiency.
- They minimize transactions needed for rebalancing. This reduces transactions costs and improves tax efficiency because the funds have the ability to rebalance with "other people's money" (using cash flows). That results in the need to only buy the underperformers, avoiding having to sell the outperformers.
- They can also rebalance using cash from dividends.
- The concept of combining multiple asset classes into a single fund can also be applied to factor-based strategies.

Single or Multi-Factor Funds

The academic evidence has led to a great increase in interest in constructing portfolios that have exposure to multiple factors. That, in turn, leads to the question of how to best build a portfolio. Is it better to create a portfolio using individual, single-factor components (thinking of them as "building blocks"), or to build a multi-factor portfolio from the security level (where scoring or ranking systems are used to select securities)? It should be intuitive that the latter approach, a bottom-up one, is superior.

One reason for this is that, if you use the component approach, you will have one factor-based fund buying a stock (or group of stocks) while another factor-based fund will be selling the same stock (or group of stocks). For example, if a stock (or an entire sector) is falling in price, it might drop to a level that would cause a value fund to buy it while a momentum fund would be selling the very same security. Investors would thus be paying two management fees and also incurring trading costs twice, without having any impact on the portfolio's overall holdings.

Jennifer Bender and Taie Wang, authors of the 2016 study "Can the Whole Be More Than the Sum of the Parts? Bottom-Up versus Top-Down Multifactor Portfolio Construction," which appears in a Special QES Issue of *The Journal of Portfolio Management*, examined which of the two approaches is more efficient. The authors observed that the bottom-up approach would seem to be a better one, because the portfolio weight of each security will depend on how well it ranks on multiple factors simultaneously, while the approach combining single-factor portfolios may miss the effects of cross-sectional interaction between the factors at the security level. The study used the equity factors of value, size, quality, low volatility and momentum, from which the authors built global portfolios from developed markets.

Bender and Wang found that the bottom-up portfolio returns were higher than any of the underlying individual component factor returns and higher than the combinations. Additionally, volatility of the bottom-up portfolio was significantly lower. For example, over the period from January 1993 through March 2015, the combination portfolio was able to return 11.1 percent, versus 12.1 percent for the bottom-up portfolio, while exhibiting higher volatility (an annual standard deviation of 14.9 percent versus 14.0 percent). As a result, the risk-adjusted return increases from 0.7 percent for the combination portfolio to 0.8 percent for the bottom-up approach.

They also found that "the bottom-up approach consistently produced better performance over the combination approach in all periods." Bender and Wang concluded "there are, in fact, beneficial interaction effects among factors that are not captured by the combination approach. Both intuition and empirical evidence favor employing the bottom-up multifactor approach."

Portfolios that provide exposure to multiple factors allow investors to diversify their holdings in more efficient ways than were previously available. And the theory and evidence demonstrate that the bottom-up approach is the more efficient way to construct a portfolio of factor-based funds—it is an improvement over single factor funds. There are now many fund families that offer multi-factor funds.

Before concluding the chapter, we have one more important implementation issue to discuss.

Cash Flow versus Total Return Approach to Spending

To meet their spending needs, retirees generally take one of two approaches. The first is to limit spending to the cash flow generated by the portfolio. That means limiting spending to the interest income generated from their bonds and the dividends generated by their stocks. The second is a total return approach, which not only utilizes the cash flow generated from the portfolio, but also considers selling financial assets when there is a shortfall between spending needs and the cash flow generated by the portfolio.

It is important to note, however, that under the total return approach, the income generated by the portfolio is the first source tapped to meet spending needs. Only when this is insufficient does the investor liquidate some holdings. Thus, when the total portfolio cash flow is equal to or greater than the annual spending requirement, the total return approach is the same as the income approach. With that said, there are two main reasons why we recommend the total return approach.

First, the main benefit of the cash flow approach is that you will not run of of money if your spending is limited in that way. However, you cannot take the assets you have accumulated with you. Nor will you live forever. And there is always the chance that you will not live to your life expectancy. Thus, limiting spending to cash flow means you are spending less today (we value spending today more than we value the same spending in the future) than you could using a prudent withdrawal strategy determined by the outcome from a Monte Carlo simulation. We want you to be able to spend as much as is prudently possible so you can enjoy your retirement.

Second, when interest rates are low (as was the case through the entire decade following the financial crisis that began in 2008), the cash flow from the portfolio may not provide sufficient cash flow to meet spending needs. To offset the shortfall, many investors will sell their safe bond investments (such as FDIC-insured CDs), Treasury securities, and high-quality (AAA/AA) municipal bonds and purchase higher yielding assets such as high-yield (or even junk) bonds, REITs, and stocks with a high dividend yield. Investors that do so allow their need to take risk to dominate the asset allocation decision, while ignoring, or not providing sufficient consideration to, their ability and willingness to take risk.

While the cash flow approach will provide more income, it can lead to taking on considerably more risk since the higher yielding assets have risks that tend to show up at exactly the wrong time—when equities are also doing poorly. To illustrate this point, we will look at returns in 2008. While five-year Treasury notes returned 8.7 percent, the S&P 500 lost 37 percent, Vanguard's High-Yield Corporate Bond Fund (VWEHX) lost 21.3 percent, Vanguard's REIT Index Fund (VGSIX) lost 37.1 percent, and the Vanguard High Dividend Yield Index Fund Investor Shares (VHDYX) lost 32.5 percent. In addition, dividends are not necessarily safe (many companies cut, or even eliminated, dividends during the crisis) and risky corporate credits can default, doing permanent damage to the ability of the portfolio to generate cash flow. These risks increase the odds of outliving financial assets.

We now turn to the topic of building portfolios which have not only been more efficient than market-like portfolios, but have greatly reduced the downside risk in bear markets. This is an especially important topic for those in the withdrawal stage of their investment life-cycle because bear markets can have a devastating effect on the odds of outliving your assets.

CHAPTER 7

Investment Strategy Part II: Reducing the Risk of Black Swans

O NE OF THE more common mistakes investors make is to treat expected returns as "deterministic"—meaning they believe they will earn that specific return—rather than as just the mean of a potentially very wide dispersion of possible returns. The following illustration demonstrates why thinking of the expected return in a deterministic way is dangerous.

In a November 2012 paper, "An Old Friend: The Stock Market's Shiller PE," Cliff Asness of AQR Capital found that the Shiller CAPE 10 does provide valuable information. Specifically, he found that 10-year forward average real returns fall nearly monotonically as starting Shiller P/E's increase. He also found that, as the starting Shiller CAPE 10 increased, worst cases became worse and best cases became weaker. And he found that while the metric provided valuable insights, there were still very wide dispersions of returns. For example:

- When the CAPE 10 was below 9.6, 10-year forward real returns averaged 10.3 percent. In relative terms, that is more than 50 percent above the historical average of 6.8 percent (9.8 percent nominal return less 3.0 percent inflation). The best 10-year forward real return was 17.5 percent. The worst was still a pretty good 4.8 percent 10-year forward real return, just 2.0 percentage points below the average, and 29 percent below it in relative terms. The range between the best and worst outcomes was a 12.7 percentage point difference in real returns.
- When the CAPE 10 was between 15.7 and 17.3 (about its long-term average of 16.5), the 10-year forward real return averaged 5.6 percent. The best and worst 10-year forward real returns were 15.1 percent and 2.3 percent, respectively. The range between the best and worst outcomes was a 12.8 percentage point difference in real returns.
- When the CAPE 10 was between 21.1 and 25.1, the 10-year forward real return averaged just 0.9 percent. The best 10-year forward real return was still 8.3

percent, above the historical average of 6.8 percent. However, the worst 10-year forward real return was now—4.4 percent. The range between the best and worst outcomes was a difference of 12.7 percentage points in real terms.

- When the CAPE 10 was above 25.1, the real return over the following 10 years averaged just 0.5 percent—virtually the same as the long-term real return on the risk-free benchmark, one-month Treasury bills. The best 10-year forward real return was 6.3 percent, just 0.5 percentage points below the historical average. But the worst 10-year forward real return was now—6.1 percent. The range between the best and worst outcomes was a difference of 12.4 percentage points in real terms.

What can we learn from the preceding data? First, starting valuations clearly matter, and they matter a lot. Higher starting values mean that future expected returns are lower, and vice versa. However, a wide dispersion of potential outcomes, for which we must prepare when developing an investment plan, still exists.

The following illustration shows the right way to think about the expected return of a portfolio or an asset class. Although stock returns do not fit exactly into a normal distribution (as the following bell curve depicts), a normal distribution is a close approximation. Thus, we think this graph will be helpful in explaining how to think about expected (forward-looking) returns.

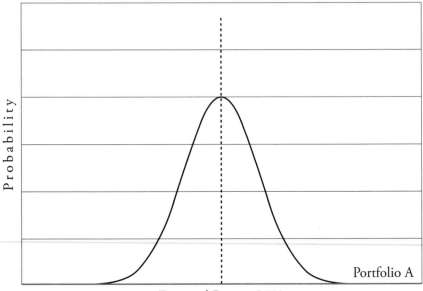

Expected Return 5.0%

In the illustration, think of Portfolio A as a market-like portfolio (such as the Vanguard Total Stock Market Index Fund). Using a 3.2 percent expected real return to stocks (based on the Shiller CAPE 10 at year end 2019) and an expected inflation rate of 1.8 percent, we arrive at an expected nominal return of 5.0 percent for the overall stock market. The right way to think about this 5.0 percent figure is as the mean (and median) of the wide dispersion depicted. In other words, there is a 50 percent chance the actual return will be greater than the expected 5.0 percent, perhaps a 30 percent chance it will be greater than 7 percent, a 10 percent chance it will be greater than 8 percent, and a 5 percent chance it will be greater than 10 percent. The possibilities are similar that it will fall on the left side of the distribution with returns below, and even well below, the expected rate of 5.0 percent.

Now consider Portfolio B, which has the same 5.0 percent expected return, but a different potential dispersion of returns. As the following illustration shows, more of the weight of the distribution (its probability density) is closer to the mean expected return of 5.0 percent than is the case with Portfolio A. It is a taller and thinner bell curve, with less of its weight in the tails, both left (bad) and right (good).

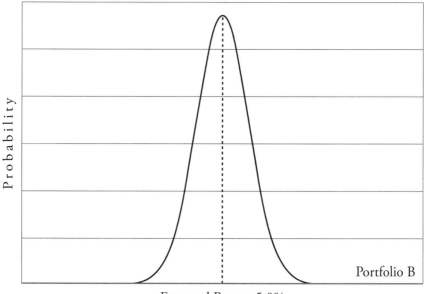

Expected Return 5.0%

Now consider both Portfolios A and B. They have the same expected return—in both cases the mean return is 5.0 percent. However, they have a different estimate of the potential dispersion of returns. In Portfolio B, more of the weight of the potential distribution is closer to the mean. And, importantly, the tails of the distribution of Portfolio B are shorter than they are for Portfolio A (there is less risk of a large loss, and less opportunity for a large gain). Thus, the odds are greater that the future return will be closer to the mean than with Portfolio A. Faced with the choice of living with the risks of the potential return dispersions in either Portfolio A or B, which would you choose?

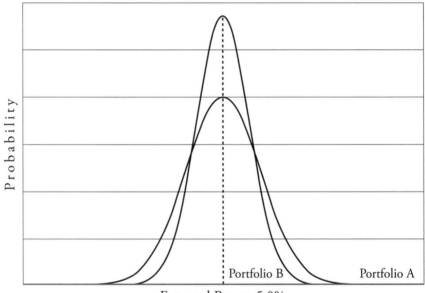

Expected Return 5.0%

If you are like most people, you would choose to live with the risks of Portfolio B. Most investors are risk averse—given the same expected return, they choose the portfolio with the lower standard deviation of returns (Portfolio B). Said another way, if you are like most investors, you are willing to sacrifice the opportunity to earn the great returns in the right tail of the distribution of Portfolio A (that are not there with Portfolio B) if you also minimize, or eliminate, the risk of the very bad returns in the left tail of Portfolio A (that, again, are not there with Portfolio B).

The reduction of left tail risk becomes increasingly important as we approach and enter retirement. The reasons are two-fold. First, in retirement we no longer have the ability to generate income to make up for equity losses, we have less time for markets to recover from bear market losses, and our tolerance for risk tends to decline. Second, the order in which investment returns occur increases in importance in retirement. Once we begin to withdraw from our portfolio, large losses in the early years of retirement can greatly increase the odds of outliving our assets.

At Buckingham Strategic Wealth, using the findings from academic research, we have been building portfolios where the distribution of potential returns looks more like Portfolio B than Portfolio A for more than 20 years. We will show you that "secret sauce."

Achieving Your Goals in a CAPM World

In a CAPM (one-factor) framework, the only ways to increase the expected return of your portfolio are to increase your allocation to stocks or to purchase higher-market-beta stocks. In either case, you are not diversifying the sources of the portfolio's return—just adding more market beta to it.

An example can illustrate this point. Let's assume equities (as represented by a total stock market fund) are expected to return 7 percent and bonds (as represented by the yield on, say, a five-year Treasury bond) are expected to return 5 percent. We will use these figures to keep the math simple. Based upon your ability and willingness to take risk, you decide that a portfolio with an allocation of 50 percent stocks and 50 percent bonds would be appropriate. Such a portfolio would have an expected return of 6 percent. However, the desired spending component of your long-term financial plan requires a 6.5 percent return. In a one-factor world, to achieve the expected return of 6.5 percent, you have to increase your equity allocation to 75 percent.

Portfolio 1: $(75\% \times 7\%) + (25\% \times 5\%) = 6.5\%$

The only other alternative would be to increase the market beta of the stocks in your portfolio. The math works out in such a way that you would be left owning a portfolio consisting basically of only very high-market-beta stocks. In either case, you would be adding more of the same market beta risk already in your portfolio. Instead of putting all your eggs in one risk basket (market beta), would it not be better to diversify your sources of risk across other baskets with unique risks? Another important consideration is that the portfolio with 75 percent stocks is riskier than the one with just 50 percent stocks—the allocation you felt was appropriate based on your risk tolerance.

As we have discussed, the academic research has shown that we do not live in a single factor world. The size and value factors have not only been shown to deliver premiums, but the correlation of their returns to each other and to market beta are low, providing diversification benefits we can utilize.

Achieving Your Goals in a Three-Factor World

From 1927 through 2019, small value stocks (as represented by the Fama-French small value research index) have outperformed the market (as represented by the S&P 500 Index) by an annualized 4.2 percentage points (14.4 percent versus 10.2 percent). Thus, if we assume stocks (the S&P 500) will return 7 percent, we might assume small value stocks will return an additional 4.2 percentage points a year for a total return of 11.2 percent. Recall our initial example of a 50 percent stock/50 percent bond allocation. (For simplicity, we will ignore implementation costs, such as a fund's expense ratio and trading costs, and how much exposure a fund has to the research index—are the stocks in a fund as small and value oriented as those in the research index?)

Instead of increasing your stock allocation to achieve the higher 6.5 percent return, you decide to divide your 50 percent stock allocation equally between the S&P 500 Index and small value stocks—25 percent each. Now the expected return is almost 7 percent.

Portfolio 2: (25% × 7%) + (25% × 11.2%) + (50% × 5%) = 7.05%

Without increasing your stock allocation, you have increased the portfolio's expected return to more than the required 6.5 percent. We did this by adding an allocation to the higher expected returning small value stocks. It is important to recognize that while your exposure to stocks basically remained unchanged (the allocation of small value stocks, while riskier, did add two new unique risk factors, providing some diversification benefit), the expected return of the portfolio increased by more than the risk (the expected standard deviation of return). However, you do not need to earn 6.95 percent. Your plan only requires a return of 6.5 percent. With that in mind, we can try lowering the stock allocation to 40 percent, again splitting it equally between the S&P 500 Index and small value stocks. Now the expected return is:

Portfolio 3: (20% × 7%) + (20% × 11.2%) + (60% × 5%) = 6.64%

You have now achieved your goal of an expected return of 6.5 percent. And you did so with an allocation to stocks of only 40 percent. Using your intuition, which portfolio, Portfolio 1 or Portfolio 3, do you think is riskier? Which portfolio would you expect to perform worse in a bear market? Intuitively, most people will say Portfolio 1.

While Portfolio 3 has the same expected return as the 75 percent equity portfolio, the risks are completely different. Portfolios with higher equity allocations have greater potential for losses. The tradeoff is that the potential upside of the portfolios with higher equity allocations is much greater. For investors for whom the pain of a loss is greater than the benefit of an equal-sized gain (probably you), reducing downside risk as the price of reducing upside potential is a good tradeoff.

Let's tackle another consideration especially important to loss-averse investors (which most are). Because bonds are safer investments than stocks, in a severe bear market the portfolio's maximum loss would likely be far lower with a 40 percent equity allocation than with a 75 percent one. 2008 provided a great example, at least if the fixed income you owned were limited to Treasuries and other high-quality bonds. While the market fell 37 percent, five-year Treasury bonds rose about 13 percent. And Portfolio 3 not only owned less of the losing stocks, but far more of the winning bonds.

Using the S&P 500 Index, the Russell 2000 Value Index (for small-cap value stocks) and the five-year Treasury, we see that in 2008, Portfolio 1 would have lost 24.5 percent, Portfolio 2 would have lost 9.9 percent and Portfolio 3 would have lost just 5.3 percent.

Thus, while the expected returns of Portfolio 1 and Portfolio 3 are the same, the portfolio with the lower equity allocation has much less downside risk. Of course, the upside potential during a strong bull market is correspondingly lower. For example, in 2003, Portfolio 1 gained 35.1 percent, Portfolio 2 gained 19.9 percent and Portfolio 3 gained just 16.4 percent.

To illustrate why reducing downside risk at the price of limiting upside potential is likely a good tradeoff, examine the following chart.

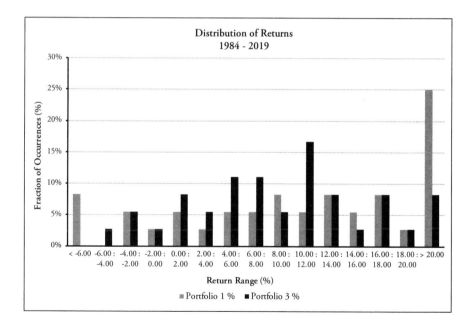

As you can see, Portfolio 1 experienced more years in which returns fall on the far left-hand side of the chart, as well as more years in which they fall on the far right-hand side of the chart—the tails were bigger.

We now turn to showing you how you can utilize what you have learned to build more efficient portfolios by combining Fama and French's work with Harry Markowitz's insight (for which he won a Nobel Prize) that you can add risky, but non-perfectly correlating, assets to a portfolio and generate higher returns without a commensurate increase in the portfolio's volatility.

Building a More Efficient Portfolio

We will begin with a portfolio that has a conventional asset allocation of 60 percent stocks and 40 percent bonds. In this case, the stock allocation is to the S&P 500 Index and the bond allocation is to five-year Treasury notes (the highest quality intermediate-term bond). The timeframe will be the 45-year period from 1975 through 2019. We chose this period because it is the longest for which we have data on the indices we need. While maintaining the same 60 percent stock/40 percent bond allocation, we will then expand our investment universe to include equity asset classes other than U.S. large-cap stocks. We will see how the portfolio performed if one had the patience to stay with this allocation for the duration and rebalanced annually. We will then demonstrate how the portfolio's performance could have been made more efficient by increasing its diversification across asset classes. We do so in four simple steps. (Indices are not available for direct investment—the investor has to invest in a fund, which has an expense ratio and trading costs, while the index itself does not have these costs.)

Portfolio 1

* S&P 500 Index: 60%
* Five-Year Treasury Notes*: 40%

1975–2019

	Annualized Return (%)	Annualized Standard Deviation (%)
	10.4	10.3

* Data source: © 2019 Morningstar, Inc. All rights reserved. Reproduced with permission.

By changing the composition of the control portfolio, we will see how we can improve its efficiency. To avoid being accused of data mining, we will alter our allocations by arbitrarily "cutting things in half."

Step 1

The first step is to diversify our stock holdings to include an allocation to U.S. small-cap stocks. Therefore, we reduce our allocation to the S&P 500 Index from 60 percent to 30 percent and allocate 30 percent to the Fama/French US Small Cap Index. (The Fama-French indices use the academic definitions of asset classes. Note that regulated utilities have been excluded from the data.)

Portfolio 2

- S&P 500 Index: 30%
- Fama/French US Small Cap Index: 30%
- Five-Year Treasury Notes*: 40%

1975–2019

	Annualized Return (%)	Annual Standard Deviation (%)
Portfolio 1	10.4	10.3
Portfolio 2	11.8	10.4

* Data source: © 2019 Morningstar, Inc. All rights reserved. Reproduced with permission.

Step 2

Our next step is to diversify our domestic stock holdings to include value stocks. We shift half of our 30 percent allocation to the S&P 500 Index to a large-cap value index and half of our 30 percent allocation to small-cap stocks to a small-cap value index.

Portfolio 3

- S&P 500 Index: 15%
- Fama/French US Large Value Research Index: 15%
- Fama/French US Small Cap Index: 15%
- Fama/French US Small Value Research Index: 15%
- Five-Year Treasury Notes*: 40%

1975–2019

	Annualized Return (%)	Annual Standard Deviation (%)
Portfolio 1	10.4	10.3
Portfolio 2	11.8	10.4
Portfolio 3	12.3	11.1

* Data source: © 2019 Morningstar, Inc. All rights reserved. Reproduced with permission.

Step 3

Our next step is to shift half of our equity allocation to international stocks. For exposure to international value and international small-cap stocks, we add a 15 percent allocation to both the MSCI EAFE Value Index and the Dimensional International Small Cap Index.

Portfolio 4

- S&P 500 Index: 7.5%
- Fama/French US Large Value Research Index: 7.5%
- Fama/French US Small Cap Index: 7.5%
- Fama/French US Small Value Research Index: 7.5%
- MSCI EAFE Value Index*: 15%
- Dimensional International Small Cap Index: 15%
- Five-Year Treasury Notes**: 40%

1975–2019

	Annualized Return (%)	Annual Standard Deviation (%)
Portfolio 1	10.4	10.3
Portfolio 2	11.8	10.4
Portfolio 3	12.3	11.1
Portfolio 4	11.9	11.0

* Data source: MSCI
** Data source: © 2019 Morningstar, Inc. All rights reserved. Reproduced with permission.

One effect of the changes has been to increase the return on the portfolio from 10.4 percent to 11.9 percent. This outcome is what we should have expected to see as we added riskier small-cap and value stocks to our portfolio. Thus, we also need to consider how our changes impacted the risk of the portfolio. The standard deviation (a measure of volatility, or risk) of the portfolio increased from 10.3 percent to 11.0 percent. Returns increased by a relative 14.4 percent while the relative increase in volatility was 6.8 percent.

You have now observed the power of modern portfolio theory at work. You saw how you can add risky (and, therefore, higher expected returning) assets to a portfolio and increase its returns more than its risk rose. That is the benefit of diversification across asset classes that are not perfectly correlated. While most investors and advisors with this knowledge have used it in the preceding manner, there is another way to consider employing it. Instead of trying to increase returns without proportionally increasing risk, we can try to achieve the same return while lowering the risk of the portfolio. To achieve this goal, we increase the bond allocation from 40 percent to 60 percent and proportionally decrease the allocations to each of the equity asset classes.

Portfolio 5

- S&P 500 Index: 5%
- Fama/French US Large Value Index (ex utilities): 5%
- Fama/French US Small Cap Index: 5%
- Fama/French US Small Value Index (ex utilities): 5%
- MSCI EAFE Value Index*: 10%
- Dimensional International Small Cap Index: 10%
- Five-Year Treasury Notes**: 60%

1975–2019

	Annualized Return (%)	Annual Standard Deviation (%)
Portfolio 1	10.4	10.3
Portfolio 2	11.8	10.4
Portfolio 3	12.3	11.1
Portfolio 4	11.9	11.0
Portfolio 5	10.4	8.0

* Data source: MSCI
** Data source: © 2019 Morningstar, Inc. All rights reserved. Reproduced with permission.

Compared with Portfolio 1, Portfolio 5 achieved the same return with far less risk. Specifically, Portfolio 5 returned 10.4 percent per year while experiencing volatility 2.3 percentage points lower (8.0 percent versus 10.3 percent). In relative terms, its volatility was 22.3 percent lower.

Now that you have a good understanding of how modern portfolio theory can be used to build more efficient portfolios, we will move to our last step. In it, we will show you how, by concentrating your equity allocation in only the highest expected returning asset classes, you can improve a portfolio's risk profile even further.

Just as the equity premium is compensation for taking risk, so are the size and value premiums. Thus, we add the usual disclaimer that the future may look different from the past. There are no guarantees in investing. Due to data limitations, the period we will now consider is the 38 years from 1982 through 2019. We will look at two portfolios, A and B. Portfolio A is again allocated 60 percent to the S&P 500 Index and 40 percent to five-year Treasury notes. Portfolio B will hold 25 percent stocks and 75 percent five-year Treasury notes. With U.S. stocks representing roughly half of the global equity market capitalization, we will split the equity allocation equally between U.S. small value stocks (using the Fama/French US Small Value Index) and international small value stocks (using the Dimensional International Small Cap Value Index).

1982–2019

- Portfolio A: 60 percent S&P 500 Index/40 percent five-year Treasury notes*
- Portfolio B: 12.5 percent Fama/French US Small Value Research Index/12.5 percent Dimensional International Small Cap Value Index/75 percent five-year Treasury notes*

	Portfolio A	Portfolio B
Annualized Returns/Standard Deviation (%)	10.3/10.3	9.4/7.2
Years with Returns Above 15%/Below −15%	12/1	9/0
Years with Returns Above 20%/Below −20%	8/0	3/0
Years with Returns Above 25%/Below −25%	2/0	2/0
Worst Year Return/Best Year Return (%)	−17.0/29.3	−3.1/28.6
Number of Years with Negative Return	6	2

* Data source: © 2019 Morningstar, Inc. All rights reserved. Reproduced with permission.

As you can see, while Portfolio A produced an annualized return 0.9 percentage points higher than Portfolio B (10.3 percent versus 9.4 percent), it did so while experiencing volatility 3.1 percentage points greater (10.3 percent versus 7.2 percent). In relative terms, Portfolio A's annualized return was only 9.6 percent greater than Portfolio B's, while the volatility it experienced was 43.1 percent higher.

In addition, Portfolio B had fewer events in the tails of the return distribution (said another way, it had both fewer extremely good and fewer extremely bad years). While Portfolio A had 12 years with returns greater than 15 percent, Portfolio B had nine. And while Portfolio A had one year with a loss greater than 15 percent, Portfolio B never experienced a loss that large. Moving the hurdle to years with 20 percent gains or losses, we see that Portfolio A had eight years with returns greater than that level and no years with losses of that size, while Portfolio B had just three years of gains that large. Moving the hurdle to the 25 percent level, both Portfolio A and Portfolio B had two years with returns in excess of that amount and no years with losses that great. The best single year for Portfolio A was 1995, when it returned 29.3 percent.

The best single year for Portfolio B was 1985, when it returned 28.6 percent. Note that while Portfolio B has just 25 percent in equities, its best year was almost as good as the best year for Portfolio A, which has 60 percent in equities. On the other hand, Portfolio A's worst single year was 2008, when it lost 17.0 percent. The worst single year for Portfolio B was 2018, when it lost just 3.1 percent. In addition, while Portfolio A experienced six years of negative returns, Portfolio B posted just two.

Portfolio B—the low-market-beta/high-tilt portfolio—with its shorter tails, looks more like our original Portfolio B from earlier in the chapter. While its best year was not as good as Portfolio A's best year, and it had fewer years in the good right tail, its worst year was much less painful than Portfolio A's worst year, and it had fewer years in the bad right tail.

There is another important point to cover, and to help make it we have reproduced the original illustration of the potential dispersion of returns for Portfolios A and B.

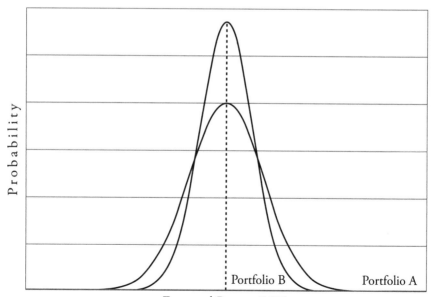

Expected Return 5.0%

Recall that your preference for Portfolio B was based on your aversion to risk—your willingness to give up the opportunity for the extreme good returns in the right tail of Portfolio A in return for minimizing the risks of the extreme bad returns in its left tail. The illustration shows that, if you choose Portfolio B, both the good and bad tails of Portfolio A are reduced equally. However, using actual returns, we saw that while Portfolio A did produce more good years than Portfolio B, and had a higher best returning year than Portfolio B, the difference in returns between their best years was just 1 percentage point, while the difference in returns between their worst years was almost 14 percentage points. In other words, bad tail risk was curtailed much more than good tail risk. If you preferred Portfolio B to Portfolio A, you should have a strong preference for a low-market-beta/high-tilt portfolio.

Before moving on, we must admit there is no way that, in 1982, we could have predicted the allocation for Portfolio B would have produced returns so similar to the allocation for Portfolio A. We might have guessed at a similar allocation, but we cannot predict the future with anything close to that kind of accuracy.

As we mentioned, Buckingham Strategic Wealth has been using this strategy of what can be called "low beta/high tilt" to build more efficient portfolios, ones with less downside risk, for more than 20 years. The "secret sauce" that produced more efficient portfolios with less tail risk was the addition of unique sources of risk (factors) that carry premiums whose returns have low to negative correlation with traditional stock and bond portfolios. Thanks to recent financial innovations we now have new tools that we can use to build even more efficient portfolios.

As you will recall from our recurring illustration, when shown the two bell curves representing the distribution of potential returns for Portfolios A and B, investors prefer Portfolio B with its narrower distribution. But what if you could create a portfolio with an even more favorable distribution of returns? Perhaps one whose distribution of returns looks more like Portfolio C as depicted in the following graph?

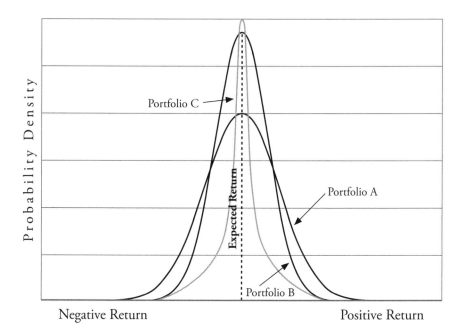

The way to create a portfolio that looks more like Portfolio C is to continue to add unique sources of risk (sources of risk that have low correlation with each other) that also have risk premiums. There are four alternative investments which we believe have equity-like expected returns, but with far less volatility and far less downside risk, while also having low to no correlation of their returns to either stocks or bonds. And the low correlation of their returns means that a portfolio of these alternatives will have even less volatility than their weighted average volatility. While the scope of this book doesn't allow for going into great detail on each of them (for those interested, this is provided in the 2018 edition of our book, *Reducing the Risk of Black Swans*), the following is a brief description of them:

1. **Alternative Lending:** Prime (higher quality) fully amortizing consumer, small business, and student loans. Our preferred vehicles is Stone Ridge Asset Management's Alternative Lending Risk Premium Fund (LENDX). We believe the expected return is about 4.5 percent above one-month Treasury bills, with volatility of about 5 percent. Note that the distribution of returns of the fund exhibits negative skewness—the left tail is larger than the right tail. We also recommend the Cliffwater Corporate Lending Fund (CCLFX) which makes loans to middle market corporations which are not large enough to issue public debt. The fund's focus is primarily on senior, first lien loans, with an average loan-to-value of under 45 percent. We

believe the expected return is about 5.5 percent above one-month Treasury bills with volatility of about 5 percent. As is the case with LENDX, the distribution of returns exhibits negative skewness.

2. **Reinsurance:** The reinsurance industry's existence presents an opportunity for investors to add an asset, through participation in the reinsurance business, with equity-like returns that are uncorrelated with the risks and returns of other assets in their portfolios (stocks, bonds and other alternative investments). Stock market crashes do not cause earthquakes, hurricanes or other natural disasters. The reverse is also generally true—natural disasters tend not to cause bear markets in stocks or bonds. The combination of the lack of correlation and equity-like returns results in a more efficient portfolio, specifically one with a higher Sharpe ratio (a higher return for each unit of risk). Our preferred vehicle is Stone Ridge Asset Management's Reinsurance Risk Premium Fund (SRRIX), a globally diversified fund. We believe the expected return is about 6 percent above one-month Treasury bills, with volatility of about 12.5 percent. Like LENDX, the fund's distribution of returns exhibits negative skewness.

3. **Variance Risk Premium (VRP):** The VRP refers to the fact that over time, the implied (ex-ante) volatility in options has tended to exceed the realized volatility of the same underlying asset. This has created a profit opportunity for volatility sellers—those willing to write options (puts and calls), collect the premiums, and bear the risk that realized volatility will increase by more than the implied volatility. Investors are willing to pay a premium because risky assets, such as stocks, tend to perform poorly when volatility increases. In other words, markets tend to crash down, not up. Thus, the VRP isn't an anomaly that should be expected to be arbitraged away. And since the risks of the VRP (selling options performs poorly) tend to show up in bad times (when risky assets are performing poorly), we should expect a significant premium. Our preferred vehicle is Stone Ridge Asset Management's All Asset Variance Risk Premium Fund (AVRPX), a globally diversified fund that writes puts and calls across more than 500 contracts across stocks, bonds, commodities and currencies. We believe the fund has an expected return of 8 percent above one-month Treasury bills, with an expected volatility of about 10 percent. Like LENDX and SRRIX, the fund's distribution of returns exhibits negative skewness.

4. **Alternative Risk Premium:** Traditional mutual funds are long-only, allowing investors to capture only a portion of the desired factor premium and leaving their portfolios dominated by market beta. By adding a long-short fund, investors are able to capture more of the premium. For taxable accounts, our preferred vehicle is AQR Capital Management's Alternative Risk Premia Fund (QRPRX), which provides long-short exposure to six factors (value, momentum, defensive [quality], carry, time-series momentum

[trend following] and the variance risk premium fund). It provides exposure to these factors across stocks, bonds, and currencies. We believe the fund has an expected return of about 4.5 percent above one-month Treasury bills and an expected volatility of about 8 percent. It too exhibits negative skewness in its distribution of returns. For tax-advantaged accounts, our preferred vehicle is AQR's Alternative Style Premia Fund (QSPRX). It is also a long-short fund, providing exposure to four factors (value, momentum, defensive [quality], and carry) and four asset classes (stocks, bonds, commodities and currencies). We believe the fund has an expected return of 5.5 percent above one-month Treasuries and an expected volatility of about 10 percent (and it exhibits negative skewness).

Importantly, while the weighted average volatility of the four strategies is about 9 percent, we believe that an equal-weighted portfolio would have volatility of only about 5 percent, while providing an expected return of about 5.5 percent above one-month Treasury bills, producing a high Sharpe ratio (risk-adjusted return). In addition, the low correlation of the returns of the four funds reduces the negative skewness found in each individual fund's returns.

The next chapter is about IRAs and other retirement/profit sharing plans and their effective use.

CHAPTER 8

IRA and Retirement/
Profit Sharing Plans

W E BEGIN OUR discussion on retirement accounts with the decision on whether to invest in a Roth IRA or a traditional IRA.

Roth versus Traditional IRA

Individual retirement accounts (IRAs) are tax-advantaged investments. The two different types of IRAs—traditional and Roth—have some similarities and some differences. The differences have implications for the development of an investment policy statement, the asset allocation decision, and the choice of the preferred vehicle.

Contributions to a Roth IRA are made on an after-tax basis and distributions are not subject to income tax. The traditional IRA is the mirror opposite. It allows contributions to be made on a pre-tax basis (on the tax return the adjusted gross income is reduced by the amount of the contribution), but all withdrawals are subject to taxation. An example will illustrate both the differences and similarities of the two accounts.

Consider two investors, John and Mary. Both are in the 25 percent federal tax bracket. Both expect to be in that same 25 percent bracket when they retire. They also have the same income and spending needs. They both invest on the same day in the same mutual fund. Each has just received a $1,000 bonus. We will start with John.

John decides he will invest his bonus in a Roth IRA. Having to set aside 25 percent of his bonus to pay federal income taxes, John makes a $750 contribution to his Roth IRA, investing that amount in a mutual fund that invests in equities. John's investments increase in value by 33 ⅓ percent. He now has $1,000. Assuming no penalty for early withdrawal, John could withdraw $1,000 with no taxes owed. Now let's consider Mary.

Mary decides to use her bonus to contribute $1,000 to her traditional IRA. She can invest $250 more than John because she doesn't have to pay the current income tax on the $1,000 invested. Mary invests her $1,000 in the same mutual fund, earning the same 33 ⅓ percent return. She ends up with $1,333. When she withdraws the funds from her traditional IRA (still assuming no early-withdrawal penalty), she will pay a tax of 25 percent ($333). Like John, she ends up with exactly the same $1,000. That tax of $333 is equal to the original tax that was deferred ($250) plus $83—the 33 ⅓ percent gain on the $250. It helps to think of a traditional IRA (or any tax-deferred account) as a joint account you have with Uncle Sam. Add your state tax collector to that if applicable. In our example, Mary owes 25 percent of account withdrawals to Uncle Sam because she's in the 25 percent federal tax bracket. Because 25 percent of her account is due to the government, she would be right to think she only really owns 75 percent of her IRA. This example demonstrates five important facts.

Five Key Facts

1. A traditional IRA is identical to a Roth IRA if the tax rate at the time of contribution is the same as the tax rate on withdrawal. Our Mary/John example proves this: Both portfolios generated $1,000 net.
2. If the same investment in either a Roth or traditional IRA results in the same amount of dollars after withdrawal, then taxes do not matter and you can consider them non-existent. Many people have a hard time understanding this. The right way to think about it is that Mary never owned 100 percent of her $1,000 investment. She owned 75 percent of it; the government owned the other 25 percent. The government let Mary invest its share of the money until she withdrew her share. At that point the government claimed its 25 percent. Mary is in an identical situation to John. Just as there was no tax on John's earnings, there really was no tax on Mary's share of the earnings.

   You may often have heard advice that you should not hold equities in a traditional IRA because doing so converts what would otherwise be capital gains into ordinary income. This is incorrect: As the example shows, there is no tax on the gain.
3. Taxes need to be integrated into investment policy. Considered in the right light, after taxes Mary owned 75 percent of her $1,000 investment. This has important implications for investment policy and the asset allocation decision. Assume Mary and John each started with $1,000 of equity holdings in taxable accounts. John invests another $750 in his Roth and Mary another $1,000 in her traditional IRA. This time they both put the money into bond funds. What are their respective asset allocations? The conventional analysis would be as follows:

- John has $1,000 in stocks and $750 in bonds. His asset allocation is thus 57 percent stocks and 43 percent bonds.
- Mary's allocation of $1,000 in stocks and $1,000 in bonds is 50/50.

However, since the Roth and the traditional IRA are the same, Mary's allocation must actually be the same as John's, not 50/50. Her allocation is the same $1,000 in stocks and $1,000 × [1 minus the 25 percent tax rate], or $750, in bonds. This is the same 57/43 allocation. If Mary wanted to have an allocation of 50/50, her holdings should have been $875 of stocks and $125 of bonds in the taxable account and $1,000 of bonds in the traditional IRA.

The tax code impacts the asset allocation of taxable accounts as well as IRAs. For example, if John had a taxable account that owned an equity mutual fund with a cost basis of $1,000 and a present value of $11,000 (assuming a long-term federal and state capital gains tax of 20 percent and no step-up in basis expected), for the purposes of determining John's asset allocation we would conclude he owns just $9,000 of equities, not $11,000. The government "owns" $2,000 of the $11,000—20 percent of the $10,000 unrealized gain.

We now turn to the issue of what drives the decision of which IRA to invest in.

4. The decision to make a contribution to a traditional or Roth IRA should be based on whether the tax rate on withdrawal is expected to be higher or lower than at the time of contribution. If lower, the preferred choice should be the traditional IRA—the government will "own" a lower percentage of the investment dollars. Here's an example.

John's tax rate is 25 percent on contribution. He expects it to be just 15 percent on withdrawal. In the original example, John invested $750 in the Roth IRA; given the 33 ⅓ percent return he would be able to withdraw $1,000. If instead he made the contribution to a traditional IRA, he could contribute $1,000, deferring the 25 percent income tax otherwise due. The $1,000 grows to $1,333. With John's income tax rate just 15 percent at withdrawal, he can withdraw $1,133 ($1,333 × [1 minus 0.15]). In terms of asset allocation, John owned 85 percent of the account, not 100 percent— Uncle Sam owns the other 15 percent.

If the tax rate at withdrawal is expected to be higher than at contribution, the preferred choice should be the Roth: You pay the government its share when the tax rate is lower. Using John again as an example, assume he's in the 25 percent bracket at contribution, but expects to be in the 33 percent bracket on withdrawal. If he invests in the Roth he can invest $750, and will be able to withdraw $1,000. If he invests in a traditional IRA he can invest $1,000 and withdraw $1,333 before taxes. However, after taxes the net amount is just $893 ($1,333 × [1 minus the 33 percent tax rate]). Thus, when the tax rate is expected to be higher at withdrawal than at contribution, the Roth is generally the preferred choice. But there is another consideration.

Maximizing the Benefits of the Tax Code

The maximum contributions to traditional and Roth IRAs are the same. For 2020, the maximum for those under age 50 was $6,000. For those over 50, the maximum was $7,000 (allowing for what is called a "catch up"). Assume Mary and John are both 40 and both have $7,500 available to invest in an IRA. John invests $6,000 in a Roth account. He retains $1,500 to pay the income tax due on the $6,000 of income. Because with traditional IRAs taxes are due on withdrawal, Mary is able to invest not only the $6,000 in her IRA, but also the additional $1,500 she has available.

Let's look at the implications of John's $6,000 investment in a Roth IRA versus Mary's $6,000 contribution to a traditional IRA. Mary does not own the full $6,000 of her traditional IRA, only $4,500 ($6,000 × [1 minus the tax rate of 25 percent]). The government is due the remaining $1,500. On her holdings, $4,500 will not be subject to any tax and $1,3500 (in the taxable account) will be subject to taxes on any gains, dividends or interest earned on the investments. Her total holdings are $5,500, just like John. However, all of John's $5,500 is in a tax-free (Roth) account. If the tax rates at contribution and withdrawal are expected to be the same, the Roth account is the preferred choice for those that can make the maximum contribution. Doing so allows them to hold more funds in a tax-free environment.

The benefit of the lower tax rate on withdrawal has to be weighed against the benefit of being able to invest more dollars in the tax-free environment. The individual needs to decide which is more valuable—contributing a greater amount to a tax-advantaged account, or having the government take a smaller share. The answer depends on tax rates at contribution and withdrawal. The greater the tax rate at the time of contribution compared to the tax rate at withdrawal, the more it favors the traditional IRA.

Given (1) tax rate differences can be large; (2) investors have access to highly tax-efficient investment vehicles (like tax-managed equity funds); and (3) the difference in the additional amount of investment dollars that can be placed in tax-advantaged accounts is relatively small, the traditional IRA would still be the choice if the tax rate is expected to be lower at withdrawal. It would still be prudent to seek expert counsel.

The issues related to the ability to maximize contributions also relate to a Roth 401(k). The difference is that the Roth 401(k) is not constrained by the same income limitations or contribution rules constraining a Roth IRA. Employees can decide to contribute funds on a post-tax basis, in addition to or instead of pre-tax deferrals under their traditional 401(k) plans. An employee under the age of 50 could defer (whether to a traditional 401(k), a Roth 401(k), or to both) up to $19,500 for tax year 2020. If over age 50, they could contribute an additional $6,500, for a total of $26,000. Note that employer contributions (employer match, profit sharing contribution) are always pre-tax; the Roth option is only available for employee contributions.

Since individuals should always try to maximize their contributions to tax-advantaged accounts, the Roth 401(k) is a valuable tool. The same issues apply to 403(b) accounts.

Pay Me Now or Pay Me Later

As seen from the examples above, it is just a case of when the government's "tax bell tolls." You do control the timing. Your choice should be based on when you think the government's percentage ownership is likely to be lower. Since you do not know for certain what future tax rates will be, one strategy is to assume your future marginal tax rate will be the same as it is today. Another strategy worth considering is diversifying the risk of changing tax rates, splitting contributions between a Roth and a traditional IRA. As your tax rate varies over time you will withdraw more from your Roth when your marginal rate is high and more from the traditional IRA when it is low.

5. While traditional IRAs require minimum withdrawals (RMDs), Roths do not: The government has already collected its toll (taxes on the income have already been paid). If an individual believes they will not need the RMD to pay for living expenses, choosing the Roth could be better even if the tax rate was expected to be slightly lower at withdrawal. Remember, too, that when estimating future tax rates, you should consider the impact of an RMD on the marginal tax rate and on the taxability of Social Security benefits.

    One more point: Due to the specific formulas for the calculation of taxes for investors likely to be subject to estate tax, the dollars accumulated in Roth IRAs are, in effect, taxed less heavily than those in a traditional IRA. The formulas are complicated. Those likely to be subject to the estate tax should seek professional estate tax advice from their CPA.

Summary

Integrating tax consequences into investment plans can be complex, especially as tax rates and investment values change. There are two ways to address this problem. The first is to tax adjust your current holdings to account for the government's share. The other approach is to use a Monte Carlo simulation with tax codes built in to determine the odds of success of your investment plan. The simulation will account for the government's share and give you the estimated odds of your plan succeeding in achieving its goal. The latter approach, the one we use, is recommended for its simplicity. Either will help you make the right decisions.

A final note: We urge caution in using software tools purporting to analyze the benefits of traditional IRA and Roth IRAs. Several we have looked at contain errors, missing some of the key points raised in this chapter.

We now turn to a discussion about conversions of traditional IRAs to Roth IRAs.

IRA Conversions

The IRS allows for conversions of traditional IRAs to Roth IRAs upon paying the appropriate tax. And there are situations when it is in your benefit to do a conversion. However, there are limitations.

Limitations

Roth IRAs restrict contribution eligibility. For 2020, investors who were married, filing jointly, saw their contribution limits phase out once their MAGI (Modified Adjusted Gross Income) exceeded $196,000. And they lost Roth IRA contribution eligibility with a MAGI above $2,069,000. For those with a filing status of single or head of household, the limits were $124,000 and $139,000, respectively. Qualifying investors can still own a Roth IRA by doing what is called a Roth conversion. This involves converting a traditional IRA into a Roth IRA. Determining if a conversion makes sense is where it gets more complicated.

When considering a conversion, keep the following factors in mind:

- Are sufficient funds available to pay the tax on the amount to be converted? (Remember, taxes are based on ordinary income tax rates.) The greatest potential for growth occurs when funds from taxable accounts are used to pay the taxes.
- An IRA inherited from a person other than a spouse cannot be converted to a Roth IRA.
- Assets must not be withdrawn from the Roth IRA within five years of the conversion. If you do, you will have to pay the 10 percent early distribution penalty, unless you are older than 59½. The five-year withdrawal limitation for IRA conversions begins January 1 of the calendar year the conversion takes place. So, if you convert to a Roth IRA in December 2020, the effective start date for the five years is January 1, 2020. That means you have only four years remaining until the withdrawal penalties disappear.

- Conversion income could push you into a higher tax bracket, increasing your total tax liability and possibly disqualifying you from other tax benefits such as the dependent child care and college tuition tax credits. The conversion income could also increase the percentage of your Social Security benefits that are taxable.

Who Should Consider a Roth Conversion?

A Roth conversion may make sense if you answer "yes" to any of the following questions:

- Do you have enough money outside your IRA to meet your needs? Unlike traditional IRAs, Roth IRAs do not have required minimum distributions at 72. If you want to pass this account untouched to your heirs, conversions can make sense.
- Do you live in a high-tax state and plan to retire to a low-tax state? Again, you would not want to pay more tax now than you would on distributions later.
- Are your heirs likely to inherit your IRA, and are they in lower tax bracket than you are now? Again, save the taxes for your family.
- Do you need to generate income to take advantage of tax credits or deductions? If you have charitable deductions, carry-forwards or other tax-favored items, but not much income one year, conversions may make sense. Not only do you get the benefits of conversion, but by forcibly increasing your income (money moved counts as income), you can take advantage of all your qualified deductions and credits. A conversion can also be helpful for investors with high medical expenses; additional taxable income helps take advantage of the full deduction.
- Will a conversion trigger stealth taxes (such as taxation of Social Security benefits and the cost of Medicare premiums) that are tied to adjusted gross income? If that is the case a careful analysis should be done to weigh the benefits of a conversion versus the negative impact in the year of the conversion.
- Is financial aid likely to be affected by a spike in income from a Roth conversion? If this is the case, timing is critical, especially when a large chunk of needed money might be at risk. While retirement accounts are generally excluded for financial aid, income is not. If you need the aid and could suffer from a spike in income, a Roth conversion may have to be put on hold until assistance is no longer needed.
- Do you anticipate needing to tap IRA funds to pay heavy out-of-pocket medical expenses in retirement (which won't be reimbursed with insurance)? If that is the case a Roth conversion is a bad choice because the medical expense deduction survived tax reform (it's limited by a 10% AGI threshold

for 2019 and later years). The deduction may be used to offset the tax on future IRA distributions. This, of course, assumes that the medical bills will be high enough to itemize, given the new expanded standard deduction.

- Do you believe your tax bracket is lower now than it will be in retirement? Conversions may be good for young investors with low income. The tax on the conversion should be low, and it is possible that when the money is withdrawn, a higher tax will later apply on taxable distributions. This would be especially true if the investors have high equity allocations in their traditional IRA. Equities have high expected returns. The account could grow to sufficiently large levels, making the required minimum distributions large enough to cause their marginal tax rate to be at a high level. The longer the investment horizon, the more important this issue becomes.

- Are your heirs likely to inherit your IRA, and are your heirs in a higher tax bracket than you? This closely relates to the last question. If your heirs are in a higher tax bracket than you are, it is to their benefit to do a Roth conversion now. You might even ask if they are willing to pay (or share) in the taxes on the conversion.

- Do you have enough money outside the IRA to pay the taxes on the conversion? Investors converting their IRAs should pay conversion taxes from taxable dollars. Doing so allows for greater growth potential.

Who Should Not Consider a Roth Conversion?

If you answer "yes" to any of the following questions, a Roth conversion may not make sense:

- Do you believe you are in a higher tax bracket now than you will be in retirement? The taxes paid to convert now may exceed the taxes paid later at the lower rate on IRA distributions, negating the benefits.

- Are you interested in leaving your IRA to a charity? There are no advantages to rolling it into a Roth and paying taxes on it now, since it will be a tax-free event for the charity when received.

Partial Conversions

A partial conversion may make more sense in the following scenarios:

- If you do not have money to comfortably pay the taxes, partial conversions over a set time period would soften the tax impact. As long as you meet the income and filing requirements you can continue to convert a portion every year.

- When you convert money from traditional IRAs to Roth IRAs, it counts as income. If the amount of the conversion would increase taxable income enough to move you into a higher tax bracket, partial conversions may be more sensible. This can be difficult to estimate, so it is important to get your tax professional involved.

Conversions from Non-Deductible IRAs

If you have only contributed to non-deductible IRAs and wish to convert, part of the conversion will be tax-free. Taxes are calculated only on the earnings from non-deductible contributions, not the non-deductible contributions themselves. However, if you own both deductible and non-deductible IRAs, the taxable portion of the IRA (or portion of the IRA you will convert) will be determined based on the proportion of taxable money in all the traditional and simple IRAs combined. If you have untaxed amounts in other IRAs, you may end up owing more in taxes on this conversion than expected. The IRS does not allow you to designate that your conversions are only from the non-deductible contributions.

Summarizing, the decision to convert traditional IRAs into Roth IRAs is not an easy one to make. You have to make assumptions regarding both your future tax situation and cash flow needs. It is important to think these things through and consult a tax expert.

We next address a question with which we frequently have to deal.

What to Do When Retirement Plan Choices are Poor

The historical record provided by academic studies is clear: The prudent investment strategy is investing in low-cost mutual funds that are passively managed—index funds, ETFs and passive asset class funds. Because of the expenses of providing and maintaining a plan, a conflict of interest can arise between what is best for the employer (least cost) and best for the employee (access to the best investment vehicles). This conflict is very often decided in favor of the employer.

The employer can save significant dollars by not having to pay for administration of the employee benefit. Management gets really interested when a fund family providing high-cost, actively managed funds proposes to the employer that they will pick up all of the plan's administrative expenses if the employer makes their fund family the exclusive (or at least dominant) provider of investment alternatives. Because high-cost, active management is a loser's game, it is the employees that lose, accumulating fewer dollars in their retirement accounts.

It would be far better for both employers and employees to choose a plan with low-cost, passive investment vehicles. If the employer could not afford the administrative costs of such a plan, the costs could be unbundled and appropriately passed on to each employee. Employees may be concerned they would be charged for a service that in the past was "free." However, through education they will learn they have been paying for administration services all along, just not being billed separately for them. The cost showed up in lower returns earned due to the higher internal expenses of the mutual funds in which they were investing. In the long term, charging employees directly for administration costs is significantly less expensive than paying both the expenses of high-cost mutual fund companies and the extra, and non-productive, trading costs of active management.

If your employer's plan does not have access to low-cost funds, you should inquire if the plan allows for an in-service distribution. If so, you can rollover your retirement plan balance to your self-directed IRA and access better options. If this option is not available you are left with choosing between the "lesser among evils."

For three reasons, the best choice is to utilize the retirement plan for fixed income assets. First, it's preferable from a tax efficiency standpoint to hold the equities in taxable accounts and fixed income assets in tax-advantaged accounts. Index or other passively managed funds should be used, though they are often not available.

Second, the expense ratios and trading costs of actively managed fixed income funds are generally lower than for actively managed equity funds. Because the turnover of fixed income funds is generally lower than for equity funds, by choosing fixed income funds you can reduce total expenses and the drag on returns.

Third, the dispersion of returns across bond funds is usually much lower than for stock funds. Actively managed stock funds are more likely to underperform by large amounts than even poor (or lucky) bond funds.

If the investor needs to hold equities in the tax-advantaged account, the first choice should be to choose index or other passively managed funds. The preference should be for domestic funds, since the foreign tax credit is lost in tax-advantaged accounts. If passively managed funds are not available, the risk of style drift by active managers must be considered. Since controlling the risk of a portfolio is of paramount importance, investors should look for funds that "stick to their knitting." Investors should also look for funds having the lowest total expenses (operating expense ratios, other fees, and the lowest turnover): Expenses incurred in selecting securities and/or timing the market are highly likely to prove counterproductive.

The bottom line is that investors should look for funds most closely resembling low-cost, passive funds. One example is Vanguard's Windsor Fund, a good choice for gaining exposure to the asset class of U.S. large value. It is low cost, low turnover, and has shown no tendency to style drift.

It is important to build a globally diversified by asset class portfolio, avoiding having all your eggs in one asset class basket (U.S. large growth). However, if your only choices are active funds and one index fund (many plans include at least an S&P 500 Index or Total Stock Market fund), invest in the index fund and diversify your equity holdings outside the plan. If the costs of the active choices allowing you to diversify are high, forgo the diversification benefits in favor of the sure savings from lower expenses.

One more point to consider: If the only two index funds in the plan are an S&P 500 Index fund and a total stock market fund, with similar expenses, choose the latter. It is more diversified.

Summary

Retirement accounts play an important role in most investors' portfolios. For many, they constitute the majority of their financial assets. Thus, it is important to both maximize their benefits, and understand the implications of choices you have available. We have provided you with the information needed to make the right decisions.

The next chapter is about Health Savings Accounts. While not originally created to serve as investment accounts, using them for that purpose is an effective strategy.

CHAPTER 9

Health Savings Accounts

RABAH KAMAL AND Bradley Sawyer of the Kaiser Family Foundation estimate that health-care costs will increase almost 5 percent per year through 2026. Thus, as you age, medical expenses are likely to be among the most significant of your costs in retirement. In fact, according to the Employee Benefit Research Institute 2017 study:

- A 65-year-old man needs $73,000 in savings and a 65-year-old woman needs $95,000 if each have a goal of having a 50 percent chance of having enough savings to cover premiums and median prescription drug expenses in retirement. If they want a 90 percent chance of having enough savings, the man needs $131,000 and the woman needs $147,000.
- A couple with median prescription drug expenses needs $169,000 if they have a goal of having a 50 percent chance of having enough savings to cover health-care expenses in retirement. If the couple wants a 90 percent chance of having enough savings, they need $273,000.

These staggering figures are why a Health Savings Account (HSA) can be among the most significant tools for retirement success.

What is an HSA?

An HSA is a tax-favored savings account used for the purpose of paying health-care expenses, available to those participating in a High Deductible Health Insurance Plan (HDHP). As a savings vehicle, the HSA has tax advantages greater than traditional retirement accounts, such as a 401(k) and IRAs, whether traditional or Roth. The reasons are:

1. Contributions are 100 percent deductible, whether or not you itemize deductions, up to the annual limit.

2. Interest and/or earnings are either tax-deferred, or tax-free if used strategically.
3. Withdrawals used to pay for qualified medical expenses are tax-free and penalty-free.

Based on whether your insurance coverage is for an individual or a family, the IRS sets limits on the amount you can annually contribute to your HSA. For 2021, the limit is $3,600 for individuals and $7,200 for family coverage. An employee age 55 or older can contribute up to $1,000 in additional "catch up" contributions. Unlike limits on certain other retirement accounts, there are no income limits related to an HSA. Also, an employer may or may not contribute to an HSA.

Tax-Free Distributions

As mentioned above, distributions for qualified health-care expenses for dependents are penalty- and tax-free. Eligible expenses are generally those necessary to alleviate, or prevent, physical or mental illness.

Expenses not eligible would typically be cosmetic in nature (such as teeth whitening or hair transplants). The IRS provides a list of eligible expenses, which you can find at www.irs.gov/publications/p502. The list is worth reviewing to be certain you will not be penalized. For example, while a gym club membership may be good for your health, it is not an eligible medical expense. Also, expenses that took place before the HSA was established are not considered qualified.

While funds in the HSA can technically be used for any purpose, you have to pay income taxes on ineligible distributions, plus a 20 percent penalty. If you are 65 or older and make a non-eligible distribution, you have to pay taxes, but there is no penalty.

Portability

Another important feature of HSAs is that they are portable—funds in the account, including employer contributions, are owned by the account owner, and remain so whether you change employers, stop working entirely, or are no longer a participant in an HDHP. And if you are no longer insured, are on COBRA, use a health insurance plan of another employer (new job or spouse's plan), or are on Medicare, you keep your HSA.

Another benefit of an HSA is that unlike with a Flexible Spending Account (FSA), typically associated with traditional health insurance plans, there is no "use it or lose it" component—if you do not spend the contributions in a given year, they can be used in subsequent years. That allows you to strategically use your HSA as a retirement savings account.

A Powerful Retirement Tool

If you have a retirement plan such as a 401(k) where your employer matches contributions, that plan should be the first place to put your investment dollars to work. With that caveat in mind, there are three key ways an HSA can serve as a powerful retirement tool. First, the triple tax benefit described earlier. Second, the potential for growth by investing your HSA contributions. Third, tax-advantaged investment growth. If you are able to fund medical expenses from your taxable accounts, you can grow your tax-advantaged HSA for use in retirement. And, as with any long-term investing plan, the sooner you are able to take advantage of an HSA, the greater the benefit of compounding.

Why Not Take Advantage of an HSA?

The first decision you have to make is whether or not an HDHP is appropriate based on your current medical and financial situation. While an HDHP can potentially work for anyone, they typically make the most sense for either the young and healthy (who are not likely to have significant medical costs), or those with the means to cover the out-of-pocket maximum should a major medical issue arise. Depending on the plan the out-of-pocket costs can vary significantly, so it is important to review your specific plan. Alternatively, if you, or a family member under your plan, incur substantial medical issues and/ or do not have outside resources to cover medical expenses, an HDHP might not be a good fit.

Determining the Right Insurance Plan

As you weigh options, consider the difference in premiums, the size of the deductible, and potential costs associated with anticipated, or unanticipated, medical expenses.

Choosing an HSA Provider

Your employer may automatically set you up with a specific financial institution to administer the HSA. If you are able to choose your own (and if it's not clear, be sure to ask), there will be variations in terms of ease of administration, fees, interest rates, minimum balances before one can invest, and investment options. Make sure you perform a thorough due diligence as there can be large differences among these factors. Working with a trusted advisor can help you determine the plan—including the right investment options for your situation—that is right for you. As a general rule, choose a bank with low fees, low costs, and index, or other passively managed, funds that allow you to diversify your portfolio.

There are a few more points we need to cover. As we note in the Social Security and Medicare chapters (12 and 13, respectively), you can no longer contribute to an HSA once you have filed for Medicare and/or Social Security. And make sure you avoid the six-month lookback rule.

If you pass away, your spouse can inherit your HSA. One word of caution: if someone other than the spouse is the beneficiary, it loses its status as an HSA plan and becomes fully taxable to the beneficiary in the year you pass away (if your estate is the beneficiary, the value of your HSA will be included on your final income tax return). However, considering the expected high cost of health care and the relatively low annual contribution amounts, it may take a substantial amount of time—and a lot of good health in later years—to have an estate planning concern when it comes to an HSA. And recall that there is no time limitation for reimbursement. For example, you can save a medical receipt from an expense incurred when you are 23 (provided you established an HSA by that time), and not reimburse yourself until you are on your death bed! The benefit is that you have the tax-free growth of the invested dollars.

Summary

With its unique tax structure, and the likelihood that substantial expenses in retirement could be health care-related, using the HSA as a savings vehicle can provide significant benefits.

The next chapter is about the all-important asset location decision. Allocating assets in the right locations can significantly improve the odds of success of achieving your goals.

CHAPTER 10

The Asset Location Decision

D URING THE ACCUMULATION phase, the choice of location (taxable versus tax-advantaged accounts) where you place your investments can have a significant impact on the odds of achieving your financial goals. And the same holds true when you begin withdrawing assets. We will begin with our recommendations for locating assets when investing.

The Accumulation Phase

When faced with a choice of locating assets in either taxable or tax-advantaged accounts, taxable investors should have a *preference* for holding equities (versus fixed income investments and alternative investments) in taxable accounts. But, regardless of whether they hold stocks or fixed income investments, investors should always prefer to first fund their Roth IRA or other deductible retirement accounts (IRA, 401(k) or 403(b)) before investing any taxable dollars. The reason is that tax-advantaged accounts are the most tax-efficient investment accounts. Thus, investors should always take maximum advantage of their ability to fund them. The one exception is the need to provide liquidity for unanticipated funding requirements.

Like all of our advice, this preference for holding equities in taxable accounts is based on the published academic literature. In this case, the paper is "Optimal Asset Location and Allocation with Taxable and Tax-Deferred Investing," by Robert M. Dammon, Chester S. Spatt, and Harold H. Zhang, which appeared in the June 2004 issue of *The Journal of Finance*. If you are interested in the mathematics behind our recommendations, see Appendix C.

There are six advantages to holding equities rather than fixed income or alternatives in a taxable account:

1. Equities receive capital gains treatment, while fixed income investments are taxed at ordinary income tax rates. And the returns from most alternative investments are generally considered either ordinary income or short-term capital gains, making them less tax efficient than equities.

2. Securities in taxable accounts receive a step-up in basis for the heirs at death, eliminating capital gains taxes, though not the estate tax. The higher expected return of equities takes the most advantage of the potential step-up, creating the preference for holding them in taxable accounts. On the downside, securities with unrealized losses in taxable accounts receive a step-down in basis at death—a good reason to harvest losses when available.

3. Capital gains taxes are due only when realized. Investors have some ability to time the realization of gains. In addition, the advent of core and multi-style funds, tax-managed funds, and ETFs has greatly improved the tax efficiency of equity investing.

4. When there are losses in taxable accounts, the losses can be harvested for tax purposes. The more volatile the asset, the more valuable the option to harvest losses. Equities are more volatile than fixed income assets.

5. Assets held in taxable accounts can be donated to charities. By donating the appreciated shares (the preference should be to donate the shares with the largest long-term capital gain), capital gains taxes can be avoided. Because equities have higher expected returns than fixed income assets, this option is more valuable for equities.

6. Taxes on dividends of foreign stock holdings are often withheld at the source. Investors can, however, claim a foreign tax credit (FTC) that can then be used as a credit against U.S. taxes. This credit is lost if the asset is held in a tax-advantaged account. We estimate that the loss of the FTC leads to a reduction of returns of about 9 percent of the amount of the dividend. This figure can change over time and across funds due to changes in withholding rates, tax treaties, and asset allocation within a fund. Remember, if the investment in international assets is a "fund of funds" structure, no portion of the FTC can be passed on to the investor by the fund of funds. However, if more than half of the fund is invested in individual foreign securities and the remainder structured as a fund of funds, the fund will qualify for an FTC.

In summary, holding stocks in taxable accounts and bonds in retirement accounts (either Roth or traditional) is contrary to the commonly held belief that bonds should be held in taxable accounts and higher-returning stocks should be held in retirement accounts to maximize the investment gains. The error in the conventional wisdom is that it overlooks the fact that the government bears part of the risk on assets held in taxable accounts.

Order of Preference

The asset allocation for some investors will require their holding equities in both taxable and tax-advantaged accounts. To make the most of tax-advantaged accounts, one should use them to hold investments that are the most tax inefficient, and then place the rest in taxable accounts. The following is our recommended order of preference for holding assets in a tax-advantaged account:

1. Reinsurance and alternative (also known as marketplace) lending.
2. Long-short Alternative Style (Risk) Premia* and commodities.
3. REITs (U.S., international and global).
4. Fixed income.
5. International small value.
6. International large value.
7. Emerging markets core, U.S. large value and U.S. small value.
8. U.S. Core and international core.

   * The preference is to hold the Alternative Style Premia Fund in a tax-advantaged account. However, if there is not sufficient space in such accounts it should be replaced with the Alternative Risk Premia Fund which is a more tax-efficient version and suitable for taxable accounts.

Ideally, all of the asset classes in the first four groups should be sheltered in tax-advantaged accounts. However, that might not be possible. A related topic is certain asset classes or strategies should be excluded if there is no room to hold them in tax-advantaged accounts. There is only one asset that we would recommend excluding from most portfolios if they must be held in taxable accounts—commodities. With that said, it is important to note that while the expected benefits of the other alternative strategies (as well as REITs) are likely large enough to consider holding in taxable accounts, especially if they are replacing fixed income assets, investors should expect relatively large taxable distributions. If the alternatives are replacing equities, while there is a loss in tax efficiency, you are still diversifying your sources of returns.

Because Roth IRAs and Roth 401(k)s are tax-free accounts, investors often wonder if they should put the highest expected return asset classes in those accounts to grow them as much as possible or to follow proper asset location order of preference instead to hold tax-inefficient strategies investments. Placing relatively tax-efficient asset classes in Roth IRA or Roth 401(k) accounts, while holding less tax-efficient asset classes in taxable accounts, generally reduces tax efficiency and detracts from long-term, after-tax return.

Traditional IRA/401(k) and Roth IRA

When making asset location decisions between traditional IRA or 401(k) accounts and Roth IRA or Roth 401(k) accounts, it typically makes sense to locate higher expected return assets in the Roth accounts and lower expected return assets in traditional accounts. The reason is that it reduces the need for required minimum distributions from traditional retirement accounts. The order of preference to fill the Roth accounts from highest expected return to lowest expected return is as follows:

1. Small value (U.S. and international).
2. Emerging markets core.
3. Core and large value (U.S. and international).
4. REITs (U.S. and international).
5. Reinsurance.
6. Long-short Alternative Style (Risk) Premia/alternative lending.
7. Commodities.
8. Fixed income.

Additional Considerations

Consider the following:

- The most tax-efficient funds should be placed in the taxable accounts.
- Tax-managed funds will generally be more tax efficient than funds not managed for tax efficiency.
- The broader the definition of the asset class, the more tax efficient the fund is likely to be. For example, a total market fund will be more tax efficient than a narrow asset class fund, such as a small-cap fund. A small-cap fund—that holds both value and growth—will be more tax efficient than a small-cap value fund.
- Large-cap funds are more tax efficient than small-cap funds.
- Marketwide and growth funds are more tax efficient than value funds.
- Multiple asset class funds (such as core funds and total stock market funds) are more tax efficient than single asset class funds due to lower turnover as stocks "migrate" from one asset class to another. For example, an international core fund holding both developed and emerging markets will be more tax efficient than holding two separate funds. In addition to the reduction in forced turnover, rebalancing costs between individual asset classes will be reduced, and the core funds will not have to trade if a country is reclassified from an emerging market to a developed one.
- The more volatile the asset class, the more valuable the ability to harvest losses.

- Because not all foreign dividends qualify for the lower tax rate applicable to qualified dividends, the amount of unqualified dividends a fund distributes is a factor that determines if it should be held in a taxable account or not.

Example

An investor has a total portfolio of $2 million: $1 million in a taxable account and $1 million in a tax-advantaged account. First determine the appropriate asset allocation based on the investor's ability, willingness and need to take risk.

Assume it is 54 percent stocks, 3 percent alternatives, 3 percent commodities, and 40 percent bonds.

1. Locate 3 percent ($60,000) allocations to both alternatives and commodities, for a total of $120,000 to the tax-advantaged accounts. That leaves $880,000 yet to be allocated to the tax-advantaged accounts.
2. Place the 40 percent of bonds ($800,000) in the tax-advantaged accounts. That leaves $80,000 of equities that can be held in the tax-advantaged accounts. Place the least tax-efficient equities in the tax-advantaged account.

Advanced Concept

Since fixed income is more attractive if you have a tax-advantaged account, you might consider maximizing that benefit by purchasing even more bonds in the tax-advantaged account. To accomplish this objective without lowering the expected return (need to take risk), lower the equity allocation (which lowers the expected return of the portfolio) and raise the exposure to the size and value risk premiums, thus restoring the portfolio's expected return to its original level. This both improves the portfolio's tax efficiency and reduces the potential dispersion of returns. You are trading a lower opportunity for outstanding returns (a reduction in the size of the good, fat right tail of potential distributions) for a lower risk of extremely negative results (a reduction in the size of the bad, fat left tail of potential distributions). One potential psychological risk is that you will increase tracking error risk.

Balanced and Target Date Funds

Balanced and target date funds are two mutual fund products that have proliferated in recent years—especially inside corporate retirement and profit sharing plans. The idea behind these products is fundamentally sound: create a fund of funds that invests in various asset classes. These funds can be structured to accommodate investors ranging from aggressive (100 percent equity allocation) to very conservative (20 percent equity allocation). They provide the following features:

- They allow investors to hold in one fund a diversified portfolio that can include both U.S. equities and international equities, including emerging markets.
- They automatically rebalance to targeted investments, which provides a disciplined approach. These funds have the ability to rebalance internally by using cash flows from new deposits and dividends. This provides a more cost- and tax-efficient way for taxable accounts to rebalance than buying and selling individual asset classes.

However, there are some important negative features:

- For investors with a choice of location (unless the fund is all-equity), combining equities and fixed income assets in one fund results in holding one of the two assets in a tax-inefficient manner. If the fund of funds is held in a taxable account, the investor is holding the fixed income assets in a tax inefficient location. If the fund is held in a tax-advantaged account, the equities are being held in a tax-inefficient location.
- If the fund is held in a taxable account the investor loses the ability to loss harvest at the individual asset class level.
- If the fund is in a tax-advantaged account, the investor loses the ability to use any foreign tax credits generated by the international equity holdings. Even in a taxable account, as a fund of funds, the investor loses the ability to utilize the foreign tax credit.
- If the fund is held in a taxable account, the equities should be in tax-managed funds. We are not aware of any lifestyle or balanced fund that tax-manages the equity portion. This makes sense, since the fund does not know which type of account it will be held. Finally, if the fund is held in a taxable account, it is likely the fixed income portion should be in municipal bonds. Otherwise, there is a loss of tax efficiency.
- If the fund is held in a taxable account, the equities should be managed for tax efficiency, including loss harvesting and not intentionally taking short-term capital gains. We are not aware of any balanced or target date fund that tax-manages the equity portion (which makes sense since the fund does not know in which location it will be held).
- If the fund is held in a taxable account, for most investors, the fixed income allocation should be in municipal bonds, not taxable bonds. Unfortunately, almost all of these funds hold taxable bonds.

There is one other important point we need to cover.

Costs Matter

The greatest benefit of mutual funds is their ability to provide broad diversification at low cost. This is an important benefit for the equity portion of the portfolio—broad diversification minimizes the idiosyncratic (and thus uncompensated) risk of owning individual stocks. The broad diversification that only a mutual fund can provide effectively is also important if your bond allocation includes risky investments such as corporate bonds, emerging market bonds, preferred stocks, and convertible bonds. However, if your bond holdings are limited to safe investments, such as Treasuries, government agencies, and FDIC-insured CDs, which is our recommendation, there is no need to incur the expense of a mutual fund. With safe investments such as these, the only benefit of a mutual fund is convenience (in the case of balanced and target date funds, the disciplined rebalancing they provide can be another benefit). Let's see how this impacts the effective cost of balanced and target date funds.

These funds have expense ratios that can run from as low as about 0.2 percent for Vanguard's retirement funds, to 1.5 percent, or more, with an average expense ratio of about 1 percent. Now consider investors who decide that they would like to have a 50 percent equity/50 percent bond allocation. Also assume that the balanced or target date fund they have chosen has an expense ratio of 1 percent. Let's also assume that their bond holdings are all in high-quality investments such as Treasuries and FDIC-insured CDs. These investments can be purchased independently at little to no cost, and without any ongoing fund expenses. Thus, the entire burden of the expense ratio of the fund is being carried by the equity portion. Thus, we should consider that the equities are really costing them 2 percent.

Now consider that our investor prefers the convenience of a mutual fund, or needs it because they want to own bonds that have credit risk that needs to be diversified. The investor can purchase the appropriate ETF or a low-cost Vanguard bond fund for as low as about 0.05 percent, resulting in an effective expense ratio for the equity allocation of 1.95 percent. In either case, it's a steep price to pay for the benefit of discipline (and possibly some tax savings due to internal rebalancing by the fund).

Summarizing, individually, each of the negative features that we discussed may provide a sufficient reason to avoid these funds. Collectively, they are very damaging. And make sure you do the "math" so that you understand the costs of these funds as compared to the alternatives.

The bottom line is that it is unlikely that these funds will be the most efficient way for you to achieve your goals. A more efficient investment strategy is to hold the stocks and bonds separately and in the most tax-efficient location.

The next chapter provides you with effective spend down strategies that can significantly improve the odds of achieving your goals, be it not outliving your assets, or leaving a large estate for your heirs or charity.

CHAPTER 11

Spend Down Strategies

I F WE LIVE long enough our financial assets can go through five phases: accumulation, transition, distribution, final spending, and legacy. Chapters 3 through 10 were all about the winning strategy in the accumulation phase. However, the knowledge required to effectively manage financial assets in the accumulation phase is not sufficient to carry you through the remaining stages. This chapter focuses on providing you with the knowledge needed to give you the best chance of achieving your life and financial goals as you pass through the various other stages.

Accumulation Phase

The accumulation phase commences when we begin our careers and start to save and invest. For those who forgo college, the accumulation phase will begin in our late teens. For others, such as doctors and lawyers, it might not begin until our late twenties. This phase is the longest one as it typically continues until we stop working full-time. The goal during this phase is to save and invest as early and as much as possible. Chapters 3 through 10 have provided you with the information needed to develop the right strategy. The strategy should include a focus on which tax-advantaged accounts should be used (traditional versus Roth IRA). Chapter 10 provides a detailed discussion on this issue. The strategies learned in this chapter continue to apply throughout your lifetime.

Each of the following phases are part of the decumulation, or withdrawal, phase. The most significant difference in strategies during withdrawal and those during accumulation is that there is a much greater emphasis on long-term tax planning during withdrawal. Taxes are often the single largest expense for investors. Thus, to ensure that you have the best chance to meet your own goals, we strive to have the IRS take the smallest share of your financial assets.

However, this does not necessarily mean paying the least amount of taxes in any particular year. Instead, the focus is on paying the least over your lifetime and possibly beyond. During accumulation, taxes are dominated by your salary and/or other sources of income. The tax strategies during this phase relate mostly to how much you can save before tax, how much after tax, and where you locate the different types of assets. However, planning during spend down presents different opportunities as you go through phases of low and high tax rates. Therefore, we break decumulation into four distinct phases.

Decumulation Phase

Transition Phase

The first phase during withdrawal, which doesn't exist for everyone, is one with low tax rates. It typically begins with your retirement, when you are no longer generating sufficient income to meet your lifestyle needs. During this time, you may not yet have chosen to receive Social Security or pension benefits and are not yet required to take distributions from your retirement accounts. Thus, you may be in a low tax bracket and can draw on your taxable assets (at relatively low tax rates), or tax-free assets, to provide the desired lifestyle.

During transition, many retirees celebrate their low taxes after years of paying large amounts with their salaries. However, as we discuss later, this might not be the best strategy.

Distribution Phase

The distribution phase is when you start spending down your tax-deferred retirement plan accounts. It typically begins the year you turn 72 and start taking your required minimum distribution (RMD). It is a period when tax rates can jump back up from the low rates of the transition period as you start receiving income from RMDs on top of your Social Security and possibly pension benefits. An individual's tax rate will often remain at this same high rate for the rest of his or her life. Although, increasingly, people move into one final phase during their lives.

Final Spending Phase

This is the phase we all hope to avoid. However, it occurs with increased frequency now, as medical advances continue to extend life expectancy. In this phase, medical and long-term care expenses can be extremely high. And given their tax deductibility, at least under current law, they can provide another period with a very low marginal tax rate—which can create new opportunities for tax-efficient strategies.

Legacy Phase

The legacy phase begins at your death, or, if married, upon the second-to-die. The goal in this phase is not only the tax-efficient transfer of your remaining wealth to heirs or charities but also preparing your heirs for the assets they will inherit. Chapter 18 covers the estate planning process, and Chapter 19 is about preparing your heirs to manage their inheritance and transferring your values.

As you move through the five stages, there are many strategies to minimize the government's share of your assets and maximize your portfolio's growth—entire books have been written on the subject. Here we provide you with examples demonstrating the important role that good financial planning has in giving you the best odds of achieving your financial goals. We will begin with an analysis of the efficient tax strategy when faced with the choice of withdrawing from taxable, tax-deferred, and tax-exempt accounts.

Tax-Efficient Withdrawal

Investors who have taxable, tax-deferred, and tax-exempt accounts can increase the longevity of their portfolio by withdrawing in the most efficient sequence.

The "conventional wisdom" has been that investors should first take withdrawals from their taxable account, then from their tax-deferred accounts (such as a traditional IRA or 401(k) plan), and finally from their tax-exempt accounts (Roth IRA). With that said, our recommendations are always based on the academic literature. So, we turn to the study "Tax-Efficient Withdrawal Strategies," published in the March/April 2015 issue of the *Financial Analysts Journal*. The authors, Kirsten A. Cook, William Meyer, and William Reichenstein, studied this issue to determine if the conventional wisdom was correct. The following is a summary of their findings:

- In general, the conventional wisdom is correct. Withdrawing first from the taxable account (TA), then from the tax-deferred (TDA), and finally from the tax-exempt (TEA), instead of the reverse order, can add about three years to the portfolio's longevity.
- A key to a tax-efficient withdrawal strategy is to withdraw funds from TDAs in order to minimize the average of the marginal tax rates on these withdrawals.

- Because withdrawals from taxable accounts can be mostly, if not entirely, tax-free withdrawals of principal, withdrawing first from the TA often results in the retiree being in an unusually low tax bracket before RMDs begin. Withdrawing funds from the TDA or converting funds from the TDA to the TEA, if these funds are taxed at an unusually low rate, increases the longevity of the portfolio in a progressive tax rate regime such as the one we have. This strategy can add about one more year to the portfolio's longevity.

The bottom line is that under our progressive tax structure, "the goal of minimizing the marginal tax rates on TDA withdrawals can be accomplished by withdrawing funds from the TDA each year so long as these withdrawals are taxed at a low marginal rate and then making additional withdrawals from the taxable account until it's exhausted. Once the taxable account has been exhausted, the retiree should withdraw funds from the TDA each year so long as these funds are taxed at a low marginal rate and then make additional withdrawals from the TEA."

The authors also note that a retiree may be in an unusually low tax bracket due to large tax-deductible expenses, such as medical costs. They make the following recommendation: "In those years, the retiree will likely be in a low, if not zero, tax bracket. Although forecasting this circumstance presents a financial-planning problem (because no one knows for certain whether they will have such high expense years), it is nevertheless desirable to try to save some TDA balances for this nontrivial possibility."

The authors also offer a Roth-conversion strategy that can extend longevity. Each year the retiree does a Roth conversion from the TDA to the TEA in an amount that pushes their taxable income to the top of the (then) marginal tax rate of 15 percent (12 percent under the 2018 tax act). At this rate, dividends and long-term capital gains are taxed at 0 percent. The authors estimate that this strategy increases the portfolio's longevity by about one year.

Finally, the authors demonstrate that the impact on portfolio longevity is greater when returns are higher, when volatility is higher, and when the returns sequences are more favorable (higher returns in the early years).

Summarizing, the authors demonstrate that the most tax-efficient withdrawal strategy can add as much as six years relative to the most inefficient one—quite an improvement considering that there are virtually no costs to the most tax-efficient approach.

The following nine examples show how to put these concepts into practice. You will note that, in general, they tend to increase income during periods of low taxes—the transition and final spending phases—while lowering income during the distribution phase when tax rates tend to be higher.

1. Proper Asset Location Saves Income Taxes Now and in the Future

Bill and Sally started saving right out of college, at age 25, by fully funding their 401(k)s and IRAs, and investing in taxable accounts for additional savings. Bill also inherited $300,000 of equities from his grandfather. They decided on an overall investment plan of 60 percent in equities and 40 percent in fixed income. Understanding the asset location issues discussed in Chapter 10, they placed all of their fixed income investments in their 401(k)s and IRAs, and their equities in the taxable accounts to the extent possible. The equities in the taxable accounts produced mostly capital gain income each year. In addition, they were able to harvest capital losses, to offset capital gains, in years when the stock markets declined.

- After 40 years of fully funding their traditional 401(k)s and IRAs, they had accumulated sizable amounts in the tax-deferred accounts. However, by keeping a large proportion of these accounts in fixed income, the growth of their total portfolio was shifted to the taxable accounts, and they paid less tax with lower RMDs.
- When Bill died at age 75, Sally received a step-up in basis on Bill's taxable account assets, to the value at that time. And when Sally died at age 85, their children received another step-up in basis for all the taxable account investments they inherited. The step-up in basis eliminated the capital gains tax that would have been due on these taxable investments.
- The children also inherited the IRAs, and they will pay income tax as they take distributions over the next ten years. However, the utilization of efficient asset location, tax strategies such as loss harvesting and step-up in basis, and managing RMDs, all contributed to a significant increase in their heirs' inheritance.

2. Minimizing Today's Tax Bill Isn't Always the Best Strategy

Steve and Jennifer had high taxable income during their working years. A year ago, at age 65, they both retired as they became eligible for Medicare. Both Jennifer and Steve plan on claiming their maximum Social Security benefits at age 70. They have sufficient funds for lifestyle needs, with substantial assets in both tax-deferred IRAs and taxable accounts. They also have small Roth IRAs.

They were able to generate their cash flow for spending by selling high-basis assets in their taxable accounts. This minimized capital gains, and they bragged about not paying any income tax the first year after retirement. They did not understand they were wasting the low tax brackets and their tax deductions.

By deferring taking taxable income now, they were building a tax-trap for later. Indeed, starting at age 72, both will be required to take higher RMDs from their IRAs, and pay higher taxes than they would now. Each year, the amount they must withdraw, and report as taxable income, will be based on the value of their account at the beginning of the calendar year and the Distribution Period per the IRS Distribution Table.

Working with an advisor, they were able to see the tax advantage of converting $1.2 million of their IRAs to Roth IRAs over the next six years. This causes $200,000 of taxable income each year, using up the lower tax brackets and enabling them to use their deductions. This strategy also has the important benefit of reducing the traditional IRA value, which reduces future RMDs when the couple will also take Social Security benefits. With graduated tax brackets, less income will be taxed at the higher tax brackets in all future years.

Another benefit of the Roth conversions is that their money will remain in tax-advantaged accounts, but all future growth in the Roth IRAs will be tax-free. They plan to leave the Roth conversion accounts untouched for many years. (Note that because Steve and Jennifer are over age 59½, the five-year rule for penalty-free distributions of converted principal won't apply. But, the five-year rule for tax-free distribution of earnings should be considered.)

By bringing taxable income into the years of the transition phase, and using up lower tax brackets, Steve and Jennifer have reduced the total amount of taxes they will pay over their lifetimes. The adage of never paying taxes now that you can defer until later can lead to more taxes over your lifetime.

Our next example is similar in that it also takes advantage of a Roth conversion. However, it has a few other nuances, including doing an IRA withdrawal at year end for tax withholding purposes, and using some of the withdrawals for spending purposes.

3. Roth Conversions to Fill Up Lower Tax Brackets

Jim and Rhonda retired last year with pension income that provides for approximately half of their spending needs. The majority of their retirement funds are in tax-deferred accounts. They are waiting until age 70 to claim Social Security to obtain the largest benefit, and they will begin taking their RMDs two years later when they turn 72. At that time, their taxable income will include their pensions, Social Security, and the RMDs. They will be in the highest tax bracket.

By letting their investments continue to grow inside the traditional IRAs, their future RMDs also increase. Projections were made to estimate how much they should withdraw from their IRAs annually until they are 72 to reduce the tax bracket in future years and the total tax over their lifetime. Since they need cash flow to support their lifestyle, they kept part of the IRA withdrawal for spending and they converted part to Roth IRAs.

Roth IRA conversions will grow tax- and penalty-free if they do not take any distributions for five years from the conversion and they are older than 59½. The five-year rule applies separately to each and every conversion.

To make their lives simpler, they will make a second IRA withdrawal at the end of the year, with federal and state income taxes being withheld from the distributions for the total estimated tax they will owe each year. This allows them to not worry about making quarterly estimated tax payments.

At the end of 2019, Congress passed the Secure Act, which introduced sweeping changes related to Individual Retirement Accounts. Our next section describes how these changes affect the planning around and opportunities available through IRAs.

4. Impact of 2019's Secure Act on a Tax-Efficient Legacy

The Secure Act introduced three critical changes for withdrawing from and saving into IRAs:

1. Required Minimum Distributions (RMDs) now must first be taken for the year the account holder turns 72, up from the previous age of 70½.
2. Non-spouse beneficiaries of inherited IRAs and Roth IRAs no longer have an RMD. However, they must withdraw all assets by the end of the tenth year after the IRA owner passed away. Taxes must still be paid for IRA withdrawals as they are made. This provision eliminates the previous "stretch" provisions that allowed non-spouse beneficiaries to withdraw the assets over their lifetimes.
3. People who work past age 70½ can now continue contributing to IRAs and Roth IRAs.

These changes impact spend down strategies in two notable ways: first, the Distribution Phase now typically begins at age 72 rather than at 70½ as previously; and second, Roth conversions might be even more attractive for legacy.

Consider the following case. Gerry and his wife, Connie, are both 63 and retired. Their portfolio is more than enough to last for the rest of their lives. Their financial advisor had run some projections for them and estimated that they had a good chance of leaving an estate of roughly $6 million to their son, Dave. About a third, or $2 million, would be in an IRA.

Until 2019, they thought that Dave would be able to spread his withdrawals from the IRA over his lifetime without too significant a tax burden. However, now he would have to take an average of about $200,000 per year into income.

When combined with his other income, it would likely push him from the 22 percent or 24 percent tax bracket into the 32 percent bracket, or even higher. Perhaps Dave can concentrate his withdrawals in years when he has lower income, but at this point, that is just pure speculation.

Gerry and Connie asked their advisor if there was anything they could do to improve this tax picture. After running some additional projections, their advisor suggested a program of annual Roth conversions until they reach age 72 and must start taking RMDs. If they convert IRA assets each year until their income reaches the top of the 22 percent tax bracket, they would be able to convert over $1 million during those nine years. He was able to show that their legacy portfolio would be much more tax-efficient for Dave, with the IRA now less than half its previous legacy value and a tax-free Roth IRA more than making up for the lower IRA value. Further, since Dave will not have an RMD for his inherited Roth IRA, he will be able to let the full account grow for ten years before withdrawing the assets tax-free.

5. Donate Appreciated Securities, Not Cash

Many people are in their highest tax brackets in the last five years of the accumulation phase. This may occur due to high earnings years or from selling a business. This is a great time to set up and fund a Donor Advised Fund (DAF), for which you receive the charitable deduction upon setup. Community foundations were the first organizations to offer DAFs. Today, financial institutions, such as Schwab, Fidelity, and Vanguard, as well as charities, offer DAFs. DAFs vary mostly in terms of their minimum contribution, minimum grant, investment options and fees. Service is also a consideration. For example, a community foundation offers a hands-on connection to local needs and initiatives.

The DAF can be used to fulfill your charitable intentions after the accumulation phase. A DAF can also be used to get children involved each year in the charitable decision-making process, teaching them your family's values and giving them a reason to get together on a regular basis.

Randy and Katie plan to give $50,000, over a five-year timeframe, to a non-profit for which Katie serves on the board of directors. They have highly appreciated securities in a living trust and were planning on selling investments to raise cash for the contribution. In lieu of donating cash, it was recommended they donate the appreciated securities approximating $50,000 into a DAF. Their tax situation, and this strategy, will allow them to fully deduct the contribution over the next couple years and avoids having to report capital gains on their tax return this year. The DAF will immediately sell the securities they received, reinvest the proceeds appropriately, and at Randy and Katie's direction each year, forward the cash to the non-profit.

6. Donating Traditional IRA Assets to Charity After 72

Dan and Kathy are married, and both are age 73. They expect to have income of $285,000 from Social Security, required distributions from their IRAs, and more than $50,000 of taxable interest, dividends, and capital gains. Over the last few years, since they started taking their RMDs from their IRAs, Dan and Kathy have exceeded the $250,000 threshold for the net investment income tax. Thus, they have had to pay an extra 3.8 percent tax on some of their investment income.

Until a few years ago, Dan and Kathy had always itemized deductions on their tax return, but the law changed in 2018. In reviewing the latest tax brackets, they noted that they now pay a marginal tax rate of 24%, down from 33% they used to pay. However, their only deductions for itemizing are currently $10,000 for state and local taxes, plus about $5,000 that they give annually to charity, for a total of $15,000 of itemized deductions. This amount is less than the standard deduction, and as a result, they no longer itemize like they used to do. With advice from their advisor, Dan and Kathy decide to use Qualified Charitable Distributions (QCDs) to gift to their charities directly from their IRAs. While the charitable donations count towards Dan and Kathy's RMDs, they are not reported as income on their tax return.

From a tax perspective, this has two benefits. First, not reporting the donations as income has virtually the same benefit as they used to get by reporting the income and then deducting it as an itemized deduction. Now, they can claim the standard deduction and still get the tax benefit for their charitable contributions on top of it. The second benefit is that since the $5,000 of QCDs count towards their RMDs, but are not reported as income, $5,000 of their investment income now falls below the Net Investment Income Tax threshold. This saves Dan and Kathy an extra 3.8 percent in tax on that $5,000. Thus, by making $5,000 of QCDs Dan and Kathy save 27.8 percent in taxes, or $1,390.

Dan, knowing a good thing when he sees it, mentioned QCDs to his brother, Rick, who could also make charitable contributions from his IRA and still benefit from the standard deduction. Rick has lower income than Dan, and he pays 12 percent on his marginal ordinary income. However, as it turns out, Rick's investment income from dividends and long-term capital gains straddles the threshold between the 12 percent and 22 percent brackets. Above the threshold, the tax on this income is 15 percent, but below, it is not taxed.

Interestingly, Rick, even at his lower tax bracket, gets almost the same benefit from QCDs as his higher earning brother, Dan. Rick's QCDs also give him two tax benefits: first, he saves the tax on the donation amount at a 12 percent rate for ordinary income, and second, because this IRA withdrawal does not show up on Rick's tax return as it would otherwise, a portion of his investment income in an amount equal to the donation falls from being taxed at 15 percent to 0 percent. Total tax rate savings on the QCD amount is 27 percent, or $1,350 on a $5,000 QCD.

In summary, QCDs are a strategy that everyone eligible should consider, no matter what your tax bracket. In most cases, they will reduce ordinary income just as itemized charitable contributions did before the tax law changed in 2018. In some cases, they can even lower tax brackets for more savings.

7. Tax-Wise Charitable Legacy

If you have charitable intentions, the efficient strategy is to leave your tax-deferred accounts to charity and your taxable accounts to family. Traditional IRAs left to family members will incur income tax as they withdraw funds over a maximum period of 10 years. IRAs left to charity escape income tax.

Upon reviewing Stan and Mary's estate documents, their advisor saw that their trust documents had provisions for $250,000 of trust assets to be left to charity. Further, they were leaving their IRAs to Sarah, their only child. Their advisor pointed out that Uncle Sam could help them fund their charitable goals and save income taxes for their daughter.

Stan and Mary revised their living trust to leave taxable accounts that would receive a step-up in basis at Stan's and Mary's deaths to Sarah, avoiding taxable gains upon sale of the assets. They then opened a new IRA for Stan, who had, by far, the larger of their IRA balances, and they split out the $250,000 targeted for their charitable legacy from his main IRA to fund the new charitable IRA. Stan named Mary as primary beneficiary and their charities as contingent beneficiaries. When the first spouse passes away, the surviving spouse will maintain this charitable IRA as a separate account with the charities then as primary beneficiaries. To keep the balance in the charitable IRA as close to their $250,000 target as possible, they would pay Stan's total RMD for both of his IRAs out of his main IRA. They can also easily transfer funds between Stan's two IRAs without taxes or penalties. And should they decide to add or remove one of the charities from their list, it is much easier to change the beneficiaries on an IRA than to change a trust document.

8. Tax-Efficient Family Legacy

Rick and Debbie are in their mid-50s. Between the two of them, they have income that puts them in the highest tax bracket. Given the size of their accounts, and their plan to work until age 70, they expect that they will remain in the highest bracket even after retirement.

This year, Rick's widowed mother, Jean, who is 85, went into assisted living. Although she does not have long-term care insurance, she has sufficient assets to meet her increased expenses. Jean's income comes from her survivor Social Security benefit of $24,000, her RMD of about $80,000, plus dividends and capital gains from security sales from assets in her taxable account. Jean has been in a 22 percent marginal tax bracket since the tax law changed in 2018.

Besides her taxable account and her IRA, Jean also has a variable annuity. It has a current value of about $200,000 and a cost basis of $110,000. Rick has never liked this annuity because of its high expenses. However, he did not want to liquidate it because it would give Jean a large tax liability. In addition, it had a $400,000 death benefit. Finally, Jean and her deceased husband had purchased series EE savings bonds 18 years ago for $10,000. They are now worth over $20,000 and will continue to earn interest for the next 12 years.

As Jean's sole heir, Rick knows that, while he will inherit the assets in her taxable account without a tax liability, he will have to pay taxes on all IRA assets, and the gains in the annuity and savings bonds. Further, he understands that once he inherits the assets, the taxes would be at his higher tax rate. Rick mentioned this to his financial advisor who set up the following plan that they discussed with Jean, who understood it and agreed:

- **Tax rates:** With Jean's increased medical expenses from assisted living this year, her itemized deductions had increased to the extent that she had no taxable income. The plan called for giving Jean sufficient income from her portfolio to bring her no higher than the top of the 24 percent marginal tax bracket. The financial advisor pointed out that the extra income would mean that Jean would have to pay more for Medicare due to her higher income and estimated that it would be the equivalent of an additional 3 percent tax on the extra taxable income. However, this was more than offset by the fact the family would save about 10 percent from the 37 percent marginal tax rate that Rick and his wife pay.
- **Annuity:** Because of its death benefit, they did not think it wise to liquidate the annuity. Instead, they changed the beneficiary from Rick to his two children in their 20s, just starting their careers, and in lower tax brackets. When the two children receive their $200,000 portion of the death benefit, of which $145,000 would be taxable, they would have several options based on the annuity contract for withdrawing the proceeds in the most tax-efficient manner (such as a lump sum, spread over five years, or systematic withdrawals over life expectancy).
- **Savings Bonds:** Although Rick thought that Jean should redeem the savings bonds, realize the $10,000 of income, and invest the proceeds into a higher yielding investment, Jean likes having them as a remembrance of her late husband and wants to keep them. Given this, Rick arranged for Jean to report all of the income earned on the bonds to date for her tax return this year. She must continue to report income earned on the savings bonds

every year. Consequently, Rick will inherit the bonds with only a minimal tax liability.

- **IRA:** Each year going forward, Rick will work with his and Jean's accountant near year end to get a good estimate of what her taxable income will be and how much additional income she can have to bring her to the top of the 24 percent tax bracket. They will then do a Roth conversion for the determined amount. They estimate that they will be able to convert over $100,000 of IRA assets each year to a Roth IRA, saving the family over $10,000 in tax liability and getting tax-free growth in the future.

9. Shifting Future Growth Out of the Taxable Estate

Joe and Sandy had recently sold their business. The proceeds were large enough that the assets in their estate exceeded the amount that could be excluded from taxes. They had two young children and had decided to start a new business. Anticipating the future success of the new business, they gifted their interests in it to their two children. Since the company was just formed and had no assets, it had no value. Thus, gifting their interests in the new business to an irrevocable trust for their two children did not use up any of their estate tax exemption. In addition, if the venture becomes successful, all the future growth in value would occur outside of their estate.

10. Gain Harvesting

Jake recently retired from full-time work at age 65. He has decided to wait to claim his Social Security benefit until age 70. Until then, his portfolio, consisting of a $100,000 traditional IRA and $900,000 in a taxable brokerage account with a cost basis of $800,000, will provide the cash needed to meet his spending needs. In December of his first year of retirement, Jake and his advisor estimate his taxable income to be $10,000. Thus, Jake had more than $30,125 remaining in his 12 percent federal income tax bracket. His advisor discussed two alternative strategies. He showed Jake that he could convert $30,125 of his traditional IRA dollars to a Roth IRA at the 12 percent ordinary income tax rate. Alternatively, he could choose to "harvest long-term capital gains" within his taxable account of the same amount and lock in the zero percent federal long-term capital gain rate that applies when taxable income does not exceed $40,125 for single filers (as of 2020 tax brackets).

Jake evaluated the difference between the rates for these two different kinds of income that he has the option to pay now, versus the rate at the next highest bracket. In the case of ordinary federal rates (applicable to Roth conversions), the next bracket above 12 percent is 22 percent—a 10 percent difference. In the case of long-term capital gain rates, the next bracket above zero percent is 15 percent—a 15 percent difference. Favoring the larger difference, Jake chooses to harvest gains within the zero percent federal long-term capital gain bracket. Jake will likely be able to engage in the same strategy for a few years before running out of capital gains to harvest. At that point, he will switch to Roth conversions to fill up his 12 percent ordinary income federal bracket in continued pursuit of paying the least amount of total tax over his retirement.

Summary

As you pass through the various phases of the decumulation process, you will be presented with opportunities that, if exploited, can significantly improve the odds of achieving your goals. Efficiently managing your assets during the withdrawal phase requires not only that you take the long-term view (not trying to minimize taxes in any one year, but minimizing them over your lifetime and beyond), but also that the investment management, estate planning, and tax management be fully integrated. Therefore, it requires that someone with expertise in all three areas act as the quarterback on your financial services team. In the next chapter we move on to maximizing your Social Security benefits.

CHAPTER 12

Social Security

I F WE TOLD you that you could receive guaranteed income that is inflation-adjusted, investment risk-free, as much as 100 percent tax-free, provides longevity protection, and comes with a spousal death benefit, you would not only want to take advantage of it, but also want to maximize that income stream.

These are all features of Social Security retirement benefits. However, because the rules are incredibly complex, and many people have a "bird in the hand" mentality, far too many do not take full advantage of this government benefit. Because Social Security benefits are often a significant source of retirement income—the Social Security Administration (SSA) indicates that these benefits represent over one-third of income for the elderly—it is important to know when it is optimal to begin payments. The right advice can literally add tens of thousands of dollars' difference in lifetime benefits.

The ideal time for filing for your benefits is specific to your unique circumstances. Factors such as age, earnings history, marital status, and disability all play roles in determining the proper strategy. Life circumstances also play a part in ways that can make the solution anything but black and white.

Unfortunately, you cannot rely on the SSA to provide the best strategy for you because they do not know your entire financial situation. This chapter provides an overview of Social Security. Our goal is to both make you aware of issues that may impact your decision and provide you with strategies to consider. While we hope this will be of significant help, there are many situations that fall outside the scope of this book. Indeed, there are entire books dedicated to this subject alone. Robust Social Security planning software—and even better, an advisor who is well versed in Social Security and keeps up with changes in its provisions—can be well worthwhile.

Overview

Although filled with complexities, the following are some basic concepts and figures you need to understand.

Social Security was established to provide retirement, survivor and disability insurance to qualified individuals. Benefits are calculated based on the individual's year of birth, benefits start date, and lifetime earnings. For the average salaried worker, you and your employer both pay into the system by having a certain amount of your paycheck withheld in the form of "FICA," or Social Security and Medicare, taxes.

Most people need to have 10 full working years—or 40 quarters—of paying into Social Security to be eligible for retirement benefits. To determine your benefit amount, the SSA will calculate your highest 35 years of earnings, with earnings for years before age 60 indexed to reflect increases in U.S. workers' average wage level. For example, if the average level in the U.S. is twice as high when the individual is 60 than when he was 40, the formula doubles the age-40 earnings.

Important Benefit Filing Ages

Once you reach your Full Retirement Age (FRA), you are eligible to receive a full—or unreduced—retirement benefit. This full benefit amount is called your Primary Insurance Amount, or PIA. Your FRA depends on your year of birth:

If you were born in	Your full retirement age is
1943–1954	66
1955	66 and 2 months
1956	66 and 4 months
1957	66 and 6 months
1958	66 and 8 months
1959	66 and 10 months
1960 and later	67

You can file for retirement benefits as early as age 62. However, there are significant reasons to wait. By filing early, your benefits are substantially—and permanently—reduced. For example, if your FRA is 66 and you start to receive retirement benefits at age 62, the benefit you receive is reduced to 75 percent;

if you are the spouse, your spousal benefit is reduced from 50 to 35 percent. (The SSA provides a table showing the impact of taking benefits early at their website www.ssa.gov/oact/quickcalc/earlyretire.html. More detail on spousal and other couples' benefits later in the chapter.)

It is also important to understand the concept of "deeming." In most cases, if you are eligible for retirement and spousal benefits and file for either one prior to reaching FRA, you are "deemed," or required, to file for the other as well. When you file for both, you effectively end up receiving the higher of the two benefits. More on spousal benefits later in the chapter, as well as exceptions to the deeming rule in the section titled "A Closed Loophole and a Limited Opportunity" (see page 143).

Another reason not to take benefits early is that you could be subject to the earnings test—if you file prior to your FRA, Social Security will deduct $1 for every $2 of benefits of income you earn that is over a specific amount ($18,240 in 2020). If you reach FRA in 2020, Social Security will deduct $1 in benefits for every $3 you earn above $48,600 up to FRA. Importantly, earnings are only counted prior to the month you reach your FRA. Thus, if your birthday is early in the year, or you do not have substantial earnings the year you reach FRA, you may not be impacted. And starting in or after the month you reach FRA, there is no such limit—you can earn any amount of salary and still receive full benefits.

Taking benefits early can also impact survivor benefits. If you are single and encounter an illness that reduces your life expectancy, it may make sense to file as soon as possible. However, for married couples, when one dies, only the higher benefit amount remains for the surviving spouse. Thus, if you are the higher earner, but take your benefits early, that not only means a reduced retirement benefit during your lifetime, but a reduced survivor benefit if you have a spouse who outlives you. The bottom line is that if you are the higher wage earner of a married couple you must consider that you are not just filing for yourself. Instead, you are filing for the couple's joint lifetime.

After reaching FRA, you can receive "delayed retirement credits" (DRCs) for an increased benefit of 8 percent of your primary insurance amount (PIA)—the level of monthly Social Security benefits if begun at the individual's FRA—per year up until age 70 for a total potential increase of 32 percent. These DRCs are pro-rated—meaning the benefit increases two-thirds of one percent of PIA for each month benefits are delayed after FRA.

DRCs are an important consideration, and key to an optimal filing strategy. Because Social Security benefits are actuarially neutral (assuming a 3 percent real return on Treasury securities and life expectancies in 1983), delaying benefits is like buying longevity insurance without having to pay a premium to an insurance company—as you would if you purchased an annuity. While the trade off for the 8 percent increase is losing one year of benefits, this strategy is more efficient than buying an annuity. In addition to helping avoid the earnings test and a reduced survivor benefit, the difference between filing at age 62 and age 70 for someone with an FRA of 66 is a 76 percent increase in benefits! It's even greater at higher FRAs.

There is one last point to consider when deciding when to begin taking Social Security benefits. Because Social Security benefits are based on your highest 35 years of earnings, working more years later in life when your income is generally higher, you can replace lower earning years with higher earnings ones, increasing your benefit. Thus, working longer may not only allow you to delay taking benefits to replace your salary, continuing to work can also increase your benefits.

When Should I File?

It is actuarially true that if you live to average life expectancy, taking benefits at any age should provide roughly the same cumulative amount of benefits. From that perspective, if your life expectancy is less than average, you should consider filing early, but only after taking into account the survivor benefit mentioned earlier. If it is greater than average, it may still make sense to file somewhere between your FRA and age 70. Further, if you face unexpected early retirement for health or other reasons and need the income, you may not have much of a choice.

If you are forced into early retirement for health reasons prior to FRA, consider applying for Social Security disability benefits. If you qualify, you could receive a benefit equal to your PIA. Once you reach your FRA, your benefit automatically converts to your FRA benefit, without any reduction. Also, you can suspend your benefits upon reaching FRA, allowing for that 8 percent growth per year until age 70.

Therefore, while you need to take into account both your immediate income needs and your health, viewing Social Security as longevity insurance—rather than from an actuarial perspective—provides a powerful reason to delay, if at all possible.

Be careful not to automatically assume that if you stop working you should file for Social Security benefits. We have run retirement analyses that depict a more successful plan if you withdraw money from your portfolio early in retirement while allowing your benefits to grow. Of course, this may not apply in your particular situation.

Longevity: A Deeper Dive

If we knew exactly when you and anyone receiving benefits based on your record would die, all these analyses would be straightforward. However, no one has a clear crystal ball.

As mentioned in the introduction, actuarially, a 65-year-old male has a life expectancy of 85. For a female, it is 88. But, these are just averages. And since, by definition, we expect half the population will live longer than average, do you want to run the risk that you or your spouse may live longer than average? As you consider this, and any other type of "bet," the prudent approach is to understand that the consequences of our decisions should always dominate the probabilities of the outcomes—no matter how confident we are in our estimates of the odds. Being alive without sufficient assets to support an acceptable lifestyle is almost unthinkable for most people. Protecting for longevity always weighs the decision towards filing as late as possible.

Married Couples: Spousal Benefit

If you are married, you are eligible to receive benefits based on your spouse's work history even if you have not worked a single day—or if you have worked but these spousal benefits are higher than your own retirement benefit. In order to qualify for spousal benefits, you need to have been married for more than one year, and the spouse with the earnings record will need to have filed for his or her own retirement benefit.

The spousal benefit represents as much as one-half of the worker's FRA benefit. The following table shows the percentage of benefits someone born prior to 1955 receives in retirement and spousal benefits depending on the ages filed.

Filing Age	Retirement Benefit Percent of Primary Insurance Amount	Spousal Benefit Percent of Spouse's Primary Insurance Amount
62	75%	35%
66 (Full Retirement Age)	100%	50%
70	132%	50%

As you can see, while it can pay to delay retirement benefits at least until FRA, one cannot receive higher spousal benefits by waiting longer than his or her FRA. While it otherwise may make sense to file for spousal at FRA, it may be more beneficial to wait until the higher earning spouse—who must file first—has reached age 70, when retirement benefit is at its maximum. Age difference and earnings history for each spouse dictate different strategies.

Married Couples: Survivor Benefits

As mentioned earlier, when a spouse passes away, the surviving spouse receives the higher of the couple's benefits and loses the lower. In order to be eligible for this benefit, the couple needs to have been married for more than nine months. If the worker has not yet filed for benefits before passing away, the full survivor benefit will be at least the decedent's FRA benefit. If he or she passes away after FRA, but before filing, the benefit will include the increased benefit due to Delayed Retirement Credits. For example, if the worker passes away at age 68, the survivor benefit will be the age 68 retirement benefit.

While retirement or spousal benefits generally start as early as age 62, one can receive survivor benefits as early as age 60. However, like early retirement or spousal benefits, there will be a reduction in benefits for filing before FRA. The benefit does not increase after your FRA. Thus, it does not make sense to file any later than this.

If you do have a substantial earnings record, it may make sense to file only for survivor benefits as early as possible, getting "free" benefits while allowing your own retirement benefits to grow. Then at age 70, you can take your increased retirement benefits. If you remarry before age 60, you cannot claim survivor benefits on your deceased spouse. However, if you remarry after age 60, you can claim the higher of your survivor benefits from your previous marriage, or your spousal benefits from your current marriage.

Divorced Couples: Ex-Spouse Benefit

You can receive an ex-spouse benefit if you meet several criteria. Specifically, you need to be divorced after being married for at least 10 years, and you cannot have remarried. Also, your ex-spouse must be at least age 62 and be eligible either for retirement benefits or disability benefits. Subject to restricted filing as described in the next section, your benefit based on your own worker record must be less than what your ex-spouse benefit would be. You would also need to be at least age 62. However, like spousal or survivor benefits for a married couple, the benefits would be reduced if you file before your FRA. Also similar to spousal benefits, your ex-spouse benefits would be 50 percent of your ex-spouse's full retirement benefit if you start receiving benefits at your own FRA.

If your ex-spouse benefits are higher than what your own retirement benefits would be, there is no reason to delay benefits beyond your FRA, as the benefit you can receive will not be greater than 50 percent.

There are two unique features of ex-spouse benefits. First, you can file even if your ex- has not filed (and vice versa). This is possible if you have been divorced for two or more years. And if your ex- has filed, the two-year rule does not apply.

Second, unlike couples that are still married, both can potentially file for just their spousal benefits.

If you remarry, you can no longer collect ex-spouse benefits, unless your subsequent marriage ends by death, divorce, or annulment. Upon remarriage, your benefits would be based on the new spouse's circumstances.

If you collect an ex-spouse benefit, it does not affect in any way the benefit that your ex-spouse receives.

Finally, divorced spouses may also be eligible to receive survivor benefits upon the passing of their ex-spouse. The ex-spouse survivor benefits mirror that of a married individual's survivor benefits.

A Closed Loophole and a Limited Opportunity

As a result of the Bipartisan Budget Act of 2015, what many considered a loophole was abruptly closed. In effect, the so-called loophole allowed the higher earner to file and immediately suspend benefits at FRA, allowing for the 8 percent growth per year until age 70. The lower earning spouse was then eligible to file for a spousal benefit. This strategy was commonly referred to as "file and suspend."

As a result of the 2015 Act, now if someone suspends retirement benefits, anyone receiving benefits based on the worker's record will also have their benefits suspended. All parties only begin receiving benefits again once the worker reinstates his or her benefits. The only exception is if someone was born before May 1, 1950, who reached FRA and suspended before April 29, 2016. Since that time, the only way to get spousal benefits (other than ex-spousal benefits) is for the worker spouse to file and receive his or her retirement benefit.

The Act also limited another strategy. The "restricted application" strategy allows someone who has reached FRA to receive his or her spousal benefit without having to take the retirement benefit. This allows the retirement benefit to grow with DRCs, letting them receive that higher retirement benefit at age 70. For those born after January 1, 1954, you cannot file a restricted application to receive only spousal benefits. If you are eligible for both retirement and spousal benefits, you will always receive the larger of the two when you file.

Along with those who were grandfathered into the previous rules and have already filed and suspended, there are limited exceptions you may be able to take advantage of:

1. If a spouse who is eligible to file a restricted application due to a birth date on or before January 1, 1954, and both spouses have an earnings history, there may be opportunity to reap additional benefits. Here are examples depending on age and earnings history:

    *   Assume the wife is the lower earner. She may be able to file early, allowing the higher earner to pick up spousal benefits at his FRA. This allows his own retirement benefits to grow until age 70. While her benefits are permanently reduced, it may benefit the overall situation to have them receive some benefits while the higher earner maintains the ability to maximize his retirement benefit, especially if the wife's spousal benefit is significantly larger than her own retirement benefit.
    *   Assume the husband is older, and the wife's earnings history is significant. The husband can file for retirement when the wife reaches her FRA. Then the wife can claim spousal benefits and allow her benefits to increase until age 70.

2. For ex-spouse benefits: if you were born on or before January 1, 1954, once you reach FRA, you can file a restricted application for only ex-spousal benefits, allowing your own retirement benefit to grow until age 70. If the growth on your own benefit is higher than your ex-spouse benefit, you can switch to the higher benefit.
3. Survivor benefits, including ex-spouse survivor benefits, are not impacted by the Act. If you qualify for survivor benefits and have a significant earnings history, you can receive "free" survivor benefits starting at your FRA (or before, if not subject to the earnings penalty), allowing your own retirement benefit to grow until age 70.

In the above instances, you will want to make sure you are filing a "restricted application" for only spousal or only survivor benefits. If you are not proactive and make sure the application is processed correctly, the SSA may either tell you this is not possible or provide you with retirement benefits instead of the spousal/survival benefit.

Couples Benefits

Beyond married couple benefits, there are some factors that are important to understand when it comes to Social Security and gender:

- Social Security is gender neutral, treating same-sex couples the same as heterosexual couples. Women with identical earnings histories are treated the same as men in terms of benefits.
- Social Security is progressive in that lower-wage earners receive a higher percentage benefit than do higher-wage earners. As discussed in Chapter 17, women often face a gender pay gap, receiving lower pay than their male counterparts. To the extent that women are low-wage workers, they actually receive more benefits in relation to past earnings than do high-wage earners.
- With longer life expectancies than men, women tend to live more years in retirement. Thus, without proper planning, they have a greater chance of exhausting other sources of income (more on retirement issues unique to women in Chapter 17). They benefit from Social Security's cost-of-living protections. As discussed above, survivor benefits may be key.

Many of these trends are shifting. Generation X and Millennial women have a higher labor participation rate than prior generations, increasing the likelihood that, if they marry, their own retirement benefits may be higher than their spousal or survivor benefits. This highlights the fact that every individual situation is unique. There is no one-size-fits-all answer as to when the best time is to file for benefits.

Taxation of Benefits

While as little as zero percent of your Social Security benefits may be taxed, at higher income levels, 50 percent, up to a maximum of 85 percent, of benefits may be subject to federal income tax. About 40 percent of people who receive Social Security benefits today have to pay some amount of taxes on their benefits. To determine how much of your benefits are taxed, you can refer to IRS *Publication 915, Social Security and Equivalent Railroad Retirement Benefits.* The 2020 publication includes a section titled "How Much Is Taxable?" and references worksheets you can use to make the calculation.

As with traditional IRA withdrawals, Social Security benefits are taxed as ordinary income. However, while a maximum of 85 percent of your Social Security benefits are taxed, 100 percent of your IRA withdrawals are taxable. Therefore, to the extent that increased Social Security benefits offset spending that otherwise would be taken from an IRA, you will save on taxes.

Social Security/Retirement/Medicare

It is important to understand that when you file for retirement benefits does not have to be the actual date you retire. In fact, depending on your situation, applying for Social Security and Medicare should be done at different dates.

We will go into much greater detail in the following chapter on Medicare, but it is worth highlighting this distinction. You and your employer both pay into Social Security and Medicare from amounts withheld from your paycheck. And you file for both Social Security and Medicare through the SSA. However, this is mostly where the similarities end. The major difference is what the benefits provide for, and when you can receive them.

As we have discussed, Social Security provides monthly payments—depending on your eligibility and circumstances—for retirement, disability, or survivor benefits at varying ages. On the other hand, Medicare provides health insurance for those 65 and older, and for certain younger people with disabilities.

Also, while Social Security gives you a benefit for later filing, Medicare actually penalizes you for late filing if you do not have other health insurance.

There is one other important point we need to cover. As we noted in the Health Savings Account chapter, when you enroll for either Social Security or Medicare, you are no longer allowed to contribute to an HSA. You may also receive a six-month retroactive Medicare benefit, which could result in penalties by the IRS if the retroactive feature has caused you to exceed contribution limits. Be mindful of these important dates when you apply for either benefit.

The Future of Social Security

Unlike your IRA or 401(k), where you contribute to your own account to draw from in retirement, the SSA doesn't put the Social Security and Medicare taxes collected into an account designated just for you. Your FICA taxes are used to pay benefits for people getting benefits today, just as your future benefits will be paid for by future workers.

In the introduction to this book, we noted solvency issues with Social Security. When people refer to Social Security "going bankrupt," it gives the wrong impression. Benefits will not disappear. Instead, they would decrease to the level that can be sustained by then current contributions. It is currently estimated that if no changes are made, benefits could be cut as much as 25 percent. It's important to keep in mind that this shortfall is projected to be essentially stable after 2035. There are many ways to shore up the system (such as having benefits be need-based tested or otherwise reduced, raising the age you are eligible for retirement benefits, and increasing the tax rate on both employees and employers). However, the problem is so large that it seems likely that some combination of all three will be necessary to eliminate the deficit. What we do not know is how, or when, or even if, the government will address the problem. What we do know is that the longer they wait to make changes to maintain solvency, the more painful the changes will be.

How might you plan in light of the uncertainty? If you are already at least in your 60s, you will likely face little to no impact. For those approaching retirement, we have run analyses to determine how the potential impact for reduced benefits may change the filing strategy. From the cases we have run, we have found that the same strategy still applies (although perhaps one might file a month or two earlier than they otherwise might if there were no reduction). While the actual amount of the maximum benefit changed, the strategy to get the most out of your benefits did not.

However, for people in their 50s, and certainly in their 40s or younger, it makes sense to remain conservative in your planning. While it appears that many Millennials and Gen Xers are assuming that they won't receive any benefits, this is too conservative an approach. The reason is that, as mentioned above, without any changes Social Security is about 75 percent funded. Thus, it seems likely that at most benefits would be reduced 25 percent if no actions are taken. With that said, being conservative has its benefits. However, it may cause you to defer spending more than necessary.

How to File for Benefits

The SSA recommends that you apply for benefits three to four months before you want them to start. You can typically apply for benefits in person at a local office, over the phone, or online at www.ssa.gov/benefits/retirement. This link will take you to a Retirement Benefits page with a wealth of information, including a Retirement FAQ, guidance for filing online, and ultimately a checklist of items you will need for Online Medicare, Retirement, and Spouses Applications. Even if you prefer to apply in person, the Social Security website—ssa.gov—serves as a useful resource.

The good news is that the SSA has made it relatively painless to file online. It should take about 15 to 30 minutes to complete the application process. Filing online helps you avoid potentially long waiting times at a local office. For the most up to date guidance on how to file for your benefits, visit www.ssa.gov/benefits/retirement/apply.html.

When Do I Receive My First Payment?

Social Security payments are paid one month in arrears. For example, if you file for July benefits, you will receive the July benefit in August. Deposits are made to your bank account based on your date of birth. If your birthday is on the 1st through the 10th of the month, you will receive your payment on the second Wednesday of the month. If your birthday is on the 11th through the 20th, you will receive payment on the third Wednesday. And if your payment is on the 21st through the end of the month, you will receive payment on the fourth Wednesday.

What if I Did Not Receive a Payment?

If you miss a Social Security payment, you could be the victim of identity theft. If this is the case, you should act quickly to correct the problem. You can submit a report by filling out the form or using the other contact information found at oig.ssa.gov/report.

To protect against identity theft, know that you should never receive emails from the SSA. And if they call you, they will never require that you provide your Social Security number to identify yourself. Finally, if you have not already established a Social Security account online, we recommend you claim your account so that someone else cannot establish an account in your name and attempt to fraudulently collect your benefits.

Adjusting Benefits if You Change Your Mind

If you filed early and have changed your mind, you have two options:

1. If you have filed within the past 12 months, you can submit a Form SSA-521 "Request for Withdrawal of Application." This form can be found by searching online for "Request for Withdrawal for Application—Social Security." With this action, you can complete a one-time "do-over." You will need to pay back any benefits you received (interest-free), and you will have one more opportunity to file.
2. You can also choose to suspend your benefits upon reaching FRA. Remember that in most cases, suspending your own benefits means that anyone receiving benefits based on your record (such as spousal or child benefits) will also have their benefits suspended until you reinstate them. Also remember, if you suspend benefits but were deducting Medicare premiums from your Social Security benefit, you will have to make other arrangements to pay those premiums.

Summary

Social Security was never meant to cover all retirement expenses. It was created to be a "safety net," bolstered by company pensions (which most employers have done away with) and personal savings. We have shown that as long as you have the flexibility to delay receiving Social Security payments, doing so will generally maximize benefits.

As we have discussed, there are a plethora of rules, provisions, caveats, and differing situations. And we have not even covered all of them that may apply to you, such as whether you are a government employee receiving a pension from a job not covered by Social Security taxes, whether you have a child under age 18 or disabled before 22, and others. Given all the variables, the best advice we can give is to seek out the advice of an expert. Do not rely on guidance from a friend, relative, or something you read online. Even if well intentioned, the way they filed or suggest that you file may not be appropriate for your situation. And while many representatives at the SSA can be helpful in answering questions, they are not necessarily the best resource. We have encountered situations where our clients may not have been given correct information (or the person filing isn't using the proper language and therefore may be filing incorrectly). You may need to arm yourself with provisions that you can point to when you speak to a supervisor to resolve an issue and make sure you are filing as intended.

In fact, in 2018 a government audit found that the SSA underpaid 82 percent of dually entitled widows and widowers because they failed to notify these individuals that they could apply for survivor benefits while taking advantage of delaying their own retirement benefit until 70 for potentially a substantially higher lifetime benefit.

The lesson is that you need to be in charge of ensuring that you are maximizing your benefits. Find comprehensive software (not just what's free), or a good advisor (one who truly understands the permutations of Social Security), as they can play a critical role in helping you understand how to apply for the optimal benefit. There are several online calculators, and the benefits they provide in determining the best strategy can far outweigh their costs. In our due diligence, we have found www.maximizemysocialsecurity.com to be a very good solution. A good advisor will not only determine the ideal filing strategy, but can also integrate this into a larger plan, since even the so-called "optimal" strategy might not work with your actual circumstances. The right analysis will help you make the right decisions when factored into the big picture. For example, perhaps working one year more than expected, or working part-time during retirement, can greatly increase your chances of retirement success.

We now turn to Medicare.

CHAPTER 13

Medicare

Medicare Overview

MEDICARE IS THE federal health insurance program that provides coverage to seniors and the disabled. The program was signed into law on July 30, 1965 by President Lyndon Johnson. By 2017, the program has grown to provide benefits to approximately 60 million Americans. As the Baby Boomer generation has started to enter retirement, this number is expected to continue to rise, with an estimated 10,000 Americans enrolling in Medicare every day.

Medicare is available to those 65 and older, those younger than 65 with disabilities, and those suffering from End Stage Renal Disease (ESRD). If you or your spouse have worked for at least 10 years and paid Medicare payroll taxes, you will qualify for Medicare. Those individuals deemed disabled by Social Security become eligible for Medicare benefits after receiving 24 months of disability benefits. One exception to this rule is for those suffering from ALS— Lou Gehrig's disease. In those cases, Medicare benefits will start when you are deemed disabled. For those suffering from ESRD, the wait period will vary depending upon your circumstances and when you start dialysis.

Medicare Components

There are five main components of Medicare, each providing a different set of benefits and coverage. Some of the components are managed by the federal government through the Centers for Medicare and Medicaid Services (CMS). Others are provided through private insurers.

There are two main avenues for receiving your Medicare benefits. The first is what we'll call Original Medicare, consisting of Parts A, B, D, and a Medicare Supplement. The second option is a Medicare Advantage plan, which is Medicare Parts A, B, and C. Let's look at what each section covers.

Medicare Part A: Hospital Insurance

The first section of Medicare is Part A. This is hospitalization coverage. The program is administered by the federal government through the CMS. It provides coverage for in-patient hospital stays, hospice care, skilled nursing care, and home health care. If you are receiving Social Security or Railroad Retirement Board benefits when you turn 65, you will be automatically enrolled in Part A. If you are not receiving Social Security, then you would need to opt in to Part A at 65.

For a majority of recipients, there is no cost or premium for Part A, since the premiums are covered through payroll taxes. You qualify for premium-free Part A if you, or your spouse, worked for at least 10 years, or 40 quarters, and paid Medicare payroll taxes. However, if you or your spouse failed to pay Medicare taxes for at least 10 years and enrolled in Part A, you would be required to pay a monthly premium for the coverage. Your premium would depend on the number of quarters you worked and paid into Medicare. For 2020, the premium for Part A for those who worked less than 30 quarters is $458 per month and for those who worked 30–39 quarters it is $252.

You are not required to enroll in Medicare Part A when you turn 65. If you plan on continuing to work and are covered by a large employer group plan when you turn 65, you have options available to you. You may delay enrolling in Medicare completely and stay on your group plan until you retire. Alternatively, you can choose to remain on your group plan and enroll in Part A only. In this scenario, the group plan would be your primary insurance and Part A would be a secondary payer if you became sick and required a stay in the hospital.

A caveat to this strategy is if you plan on contributing to an HSA plan. Medicare regulations forbid Medicare recipients from making any additional contributions to an HSA plan after their enrollment. If you were to enroll in Part A only, you would then be unable to make any further HSA contributions. In addition, depending on your circumstances, you may receive Medicare benefits up to six months retroactive to your enrollment if you are older than 65. If you have been contributing to an HSA plan, this could result in excess contribution penalties by the IRS. You should consult Medicare or your financial professional prior to enrolling for guidance on how to avoid this situation.

Medicare Part B: Medical Insurance

The second part of Medicare is Medicare Part B. It provides coverage for "medically necessary services", such as doctors' services, outpatient services, preventive care, medical testing, and durable medical equipment. Similar to Part A, if you, or your spouse, are receiving Social Security or Railroad Retirement Board benefits when you turn 65, you will automatically be enrolled in Medicare Part B.

Just as with Medicare Part A, you can delay enrolling in Part B if you plan on continuing to work past age 65 and are covered by a large group plan. In this situation, you will be able to enroll in Part B upon your future retirement. More on this later.

With Part B, you pay a monthly premium. Beginning in 2020, the base Part B premium starts at $144.60 per month per recipient. Medicare Part B only covers 80 percent of the costs for your medical claims. The remaining 20 percent is a coinsurance requirement that each recipient is responsible for covering. In addition, there is an annual deductible for Part B—in 2020, this is $198.

For recipients who started receiving Medicare benefits prior to 2018, your monthly premium may be slightly lower. If your income is higher than certain thresholds, your monthly premium will be higher due to an Income Related Monthly Adjustment Amount (IRMAA). For a married couple filing a joint return, any IRMAA charges would be assessed on each recipient, not the couple.

To determine if you will be assessed an IRMAA, Social Security reviews the tax returns for each recipient from two years ago. For example, for 2020, they look back at your 2018 tax return. If your Modified Adjusted Gross Income (MAGI) is greater than certain thresholds, you would be assessed the IRMAA amount on top of your monthly premium of $144.60. Below is a table of the income thresholds and the corresponding IRMAA amounts for 2020 for each of the tax filing statuses.

Modified Adjusted Gross Income (MAGI)	Part B Monthly Premium Amount	Prescription Drug Coverage Monthly Premium Amount
Individuals with $87,000 or less Married couples with $174,000 or less	2020 standard premium = $144.60	Your plan premium
Individuals above $87,000 up to $109,000 Married couples above $174,000 up to $218,000	2020 standard premium + $57.80 = $202.40	Your plan premium + $12.20
Individuals above $109,000 up to $136,000 Married couples above $218,000 up to $272,000	2020 standard premium + $144.60 = $289.20	Your plan premium + $31.50

Modified Adjusted Gross Income (MAGI)	Part B Monthly Premium Amount	Prescription Drug Coverage Monthly Premium Amount
Individuals above $136,000 up to $163,000 Married couples above $272,000 up to $326,000	2020 standard premium + $231.40 = $376.00	Your plan premium + $50.70
Individuals above $163,000 up to $500,000 Married couples above $326,000 up to $750,000	2020 standard premium + $318.10 = $462.70	Your plan premium + $70.00
Individuals above $500,000 Married couples above $750,000	2020 standard premium + $347.00 = $491.60	Your plan premium + $76.40

For married filing separately, the 2020 income tiers and adjustments are:

Modified Adjusted Gross Income (MAGI)	Part B Monthly Premium Amount	Prescription Drug Coverage Monthly Premium Amount
Individuals with $87,000 or less	2020 standard premium = $144.60	Your plan premium
Individuals above $87,000 up to $413,000	2020 standard premium + $318.10 = $462.70	Your plan premium + $70.00
Individuals above $413,000	2020 standard premium + $347.00 = $491.60	Your plan premium + $76.40

Since Social Security reviews the tax returns each year, your Part B premium may vary from year to year if your income varies. If Social Security deems that you are subject to an IRMAA charge, and you are affected by a limited number of life-changing events, you may appeal this decision. The life-changing situations include:

- Marriage
- Divorce
- Death of a spouse
- Retirement or work reduction
- Loss of income

Note that a large capital gains event, such as a business or stock sale, will not qualify as a life-changing event. If Social Security grants your appeal, the IRMAA charges would be rescinded, but they will not retroactively refund any additional premiums that you have paid.

Medicare Supplement

As just mentioned, Part B only covers 80 percent of your medical costs. This is where the third component of Original Medicare steps in to fill this gap. This component is a Medicare Supplement plan—commonly called a Medigap policy. These plans are sold and run by private insurers.

Beginning on January 1, 2020, federal law was changed to prevent any Medigap plan from paying the Medicare Part B premium. For anyone who becomes eligible for Medicare as of January 1, 2020, there are eight different Medigap plans to choose from, labeled Medicare Supplement Plans A through N—compared to 10 plans prior to that date.

The benefits provided by each plan are strictly regulated by Medicare. Insurers are prevented from altering or modifying the benefits offered by the plans in any way. However, they do set the premiums. Plans with the same letter are identical, allowing for an apples-to-apples comparison between plans. For example, a G supplement plan from one insurer will be identical to a G plan from another insurer. Here is a listing of the plans and their benefits available in most states as of 2020.

Medigap Benefit	Medigap Plans*							
	A	B	D	G	K	L	M	N
Part A coinsurance and hospital costs up to an additional 365 days once Medicare benefits have exhausted	Yes	Yes	Yes	Yes	Yes	Yes	Yes	Yes
Part B coinsurance	Yes	Yes	Yes	Yes	50%	75%	Yes	Yes

Medigap Benefit	Medigap Plans*							
	A	B	D	G	K	L	M	N
Blood (1st 3 pints)	Yes	Yes	Yes	Yes	50%	75%	Yes	Yes
Part A hospice care coinsurance	Yes	Yes	Yes	Yes	50%	75%	Yes	Yes
Skilled nursing care coinsurance	No	No	Yes	Yes	50%	75%	Yes	Yes
Part A deductible	No	Yes	Yes	Yes	50%	75%	50%	Yes
Part B deductible	No	No	No	No	No	No	No	No
Part B excess charge	No	No	No	Yes	No	No	No	No
Foreign travel exchange	No	No	80%	80%	No	No	80%	80%
Out-of-Pocket limit**	N/A	N/A	N/A	N/A	$5,240	$2,620	N/A	N/A

* Plans in Massachusetts, Minnesota, and Wisconsin are regulated differently.
** Once the annual out-of-pocket limit and Part B deductible have been fully met, the plan pays 100% of the covered services for the rest of the calendar year.

In most circumstances, it is extremely difficult to change Medicare Supplement plans once you have enrolled in them. This is because, outside of your initial enrollment where you have guaranteed acceptance by all the carriers, the carriers are not required to offer this. If you want to change your Medigap policy from a D plan to a G plan several years later, you may be required to undergo underwriting by the insurance company.

As a result of a new law, named MACRA, Medigap plans, in particular plans F and C, are no longer allowed to be sold to new enrollees who become eligible for Medicare as of January 1, 2020. Enrollment in a Plan F or C is still possible for anyone who was eligible for Medicare prior to that date, such as someone who continued to work till age 70 and was covered by their employer's group plan.

With the new MACRA law in place, the vast majority of recipients will likely opt for a G plan, since it offers the widest range of benefits. All existing Plan F enrollees will be grandfathered in and stay on the plan, but newly eligible enrollees to Original Medicare after January 1, 2020, will not have Plan F as an enrollment option.

Plan F currently pays the Part B annual deductible. By phasing out Plan F, new recipients will be forced to pay the annual Part B deductible out-of-pocket and have skin in the game with regards to their health care. Costs for all Medigap plans will vary and can be affected by plan type, carrier, state of residence, and age.

Medicare Part D: Drug Coverage

The final part of Original Medicare is Part D, which provides prescription drug coverage. Of the four sections of Original Medicare, this is the most customizable section for recipients, since everyone has differing prescription drug needs. These plans are provided by private insurers and plan offerings are dependent on your geographical region.

In many instances, insurers will offer several plans in a given region with differing levels of coverage. Think of them offering gold, silver, and bronze plans with their associated premiums on a sliding scale. Those that have more prescriptions, especially brand name and specialty drugs, would likely require a higher level plan with a higher monthly premium.

Unlike with a Medigap plan, you have the ability to easily change your plans once a year during the Open Enrollment Period. This is because prescription drug needs change over time and Medicare allows for some flexibility and understanding for this. In addition, insurers change their drug formularies, i.e., the system that determines whether a drug is covered and at what co-pay.

Retiree Coverage

In some situations, you may receive retiree healthcare benefits from your previous employer or union. Some examples of these plans would be government employee plans, TRICARE, or union retiree healthcare benefits. These plans often fill in as a Supplement and/or Part D option for the eligible recipients. If you are eligible for one of these plans, you still need to be enrolled in Medicare Parts A and B. You should check with your benefits coordinator to see how these plans will work with Medicare and how they will compare to Medicare Supplement, Part D, and Medicare Advantage plans.

Medicare Part C: Medicare Advantage Plans

As we mentioned earlier, there are two paths to obtaining Medicare. The second option is with a Medicare Advantage plan. With these plans, you still have Medicare Parts A and B, like with Original Medicare. However, instead of having a Medigap and Part D plan, you would have a Medicare Advantage plan. The Advantage plans combines the Medigap and Part D plans into a single plan.

Like Part D plans, these plans are offered through private insurers and vary widely by geographic region. The plans typically operate like an HMO, with networks of doctors and hospitals. Like an HMO, copays are lower for using in-network providers than out-of-network. The plans also usually have out-of-pocket maximums to cap your annual healthcare costs. Enrollees usually are required to have a primary care physician and must get referrals for specialist visits. In addition, some plans offer additional benefits, such as dental, vision, or even gym memberships, that are not available through Original Medicare.

Monthly premiums vary depending on the plan you choose. Often, these plans are advertised with low or zero cost monthly premiums. The trade-off is that you are limited to the plan's in-network providers, in order to get the lowest cost. The plans are not guaranteed from year to year, nor are their in-network providers. Plans can and do change their lineups of doctors and hospitals within their networks. For these reasons, Advantage plan enrollees should review their plans annually to ensure they continue to be the best fit.

It is important to keep in mind that Medicare doesn't cover all medical expenses. Costs not covered come out of your pocket, unless there is other insurance that will cover them. The following are some of the more common services or items that Medicare doesn't cover:

• Dental care
• Vision care
• Dentures
• Hearing aids
• Routine foot care
• Cosmetic surgery
• Long-term care
• Acupuncture

As was mentioned, some Medicare Advantage plans will offer coverage for some of these items, such as dental and vision services. You need to carefully review each plan's list of benefits to determine this.

Medicare Enrollment

One of the most important decisions one can make concerning Medicare is the timing of when to enroll for benefits. Provided you enroll within the right timeframes, new enrollees receive guaranteed acceptance for all sections of Medicare. It is recommended that you sign up for each section of Medicare during one of your available windows. Failing to do so can result in significant and costly consequences, including loss of healthcare coverage and lifetime premium penalties. Depending on your situation, there are different enrollment periods to keep in mind.

Initial Enrollment Period

The first enrollment period is your Initial Enrollment Period (IEP). This is the window available to everyone when they turn 65. The IEP is a seven-month window that includes the three months prior to your birth month, your birth month, and the three months following your birth month. Medicare coverage always begins on the first of the month. If you sign up for Medicare in the three months prior to your birth month, your coverage will begin on the first day of your birth month. If you sign up for Medicare in either your birth month, or the three months following it, your coverage will be delayed by up to three months.

For example, if your birthday is July 15, your IEP will run from April 1 through October 31. If you sign up for Medicare any time in April through June, your Medicare coverage will begin on July 1. If you enroll on August 3, your coverage will begin on October 1. An exception to this is if you are born on the first of the month, in which case your window gets pushed forward one month. In the example above, if your birthday was on July 1, your IEP would run from March 1 through September 30. Enrolling anytime in March through May will result in your start date being June 1.

Special Enrollment Period

Many people plan on continuing to work past age 65 and are eligible to receive healthcare coverage through their employer's group plan. If you are in this situation and your employer has 20 or more employees, Medicare allows you to skip your IEP without incurring any penalties and delay your enrollment until you retire or terminate from your employer's plan.

The second opportunity to sign up for Medicare is called your Special Enrollment Period (SEP). This is an eight-month window that starts on the first of the month following your official termination from your group health insurance. During this window, you are guaranteed enrollment in all parts of Medicare and cannot be denied coverage for any reason, same as with your IEP.

Two items to consider with your SEP. First, your employer must have at least 20 more employees. If it does, your group plan would act as your primary insurer and Medicare would be your secondary. However, under current law, if your employer has fewer than 20 employees, the roles are reversed and Medicare will be your primary insurer. Because your employer plan would be secondary, it would likely not pay on claims unless you were enrolled in Medicare.

The second item to consider is if you are eligible for COBRA benefits. Regardless of whether the IEP or SEP is concerned, COBRA coverage is not taken into consideration by Medicare when reviewing your enrollment windows. Should you continue on COBRA through your enrollment window, you will have to wait until the General Enrollment or Open Enrollment periods to sign up for Medicare—and your enrollment options might be limited. In the interim period, you would likely be without any coverage at all.

General Enrollment Period

If you miss both your IEP and SEP windows to enroll in Medicare, you have another opportunity to sign up for coverage. This is called the General Enrollment Period and it runs annually from January 1 through March 31. If you enroll during this period, your coverage will start on July 1. As was stated before, if you sign up during this window, you may have a loss of coverage until Medicare coverage kicks in on July 1.

Medicare Part C and D Enrollment

Both Part C and D have Initial Enrollment Periods (IEP) and Special Enrollment Periods (SEP), similar to Parts A and B. The IEP for Parts C and D corresponds to the IEP for Parts A and B, the seven-month window that runs from the three months prior to your birth month, your birth month, and the three months following your birth month. Starting dates for these coverages would follow the same schedule as for Parts A and B.

While there are numerous SEPs to enroll in Parts C or D, depending on the circumstances, we'll focus on the most common ones. For most people who don't enroll in their IEP, they will qualify for a SEP at any point while they are covered by their, or their spouse's, employer plan for two months following the month when their coverage officially terminates in the group plan.

The second common SEP is triggered when you are already enrolled in a Part C or D plan and you move out of your current coverage area. Since Part C and D plans are geographically specific, you must be enrolled in a plan that operates in your region to get in-network benefits. If you notify your plan prior to your move, your SEP window will be from the month prior to your move, the month you move, and continue for the two months after your move. If you notify your plan after you move, the window is the month you move through the two months after your move.

Medigap Open Enrollment

Medigap policies also have specific enrollment windows during which you are guaranteed to receive coverage, regardless of your health history. The Medigap Open Enrollment window starts the month you turn 65 and are enrolled in Part B and runs for six months. You are eligible for this window regardless of whether you enrolled during your IEP or SEP.

Open Enrollment Period

Finally, because Medicare Advantage and Part D plans change annually and/ or when your health needs change, Medicare has an annual Open Enrollment Period (OEP) where you can review your plans and change without a penalty. The OEP runs from October 15 to December 7 each year with new plans going into effect on January 1. During the OEP, those with Parts A and B can opt into a Medicare Advantage plan and vice versa. You can also change between Part D and Medicare Advantage plans.

Penalties

As we mentioned earlier, there are significant penalties you will incur if you fail to enroll for Medicare in a timely manner. Late enrollment penalties are assessed on Part A, B, and D. The late penalty for Part A applies to those who don't qualify for premium-free Part A. For every year you don't have Part A, but could have, you may face a 10 percent penalty on your monthly premium. The penalty will be assessed for twice the number of years you could have had Part A, but didn't.

The second penalty we'll discuss is for Part B late enrollment. For every full 12-month period that you could have had Part B, but did not, Medicare will assess a 10 percent late penalty on your monthly premium. The penalty will remain in place as long as you have Part B. Keep in mind, if you qualify and enroll for Part B in an SEP, you'll avoid the late penalty.

Finally, you can face a late enrollment penalty on Part D. For Part D, you'll be assessed a penalty of 1 percent of the "national base beneficiary premium" times for every full month you aren't enrolled in a Part D or receiving credible prescription drug coverage, in addition to your monthly premium. In 2020, the "national base beneficiary premium" is $32.74. The penalty is rounded to the nearest $0.10 and will be applied as long as you receive Part D benefits.

How to Enroll in Medicare

Enrollment for Medicare is done through Social Security and can be done either online, by phone, or at your local Social Security office. The easiest and least time consuming of the three options is to do it online. This option is best if your situation is straightforward and routine. This is done on the Social Security website at www.ssa.gov.

If your situation is more complicated or unusual, you may want to consider either calling Social Security or making an appointment at your local office. Both of these options will likely take longer to complete the process. If you have filed an appeal with Social Security concerning an IRMAA adjustment to your Medicare premiums, you will be required to submit the appeal in person at a local Social Security office.

Summary

Along with Social Security, Medicare is a retirement benefit that affects almost all Americans, regardless of one's personal financial situation. It is the primary, and in many instances the only, way for one to obtain adequate health coverage past age 65. It is extremely important to ensure you are aware of, and meet, all of the enrollment requirements for Medicare. Failure to do so can result in a loss of coverage and/or significant financial consequences that can adversely affect your retirement goals and plans.

CHAPTER 14

Longevity Risk: The Role of Annuities

W E BUY INSURANCE to protect our homes, cars, and lives, transferring risks we prefer not to bear ourselves. Thus, buying insurance is really about diversifying risks we find unacceptable to bear, because the costs of not being insured and having the risks "show up" are too great. The same logic applies to the purchase of payout annuities, the payments of which can be fixed or inflation-adjusted (at least to some degree) dollars.

Each of us faces two risks related to life expectancy. The first is the risk of premature death, resulting in the loss of our human capital (defined as the present value of a person's future earnings). The second risk, longevity risk, is the risk of living to an advanced age and outliving our assets.

While most of us are familiar and comfortable with protecting against the first risk by purchasing life insurance, many are not aware that insurance companies also sell products that can protect against longevity risk. At its most basic level, deciding to purchase a payout annuity is a decision to insure against longevity risk—the economic consequences of outliving a portfolio of financial assets tasked with providing lifetime income. As the pain of outliving one's financial assets is extremely high, for individuals running significant risk of that occurring, purchasing a payout annuity makes sense.

Increasing Life Expectancy

Longevity risk is coming into focus because people are living longer—with the research showing this is especially true for wealthier individuals. The table overleaf reports the probability of at least one of a 65-year-old couple living to age 95.

	Male	Female	Both	One
Average American	7%	13%	1%	19%
Healthy American	20%	29%	6%	43%
Healthy American in 2028	25%	33%	8%	50%

An average 65-year-old couple has a 19 percent chance that one of them will live to age 95 or beyond. A healthy 65-year-old couple has a 43 percent chance that one of them will live to at least age 95. At current projections, a healthy 65-year-old couple in 2028 will have a 50 percent chance that one of them will live to at least age 95.

The reason that many are unfamiliar with hedging against longevity risk is that for most of the 20th century, workers had defined benefit (DB) pension plans through their employer. In addition, Social Security protected them against this risk. However, the percentage of workers covered by DB pensions has declined sharply. And depending upon one's spending rate, Social Security may not cover a large enough percentage of retirement spending needs. As a result, many are now largely responsible for hedging their own longevity risk, just as they have been responsible for hedging the risk that they die at a young age.

The academic evidence argues that most should annuitize at least some portion of their assets to protect against longevity risk. Despite this evidence, few retirees opt to annuitize some portion of their assets. This chapter is about educating you on the benefits of annuitization. We will begin with a discussion on the two types of income annuities (the only types you should consider) you can purchase—a single-premium immediate annuity and a deferred-income annuity (also known as a longevity annuity).

The Two Types of Income Annuities

Single-Premium Immediate Annuities (SPIAs)

Immediate annuities are the most basic of annuities. An insurance company provides a contract that allows for an annuitant to immediately receive fixed payments over a specified period of time, usually over the life of the individual, in exchange for an up-front cash outlay. Over the last several years, SPIAs in their most basic form have become more commoditized and less expensive—making them an appropriate and simple option to generate stable income.

Deferred Income Annuities (DIAs)

Longevity annuities are a recent product that begins payments after a specific age, say 85 (most contracts allow choice of payout age from 50–85). The benefit to having payments occur after the annuitant reaches 85 is lower costs for larger payouts. The higher payouts are due to increased mortality credits at the end of life and the extended period of time before an annuitant begins to receive the deferred payments. Thus, the later the start date, the higher will be the payments. Simply put, the insurance company knows that many people who purchase a DIA will die before they collect much, or anything, from the annuity. This allows for large payouts to those who do live beyond an average life expectancy. Those who do not live as long as expected subsidize those who do. And those that do not live as long as expected won't need the assets anyway.

Deferred-Income Annuity versus Single-Premium Immediate Annuity

In a typical SPIA, the purchaser (or annuitant) might spend $100,000 at age 65 to guarantee lifetime income of $7,000 per year. In contrast, in a DIA, a 65-year-old male might spend $100,000 for an income of $36,000 per year starting at age 85. With both the DIA and SPIA, once the purchaser dies, the income stops. The DIA offers a higher payout than the SPIA because the income stream begins much later. DIAs tend to do a better job of protecting against longevity risk than SPIAs.

A DIA is "pure" protection against longevity risk, as the income does not begin until the purchaser is at an advanced age. A simple way to think about it is that we only insure against the risks we cannot afford to take. For example, when we buy car insurance we choose the size of the deductible based on our ability to cover that cost in the event of an accident. The greater the deductible, the lower the cost of the insurance. The logic of a DIA works the same way. You can think of the deferral period, the age until payments begin, as the deductible. The longer the wait, the lower will be the premium paid and the higher will be the payments received. Since we are trying to protect against the risk of living beyond our life expectancy, economically it makes the most sense to only insure against that risk. That is what makes the DIA attractive—avoiding the cost of paying for protection we do not need.

A study by Jason Scott, "The Longevity Annuity: An Annuity for Everyone?", which appeared in the January/February 2008 issue of the *Financial Analysts Journal*, found that for the same spending benefit, a 65-year-old with $1 million in financial assets purchasing an immediate annuity would have to annuitize more than 60 percent of his/her retirement assets, versus just 11 percent of his/her assets for a longevity annuity with the payouts beginning at age 85. Scott also found significant improvements in spending benefits. He calculated a "longevity annuity benefit multiple," defined as the ratio of longevity annuity spending improvement to immediate annuity spending improvement. He found that for men, the benefit ratio in terms of nominal spending favored the longevity annuity by more than 6:1, and for women by more than 5:1. You'll be able to see the benefits of the DIA yourself when we review the results of a Monte Carlo simulation.

Ability to Customize

Both types of annuities offer optional riders that allow investors to customize some aspects of the payments. However, any riders that are added can lead to a reduction in the income and move the product further away from pure longevity insurance. Of these riders, there are only two we recommend considering. First, a rider can allow the income to continue to the last surviving spouse. Second, an investor can purchase inflation protection, so the income stream increases at 1 percent, 2 percent, or is indexed with changes in the Consumer Price Index (CPI). Note that these products are completely different from variable annuities (which we do not recommend), as there is no variable investment component of DIAs or SPIAs. DIAs and SPIAs also generally have much lower fees than variable annuities.

The Value of DIAs and SPIAs

The easiest way to think about DIAs and SPIAs is as mortality-linked fixed income. Using this framework, the two factors that influence annuity pricing are interest rates and mortality rates. If long-term interest rates move higher, you would expect to receive a greater income stream per dollar of premium (and vice versa). For a simplified example of how mortality rates affect the income stream, imagine a hypothetical group of 50 85-year-old males who each agree to contribute $100 to a pool of investments earning 5 percent. They further agree to split the total pool equally among those who are still alive at the end of the year. Also, assume that five of the 50 will die by the end of the year. This means the full pool, now $5,250 ($5,000 principal plus $250 interest), will be split among only 45 people. Each will receive $116.67, or a return on investment of 16.67 percent. If, instead, each person had invested independently of the pool, the total amount of money earned would have been $105, or a 5 percent return on investment. The difference is known as mortality credits. It is those mortality credits that provide the attraction. The older the investor, the higher the mortality rate for the pool. As a result, older investors receive a greater income stream per dollar of premium than younger investors.

With Low Interest Rates, Should I Wait for Rates to Rise Before Purchasing a DIA or SPIA?

Waiting for annuity rates to get cheaper is risky for three reasons:

1. Your forecast may be wrong. We do not pretend to have the ability to forecast interest rates, and we do not think anyone can do it reliably.
2. Mortality rates could change in addition to interest rates. If people start living longer, this would reduce the income stream from an annuity.
3. The purchaser of a DIA would miss out on mortality credits during the waiting period.

It generally makes sense to purchase a DIA sometime between age 65 and 70, and there's no real benefit to waiting until later to purchase the DIA.

Impact on Retirement Planning Scenarios Using Monte Carlo Analysis: A Case Study

The value of DIAs and SPIAs can be quantified by looking at retirement planning scenarios. Before jumping into the full results, we can start by looking at a hypothetical case study. In our example, we have a 65-year-old male with $2 million of investable assets. He is withdrawing $80,000 (inflation-adjusted) per year from his portfolio, which is invested in a 50 percent equity/50 percent fixed income portfolio. His advisor has run a Monte Carlo analysis and finds that the investor has an 80 percent chance of having money left at age 95. Not comfortable with those odds, the advisor does a sensitivity analysis and discovers that if the investor cuts spending by 10 percent, the odds of success increase to 89 percent.

If the advisor would re-run the initial analysis to age 90 instead of age 95, the advisor would see that the odds of success jump from 80 percent to 90 percent. This is not an argument for reducing the length of the analysis. Instead, it is an argument for insuring against longevity risk. Rather than cut spending by 10 percent, our hypothetical investor could allocate $200,000 (or 10 percent of his portfolio) to a DIA with $92,000 of non-inflation-adjusted income starting at age 85. Allocating to a DIA in this manner increases his odds of success at age 95 from 80 percent up to 92 percent. Many investors would rather allocate to a DIA than cut annual spending by 10 percent. Note that any change to Monte Carlo results of 5 percent or more is significant. In this case, results improve by 12 percent.

Expanded Results

The tables that follow depict the results for different ending ages and initial withdrawal rates. Table 1 analyzes a DIA with income starting at age 85. Table 2 analyzes an SPIA. The initial withdrawal rate is adjusted for inflation after Year 1. For example, an investor with a $1 million portfolio and a 4 percent withdrawal rate spends $40,000 in Year 1, and that $40,000 is adjusted for inflation each year. Panel A in each table depicts the results assuming the investor does not annuitize, Panel B assumes the investor allocates 10 percent to an annuity, and Panel C is the difference in success rates between Panels A and B.

Table 1: DIA Results

Panel A: No Annuitization, 65-Year-Old Male, 50–50

Probability of Having $1 Left for 30-Year Horizon

Ending Age	2.0%	3.0%	3.5%	4.0%	5.0%
75	100%	100%	100%	100%	100%
80	100%	100%	100%	100%	99%
85	100%	100%	99%	98%	87%
90	100%	99%	97%	90%	68%
95	100%	97%	91%	80%	51%

Panel B: 10% Allocation to DIA, 65-Year-Old Male, 50–50

Probability of Having $1 Left, Income Starts at age 85

Ending Age	2.0%	3.0%	3.5%	4.0%	5.0%
75	100%	100%	100%	100%	100%
80	100%	100%	100%	100%	96%
85	100%	100%	99%	96%	78%
90	100%	100%	99%	94%	70%
95	100%	100%	99%	92%	61%

Panel C: Panel B – Panel A

Probability of Having $1 Left for 30-Year Horizon

Ending Age	2.0%	3.0%	3.5%	4.0%	5.0%
75	0%	0%	0%	0%	0%
80	0%	0%	0%	0%	–3%
85	0%	0%	0%	–2%	–9%
90	0%	1%	2%	4%	2%
95	0%	3%	8%	12%	10%

Table 2: SPIA Results

Panel A: No Annuitization, 65-Year-Old Male, 50–50

Probability of Having $1 Left for 30-Year Horizon

Ending Age	2.0%	3.0%	3.5%	4.0%	5.0%
75	100%	100%	100%	100%	100%
80	100%	100%	100%	100%	99%
85	100%	100%	99%	98%	87%
90	100%	99%	97%	90%	68%
95	100%	97%	91%	80%	51%

Panel B: 10% Allocation to Fixed SPIA, 65-Year-Old Male, 50–50

Probability of Having $1 Left, Income Starts at Age 65

Ending Age	2.0%	3.0%	3.5%	4.0%	5.0%
75	100%	100%	100%	100%	100%
80	100%	100%	100%	100%	99%
85	100%	100%	100%	99%	89%
90	100%	100%	99%	93%	71%
95	100%	99%	94%	84%	54%

Panel C: Panel B – Panel A

Probability of Having $1 Left for 30-Year Horizon

Ending Age	2.0%	3.0%	3.5%	4.0%	5.0%
75	0%	0%	0%	0%	0%
80	0%	0%	0%	0%	0%
85	0%	0%	1%	1%	2%
90	0%	1%	2%	3%	3%
95	0%	2%	3%	4%	3%

Key Conclusions from Expanded Results

- DIAs can significantly improve Monte Carlo results. Assuming an initial withdrawal rate of 3.5 percent to 5.0 percent, DIAs improve results at an ending age of 95 by 8 to 12 percent.
- Investors with initial withdrawal rates of 5 percent or higher do not have desirable Monte Carlo results (less than 55 percent), regardless of whether they use a longevity annuity. However, reducing spending by 20 percent (from a 5 percent withdrawal rate down to a 4 percent withdrawal rate) in conjunction with using a DIA moves these investors to a much better Monte Carlo result (84 percent). Without using a DIA, these investors would need to cut spending by 30 percent (from a 5 percent withdrawal rate down to a 3.5 percent withdrawal rate) for their results to exceed 80 percent.
- Both SPIAs and DIAs can improve Monte Carlo results, but DIAs tend to have a greater impact than SPIAs.

It is important to note that while the above examples demonstrate the valuable role annuities can play, your unique circumstances should be considered to determine if their use is right for you. For example, if your Plan B includes the possibility of selling a second home, a downsizing of your home, or moving to a lower cost of living location, this might be enough to reasonably protect you from longevity risk.

Evidence from Behavioral Finance

Despite the evidence showing their risk reduction benefits, most individuals still hesitate when it comes to buying annuities. This is referred to as the "annuity puzzle." We will discuss likely explanations for the puzzle.

First, many investors exhibit what is called "loss aversion." They feel converting to an annuity "gambles away" their assets should they die earlier than expected, thus leaving their heirs a smaller estate. Another reason is that some investors dislike giving up control of their assets, believing they might do better if the money remained and grew in their investment accounts.

In addition, investors can be deterred by the financial restrictions of some annuities. Because most annuities are illiquid and irreversible, assets can't be accessed should unexpected needs, such as health-related costs, arise. And once assets are converted, the payouts often cease when the annuity holder dies, leaving nothing for bequest purposes. (Note that annuities can be structured to have minimum payment periods, though this increases their costs.) Unless specific inflation-protected annuities are purchased, fixed payouts may not keep up with inflation. The cost of certain annuities can also be prohibitively high due to a mix of add-on benefit riders, commissions, and management and administrative expenses.

We will now examine the findings of two academic papers. The first is the 2008 study, "Why Don't People Insure Late Life Consumption: A Framing Explanation of the Under-Annuitization Puzzle," by Jeffrey R. Brown, Jeffrey R. Kling, Sendhil Mullainathan, and Marian V. Wrobel. They found that: "Framing matters for annuitization decisions: In a consumption frame, annuities are viewed as valuable insurance, whereas in an investment frame, the annuity is a risky asset because the payoff depends on an uncertain date of death. Survey evidence is consistent with our hypothesis that framing matters: The vast majority of individuals prefer an annuity over alternative products when presented in a consumption frame, whereas the majority of individuals prefer non-annuitized products when presented in an investment frame. To the extent that the investment frame is the dominant frame for consumers making financial planning decisions for retirement, this finding may help to explain why so few individuals annuitize."

Constantijn W. A. Panis, author of the chapter "Annuities and Well Being" in the 2004 book, *Pension Design and Structure: New Lessons from Behavioral Finance*, conducted an extensive survey looking at investors who decided to annuitize versus those that did not and found: "Those with greater annuitization were more satisfied in retirement, and they maintained their satisfaction throughout retirement. By contrast, retirees without lifelong annuities have become somewhat less satisfied over the years. The guaranteed income benefits may reduce anxiety about the risks of outliving one's savings and ending up in poverty."

Logical Explanations

There is a logical economic explanation for why most investors do not (or should not) purchase immediate annuities. Investors can replicate a payout annuity themselves more efficiently, at least until they reach an age when the mortality credits inside the policy are great enough to offset the issuance costs and the required profit margin of the issuer.

By way of example, the 2001 study, "Optimal Annuitization Policies: Analysis of the Options," by Moshe Milevsky concluded that a 65-year-old woman has an 85 percent chance of being able to beat the rate of return from a life annuity until age 80. For men, the figure was 80 percent. (Keep in mind that the insurance companies that issue these policies are aware they are being adversely selected, meaning that the most likely buyers of longevity insurance are those with good reason to believe they will live a longer-than-average life.)

Longevity annuities are like traditional forms of insurance that individuals purchase for protection and may never receive any benefits. That the longevity annuity can greatly reduce the amount of an individual's portfolio assets explains the two main reasons why individuals have not purchased annuities: The loss of a large part of their estate and the loss of liquidity to address unexpected spending needs. And that should help solve the annuity puzzle.

Tax Treatment of DIAs and SPIAs

If the annuity is purchased with tax-deferred dollars, the payouts will be taxed at ordinary income rates. If the annuity is purchased with taxable dollars, a portion of the payout will be a tax-free return of principal and a portion will be taxed at ordinary income tax rates. Since the return on these annuities is taxed at ordinary income rates, we generally recommend using tax-deferred dollars to purchase them.

Purchases with Taxable Dollars

The money invested in an annuity is returned in equal tax-free installments over the payment period. For example, let's assume the investor spent $100,000 on an SPIA in return for an annual income of $7,000. If the IRS considers the investor's life expectancy to be 20 years, you would divide the $100,000 by 20 to determine how much of each payout will be a tax-free return of investment. In this case, $5,000 of each $7,000 payout would be tax-free and $2,000 would be taxed at ordinary income rates. If the investor lives beyond the calculated life expectancy, the annuity payments will become fully taxable when the full initial investment has been paid out. This would work similarly with a DIA, except that the taxes wouldn't be assessed until payments start.

Qualified Longevity Annuity Contract (QLAC)

In July 2014, the U.S. Treasury Department allowed DIA purchases in tax-deferred accounts. Prior to this regulatory change, tax-deferred accounts could not hold a DIA with payouts that started later than age 70½. A DIA with income starting after age 70½ is called a Qualified Longevity Annuity Contract (QLAC). There are a few key limitations that come with purchasing a QLAC:

- The income stream must begin before age 85.
- The premium cannot exceed the lower of $125,000 or 25 percent of all IRA dollars (based on the December 31 value of the year prior to purchase). The 25 percent calculation does not include 401(k) or 403(b) accounts. For example, if an investor had $1 million in a 401(k) and $100,000 in an IRA, the limit would be 25 percent of the $100,000 IRA balance (or $25,000). QLACs cannot be funded with inherited IRAs.
- The policy cannot provide a cash value.
- The policy can have either no death benefit or a death benefit equal to the amount of the premium.
- The contract must state that it is intended to be a QLAC.
  We will now address some common concerns with DIAs and SPIAs.

Common Concerns with DIAs and SPIAs

Credit Risk

When an insurance company runs into trouble, insurance regulators typically intervene before bankruptcy occurs and assist in transferring the policyholders' assets to a healthy insurance company that takes over the responsibilities. However, some insurance companies have gone bankrupt over the years. For example, in September 1983, an insurance company named Baldwin-United filed for Chapter 11 bankruptcy protection after insurance companies in Arkansas and Indiana took over management of its insurance subsidiaries. More than 165,000 policyholders had purchased annuities from Baldwin-United, and the money was frozen for more than three years while regulators and the courts handled the mess. Eventually the assets were transferred to Metropolitan Life and purchasers were made whole.

State Guarantee Associations

Investors are now protected by state guarantee funds. The National Organization of Life and Health Insurance Guaranty Associations (NOLHGA) is a voluntary association of all 50 states, the District of Columbia and Puerto Rico. The organization was founded in 1983, when the state guaranty associations determined a need for a mechanism to help coordinate their efforts to protect policyholders when a life or health insurance company insolvency affected people in many states. Basically, the mechanism is when something goes wrong, the stronger insurance companies in the industry pool their resources and rescue the weaker company. State guarantee funds protect between $100,000 and $500,000 of premium, depending on the state in which the annuitant lives and the insurance company is headquartered. Since we never treat the unlikely as impossible, we recommend sticking to only large, high-credit-quality (AAA- and AA-rated) insurers. It is better to forgo the best quote from an income perspective to purchase from a higher-credit-quality insurer.

Illiquidity

One concern that cannot be dismissed is the lack of liquidity that comes with a DIA or SPIA purchase. Once the purchase is made, the purchaser typically cannot get the premium back. However, the concern surrounding illiquidity can be mitigated by annuitizing only a portion of one's assets. For example, in our recommendations below, we recommend a 5 percent to 10 percent allocation to a DIA as a starting point.

Recommendations

There is a specific subset of retirees for which a DIA makes sense. Specifically, for retirees who have Monte Carlo success rates between 75 and 90 percent, we recommend allocating 5 percent to 10 percent to a DIA. We generally recommend that retirees purchase the DIA in a tax-deferred account if possible, and the purchase should be made around your retirement age with income starting right before age 85.

Retirees with success rates below 75 percent will likely need to do some combination of working longer, saving more, spending less and purchasing a DIA. There are some retirees for whom purchasing a DIA would not be recommended. Retirees in poor health should not purchase a DIA. Retirees who have success rates higher than 90 percent can consider self-insuring, though it is clear from the Monte Carlo results that purchasing a DIA will not lower their rates of success. If retirees have more than 75 percent of their spending covered by Social Security and/or pensions, they likely would not need to annuitize because the pensions would serve as a sufficient hedge against longevity risk. Moreover, a retiree with a strong bequest motive may not wish to purchase a longevity annuity because he or she may leave less to heirs by purchasing an annuity.

Summary

A DIA and SPIA can be viewed as a fixed income investment without a fixed maturity date. To the purchaser, it looks like a bond that provides constant payments as long as the purchaser is alive. The periodic payments may be level, increasing at a predetermined rate, or inflation indexed. Importantly, due to the mortality credits embedded in the risk pooling, DIAs and SPIAs can provide higher yields than traditional fixed income. Therefore, it is difficult, if not impossible, for older investors to replicate this enhanced yield by using traditional bonds. That is why most economists agree that there is no better financial hedge for longevity risk than purchasing a DIA.

There are some individuals who do not need to purchase a DIA or an SPIA, either because they can self-insure against longevity risk (their Monte Carlo results show very high odds of success), or because their spending is already substantially covered by Social Security, other pensions, or other (such as rental) income.

And perhaps most importantly, the evidence is growing that retirees who purchase an annuity are happier and more content with their financial condition in retirement than those receiving equivalent levels of income from other sources. For those for whom the purchase is the prudent decision, the DIA is superior to an SPIA in terms of protecting against longevity risk.

The next chapter discusses the important role played by other types of insurance.

CHAPTER 15

The Role of Insurance: The Management of Risk

A S WE HAVE discussed, having a well-designed investment plan is only a necessary condition for investment success. The sufficient condition is integrating it into a well-designed life and financial plan that includes estate, tax and risk management planning. There are important non-investment risks to consider—mortality, disability, and morbidity (specifically the need for long-term care, and even longevity risk (living longer than expected), which we addressed in Chapter 14. If these risks are not integrated into the overall financial plan, even the best investment plan can fail. Consider this example.

John is a 32-year-old investment advisor. He is married and has two young children. He has just finished paying off his college debts and his income is now sufficient to begin saving—and investing. He has a well-designed investment plan. Unfortunately, John passes away unexpectedly in an auto accident. While he had time to implement the investment plan (e.g., asset allocation, location, and so on) he did not live long enough to execute the savings plan. If he did not have enough life insurance his family would not have sufficient resources to provide for the standard of living John desired. A mistake often made is that families consider the largest assets in their estate to be their investment portfolio, their home, and their cars. However, the largest asset for many younger families is labor capital—the present value of future earned income streams. Without that asset, or insurance to protect against the loss of that asset, a family may not be able to maintain an acceptable standard of living.

Analyzing the need for life, health, long-term care, disability, and all types of what are referred to as "personal lines" of insurance, is a critical part of the financial planning process. All types of insurance should be considered, and all existing policies should be reviewed often (every 2–3 years), if not annually, by an independent risk management specialist to ensure coverage is adequate. All policies should be reviewed after a life event such as a birth, a new home or a new job.

Let's face it, insurance is not exciting. There are so many different types (and from so many different companies) that many are left wondering, "Do I really need this? Is it worth the expense? Am I wasting my money?" The reality is that insurance is protecting us from worst-case scenarios—experiencing an event that could have catastrophic consequences for our families. While it may not be exciting, insurance plays a vital role in the planning process. This chapter will briefly discuss life insurance, long-term care insurance, disability income insurance, and briefly touch on personal lines of insurance such as home, auto, and umbrella to provide perspective on where each may fit into your overall plan.

Life Insurance

Tim Maurer, Wealth Advisor and Director of Advisor Development for Buckingham Strategic Wealth and Buckingham Strategic Partners, sums up the reason why you may need life insurance. "If anyone relies on you financially, you need life insurance." It's that simple. You buy life insurance because you love someone else and you care about their well-being. While there are many different needs that life insurance can protect, the most common is income replacement—ensuring that if an income-earning spouse were to pass away, the family wouldn't sacrifice their standard of living.

Where does the funding come from to pay for children's day care, to have the benefit of a spouse staying at home with the children, caring for an aging parent, funding the 529 plan, funding retirement? If it comes from wages, that income has to be protected. While the crowded insurance marketplace makes it confusing trying to decipher where to begin, our perspective is that life insurance discussions should start with a simple understanding of "how much coverage is needed and for how long?"

There are two main types of life insurance: term and permanent. Many use the term "whole life" to describe any type of permanent coverage, but "whole life" is a specific type of plan. An entire book could be written on the different types of insurance products, but in an effort to keep it simple, here is a quick explanation.

Term Insurance

For those looking to protect their income, term life insurance can be an inexpensive means of providing significant coverage for a window of time. This type of insurance is to provide protection against a temporary need. Term insurance plans provide a guaranteed, level premium for a specified amount of time, which is typically 10, 15, 20, 25 or 30 years. Most term policies provide a conversion privilege, which will allow a policy-holder to convert the term insurance into a type of permanent life insurance without providing evidence of insurability. Make sure that you purchase a term policy from a reputable company that allows for conversion into a high-quality permanent policy if needed.

Permanent Insurance

Permanent insurance is to provide protection against a need that is… permanent (such as providing liquidity for an estate that is subject to the federal estate tax). Options for permanent coverage can include Whole Life, Variable Whole Life, Universal Life, Variable Universal Life, Indexed Universal Life and No-Lapse Guarantee Universal Life. Going into the pros and cons of each type of coverage goes beyond the scope of this book, but those who own permanent life insurance should be sure to understand what part of the plan is guaranteed and what is not guaranteed. It sounds simple, but it rarely is. And rarely is it understood by the policyholder.

Many types of permanent insurance have a hypothetical assumption at the onset of the policy (a subaccount return, an index return, a dividend, an interest rate, etc.) that needs to come to fruition for the policy to perform as illustrated at the time of the purchase. If that hypothetical assumption doesn't come to fruition, it's the policyholder's responsibility (not the agent or the insurance company) to review the plan and make the necessary adjustments (which commonly mean additional premium contributions). For that reason, a permanent life insurance policy should never be left on autopilot. Being a policy owner goes beyond making premium payments and extends to periodic, regular reviews which will provide assurance that:

- The policy is being funded appropriately to provide coverage throughout the insured's lifetime.
- The coverage is still appropriate. Does the need that existed when the policy was purchased still apply?
- The beneficiaries listed are still the desired choices.
- There are not any unforeseen surprises in the future. Some policies have an "automatic premium loan feature," which could be advantageous, but could also lead to negative tax repercussions down the road.
- The policy is still priced appropriately. Perhaps the insured's health has improved due to cessation of smoking, significant weight loss, and so on.
- The underwriting company maintains financial stability.

Choosing only from among the highest rated insurers (only AAA- and AA-rated) is critical:

- Credit risk is positively correlated with the length of the horizon—the longer the term, the greater the credit risk. With many forms of insurance, the horizon can be decades long.
- Unlike with equity investing, in most cases it is more difficult and costly to diversify the credit risk of insurers. Thus, it is critical that you choose a highly rated company when purchasing any insurance product.

The best tool to determine financial strength is a Comdex ranking. A Comdex ranking is a composite score (1–100) averaging the ratings of the major insurance rating organizations including A.M. Best, Fitch, Moody's, and Standard & Poor's, each of which publishes their own ratings.

Many who are at, or near, retirement struggle to stay within a conservative budget. Life insurance premiums commonly stand out as a significant expense and revisiting the purpose of having the insurance and reestablishing the need is a good exercise. Many purchased permanent policies when their children were young to provide protection. Over the years, they continue to diligently pay premiums without considering that their children are now grown, with families of their own, and the need for insurance has changed. The risk to adult children shifts from their livelihoods being affected by a premature death to their livelihoods being affected by their parents' longevity. The emotional and financial impact of caring for an aging loved one is significant. In our experience, the discussion of long-term care insurance is usually very timely and, with the use of "hybrid plans" (life insurance policies with long-term-care riders), an existing permanent policy can be potentially repositioned to provide a primary benefit of long-term care insurance, while still having the death benefit coverage as a secondary, or tertiary, benefit.

There's another topic related to life insurance policies that we need to cover.

Life Settlements

Traditional life settlements offer policyholders the opportunity to access additional cash by selling policies that are no longer needed, or that they can no longer afford. In general, these types of transactions can be beneficial if there is a complete understanding of the terms of the contract. The industry has recently seen the emergence of speculator-initiated life insurance policies, or "spin-life policies," that promote the purchase of life insurance only to sell it to an investor a few years later for a single payment. A spin-life strategy is not recommended as the benefits do not outweigh the costs and inherent risks.

Background

Purchasers of traditional life settlements are generally large institutions like banks or hedge funds. The 'ideal' policyholder is an older individual (65 or older) with compromised health who can no longer afford the premiums or no longer needs the death benefits on a life insurance policy. Life-settlement investors pool the purchased policies, dividing them into life-settlement backed securities, typically sold to hedge funds, pension funds and other institutional investors.

Life-settlement brokers are also in the market. While some help investors sell their existing policies to other investors, others are taking a more aggressive approach. Some brokers seek out older high-net-worth individuals with life insurance capacity, lend them money to pay for premiums on high-value life insurance policies and prearrange to purchase the policy a few years later for a one-time cash payout (less the amount loaned for the premiums). These speculator-initiated spin-life contracts are also known as stranger-owned life insurance (STOLI) policies.

Benefits

Selling policies to fund medical care and living expenses is referred to as traditional life settlements. With anticipated changes to estate tax laws, traditional life settlements can provide investors an additional estate and financial planning tool. For example, a life settlement could be used to remove the value of an individually held life insurance policy from an estate's assets. A charitable organization receiving a donated life insurance policy can use a life settlement to receive an immediate cash benefit with no further premium obligations. The donor would receive a tax deduction from the donation and an additional amount in excess of the surrender value from the life-settlement transaction.

Risks

Life-settlement payouts are often about a third of policy value and much greater than the surrender value or cash value of the contract. There is no official guidance from the IRS regarding the tax treatment of life settlements. The IRS could consider all proceeds above the cost basis as ordinary income—not the industry's customary tax treatment. There are trade offs, as "the tax consequences to the seller of receiving a cash payment during the insured's lifetime are not as favorable (or certain) as that of receiving the policy's death benefit." You should consult a tax expert prior to arranging for a life-settlement payout.

Opaqueness of the Bidding Process

One big obstacle to completing a traditional life-settlement transaction is finding an investor. Individuals should always obtain more than one bid for their policies and request full transparency during the bidding process. There is evidence that in some cases, brokers negotiated settlements and did not pass along the full bid amounts to their clients. According to a study conducted by Deloitte, seniors completing a life-settlement transaction received just 20 cents on the dollar instead of the 64 cents on the dollar Deloitte calculated to be the intrinsic value of the policy. The (sometimes undisclosed) commissions charged by originating brokers can also play into the lower settlement amount to a client. Broker commissions can range from 4 percent to 6 percent. In addition, there may also be a fee paid to the provider.

Where policies contain personal data and medical history, sellers should verify that investors are well-established institutions that will transfer such information anonymously. If personal information is known, one can argue the insured risks a moral hazard.

Industry regulations have not been firmly established in this new industry, and there have been several well-publicized life-settlement investigations and lawsuits.

As more regulations are adopted, there may be fewer investors to offer liquidity from insurance policies, and the ability to sell policies and transfer ownership may become more difficult.

Spin-life policies are also subject to additional risks and costs that traditional life settlements do not face. There is credit risk with the investors, since the insured must both:

- Rely on funds from the investors to pay for the premiums.
- Ensure the investors will have enough capital to purchase the policy.

Carefully review contracts with an insurance expert. Some may include clauses where, if an investor cannot be found, you are not released from the debt, and interest on the debt.

Market Changes

Some states are increasing the number of contestable years for life insurance. Some 30 states are currently weighing two- or five-year waiting periods before policyholders can sell their policies. In an effort to target STOLIs directly, others prohibit the sale of a life insurance policy within five years of purchase if the insured borrowed money to pay for the premiums. Finally, a few states are contesting the legality of life settlements. To purchase insurance, one must have an insurable interest (usually in their own lives), but there are currently no laws prohibiting life settlements. Insurance lobbyists are hard at work to make those changes. This could allow insurance companies to cancel or void spin-life policies, leaving the policyholder without a policy to sell and a large amount of debt from loans on the insurance premiums.

Increases in regulations and in life insurance premiums to cover falling lapse ratios (number of lapsed policies to total number of policies in force at the beginning of the year) lead to a more restrictive life-settlements market and one with reduced individual profit. The higher premiums also make it more expensive for individuals who truly need life insurance to purchase new policies. With the legal and tax treatment of STOLI policies so uncertain, and such lack of transparency in the arrangements, these transactions cannot be recommended. However, traditional life settlements continue to be useful financial and estate planning tools. For individuals who have unnecessary policies and do not need immediate access to a lump sum of cash, there are other options. Some possible alternatives include using a 1035 exchange (the replacement of an annuity or life insurance policy for a new one without incurring any tax consequence for the exchange) to convert from an insurance asset to:

- An investment asset (such as a low-cost deferred variable annuity).
- An immediate annuity for income.
- A new life insurance policy that may eliminate the need to pay premiums while locking in a death benefit if a policy becomes unaffordable. The beneficiaries may have an interest in paying the premium to ensure the death benefit while removing the need for any type of transaction.

Long-Term Care

Most financial planners agree that there are few ways a financial plan can be more adversely affected than an extended stay in a long-term care facility. Unfortunately, long-term care insurance (LTCI) has received a lot of bad publicity due to incorrect actuarial assumptions and a "perfect storm" of factors that were unanticipated—historically low interest rates, low lapsation rates, and greater utilization than expected. However, before we throw the baby out with the bath water, let's keep in mind some important benefits that long-term care insurance provides (Medicare may cover some costs, but typically a modest amount of coverage and only for a short period of time (e.g., 100 days), while Medicaid can cover all LTC costs for life with the key being able to qualify. Medicaid planning is a specialized practice area, generally by attorneys.):

- In-home care.
- Assisted living facilities.
- Nursing home care.
- Allowing family members and trained RNs to help.

LTCI can be valuable to a family when someone they love needs care. According to a CareScout study, the cost of a private room in 2017 averaged $8,121 per month. According to the U.S. Department of Health and Human Services website (longtermcare.acl.gov) someone turning age 65 today has almost a 70 percent chance of needing some type of long-term care services and supports in their remaining years. While you can hope you do not fall into the 70 percent group, hope is not a strategy. Your financial plan should consider the risk that you, your spouse if married, or both will need care. And while 30 percent may never need long-term care support, 20 percent will need it longer than 5 years, which could be devastating for many portfolios.

Beyond the Financial Burden

Aside from the obvious financial burden that comes with needing care, the pressure put on loved ones should not to be ignored. According to EBRI, a non-partisan, tax-exempt organization on retirement benefits, for those over age 65 needing substantial help, seven in 10 family caregivers are women. Most commonly, the female spouse first provides care before it falls to the oldest daughter. While we all like to believe we would be able to care for a loved one, rather than sending them to a care facility, most underestimate the emotional and financial burden that comes with the care.

According to the Department of Health and Human Services, family caregivers are likely to spend more than 24 hours per week providing care, making it difficult for an adult child to maintain full-time employment, raise his/her own children and maintain a healthy marriage. For a parent, some would make this 24 hour a week sacrifice. However, the question is for how long can that be sustained?

According to the JAMA Internal Medicine study, "A National Profile of Family and Unpaid Caregivers Who Assist Older Adults with Health Care Activities," less than 5 percent of the time the care is for less than a year. Forty-four percent of the time the care lasts from one to four years, and 50 percent of the time, family caregiving goes beyond four years. According to the Family Caregiver Alliance, the overall cost to a female family caregiver is estimated at almost $325,000 because of lost wages and diminished working hours.

As you can see, it's critical that you consider these issues when determining whether to purchase LTC insurance.

The Role of Long-Term Care

Long-term care insurance provides an opportunity for families to offset at least some of the risk of needing care. Traditional long-term care insurance has fallen under a tremendous amount of scrutiny in the press and, in many cases, rightfully so. Many insurance agents, who sold these traditional plans, failed to communicate the lack of a guaranteed or "fixed" premium leaving seniors, who are on a fixed income, to endure major rate increases. Unfortunately, the trifecta of a historically low-interest-rate environment, higher claims, and lower lapse rates than anticipated has led to regular premium increases to existing blocks of business.

Nearly every insurance carrier has received state approval to increase rates. Yet, even with these substantial increases, these older, traditional plans are still priced far more competitively than new products today and represent a solid asset for many families (it is rarely advisable to replace a traditional LTC insurance policy). With that said, because of the uncertainty of the future of rate increases, the purchase of traditional LTC insurance products has steadily declined since 2008, while the "new normal" of longevity planning, "hybrid" Life/LTC plans, have experienced significant growth.

Understanding Your Options

There are two main types of LTCI: traditional and hybrid. The traditional type of LTCI is a standalone policy that provides coverage only for a long-term care claim. The premiums are not guaranteed and are likely going to increase in the future. While these plans are far less popular than hybrid plans today, they usually come at an initially lower premium and can be attractive to those with higher premium sensitivity (but again, the premium increases will be looming).

Traditional LTCI

Traditional LTCIs can provide for personal and custodial care for an extended period of time. Coverage is triggered by needing help with, or losing, at least two of six activities of daily living (ADLs). There are six categories: bathing, dressing, eating, transferring, toileting and continence.

The "loss of ADLs" could be the need for substantial hands-on, standby or supervisory assistance. Generally, any cognitive impairment such as Alzheimer's and dementia are automatically covered whether or not the two-ADL trigger is met.

A common misperception of long-term care is that it is only for nursing home care. While care may be received at a nursing home, typically it can also be received at an assisted living facility, adult day care with respite services, or for home-based care. Care can be defined in two ways:

1. **Care for custodial (personal) needs.** Care provided to assist with ADLs or to meet personal needs (assistance with bathing, dressing, eating or getting in or out of bed).
2. **Care for skilled needs.** Care provided by a licensed healthcare professional such as an RN, LPN, physical therapist or speech therapist. A physician must order this care.

Long-term care is a tool that can help preserve and protect financial assets. It provides flexibility in choosing the type of care and where care is received. It can help ensure high-quality care and provide financial and emotional support for the family. There are six important issues to consider when purchasing long-term care coverage:

1. How much coverage is right for you?
   - What is the cost of care in your area?
   - What daily benefit amount (DBA) would you need and want? (These may be two different answers.)
2. Where would you like to receive care?
   - Nursing home.
   - Home-based health care.
3. How would you like to receive your benefits?
   - Reimbursement: Reimbursement for actual expenses accrued on a monthly basis.
   - Indemnity: Full DBA payments when receiving licensed care whether or not maximum DBA is being used—full payment of DBA for each day of care no matter how much is spent.
   - Are you better suited to an indemnity or reimbursement plan? Are you willing to pay more to simply receive a check each month when you have qualified for a claim, or would you prefer to pay less and submit receipts?
4. How long do you want to receive benefits?
   - Typical benefit periods are two to five years.
   - With reimbursement plans, the benefit period is driven by a pool of money. Example: A $150 DBA × 365 days × 5 years = $273,750 total lifetime benefits. Even if five years have elapsed, the benefit remains until the pool of money is depleted.
5. What type of inflation protection would you like?
   - None.
   - Simple: Typically, 3 or 5 percent.
   - Compound: Typically, 3 or 5 percent.
6. How long can you wait before benefits are paid?
   - The "elimination period" is the period of time you are responsible for paying the cost of your care services.
   - A typical elimination period is 90 to 100 days.

Hybrid Plans

Most commonly these are whole life or universal life insurance plans with an LTCI rider. The most competitive products in the market offer:

- Fully guaranteed "fixed" premiums.
- Guaranteed LTC pool of funds.
- Guaranteed inflation protection.
- Guaranteed return of premium options.
- A Guaranteed death benefit.

Since 2008, sales of these plans have far outpaced traditional LTCI. According to Broker World Surveys, from 2000 through 2014, the sales of standalone LTCI policies fell about 80 percent, while the sales of hybrid polices increased about 10 times. The result was that by 2014 the sales of hybrid policies were about 10 times that of standalone policies.

These products are most commonly marketed as plans that provide benefits if you "live, die or quit." Very simply:

- **Live:** Plans provide long-term care benefits that typically grow with a guaranteed rate of compound inflation. The benefits are typically provided in yearly increments with monthly maximum limits. As they do with traditional LTC insurance, claims start when the insured can no longer perform two of six "activities of daily living" (bathing, continence, dressing, eating, toileting and transferring) or a cognitive impairment. With these hybrid plans, the LTC benefit is usually much larger than the death benefit. This allows the policy owner to best leverage their premium dollars to cover the longevity risk.
- **Die:** Each of these plans provides a death benefit that is typically much smaller than the pool of LTC funds. The death benefit will most commonly decrease dollar-for-dollar based upon any LTC claims activity. Most plans will provide a residual death benefit for final expenses (such as $10,000–$15,000) even if all of the funding is exhausted through LTC claims activity. Because this is a life insurance death benefit, the death benefit is free from income tax.
- **Quit:** These plans are not inexpensive, and this "Quit" feature is more peace of mind than anything else. Most hybrid plans allow the policy owner to surrender the plan and receive back some or all of their premium dollars, depending on the structure of the plan.

Structure of the Plan

There are a number of factors to consider when researching these plans. A good risk management company will learn your goals and objectives and then research the market to find a plan design that is most appropriate for your specific needs. The following items should be always be discussed:

- Type of Benefit: Indemnity or Reimbursement
    - Indemnity: Once you qualify for a claim, you receive a check each month for the benefit provided under the terms of the plan. For those who want family to provide care, but wish to be able to compensate them for doing so, these are considered most desirable. With all things being equal, indemnity would be the choice most people would prefer, but typically bears a substantial additional cost, making reimbursement plans more popular in today's market.
    - Reimbursement: With these plans, the policy owner submits receipts to the insurance company and the insurance company will reimburse up to the monthly maximum. With these plans, the benefit period is used more as a multiplier than a maximum amount of time that one can be on claim. For example, let's suppose we have a four-year benefit period and a $6,000 monthly benefit: 48 months × $6,000 = $288,000. If the insured individual only uses $3,000 in the first month, the remaining $3,000 would stay in the client's pool of LTC funds. Therefore, a four-year or 48-month benefit period could go longer.

Determining the Benefit Period

According to the U.S. Department of Health and Human Services website (longtermcare.acl.gov), when considering the full spectrum of care (in home, transitional, assisted living, alternative care, nursing home, etc.), the average length of care for women is 3.7 years and 2.2 years for men. For many people, that could be a good place to start. With that understanding, those who have a significant family history of Alzheimer's or dementia may wish to consider a longer period or an unlimited benefit period (which is rare in today's market, but does exist). An unlimited benefit period is the only way to ensure that you have the precise amount of care you need. The American Association for Long-Term Care Insurance 2019 report showed that the LTC policies had paid out for as long as 19 years, with payments exceeding in some cases $2.2 million.

Inflation Protection

Most LTC insurance coverage is purchased by those in their mid-to-late 50s. Because of the substantial gap between the purchase time and the likely need for care, it is typically necessary to obtain an inflation protection rider on any LTC insurance plan. At best, these inflation riders will typically allow your benefits to grow at a rate of 5 percent compounded annually. These riders are not inexpensive, so it is good practice to compare the cost of buying a higher benefit today versus a moderate benefit today with an inflation rider (in other words, a $6,000 benefit today with an inflation rider that will grow to $12,000 at the time of expected claim or simply buying $12,000 in benefits today without an inflation rider).

Elimination Period

Many plans are customizable with the elimination period. The elimination period is the amount of time you are financially responsible for your care before the LTC insurance benefit will begin. Quite typically, the longer the elimination period, the lower your premium will be. Conversely, the shorter your elimination period, the higher your premium will be. It's also important to consider how the insurance carrier counts "days." Some insurance carriers will count every calendar day towards your elimination, while others will count only "days of service."

Insurability, Leverage and Underwriting

Hybrid LTC insurance underwriting has a "pass/fail" feel to it. Though life insurance typically has 16–20 different rate classes available, hybrid plans typically offer "standard", which is average mortality/morbidity and "preferred," which is a step up. Because this is a life insurance product that also provides LTC benefits, the policy will be underwritten for both mortality and morbidity concerns.

Many people wait too long to explore LTC coverage and want it when they need it. However, anyone who uses a cane, has memory issues, is receiving disability benefits, has surgery in the near future, is using narcotic pain medication, has severe mood disorders, has had a stroke or has any muscle/joint related illness is very likely to be declined or postponed for coverage.

In addition, the leverage one can attain from these products based upon their premium dollars is much higher at younger ages. As an example:

- Married female, preferred rates, $5,000 monthly benefit, four-year benefit period, 90-day elimination with 3 percent compound inflation protection and 70 percent return of premium ("quit") option.
- Age 50: 10 premium payments of $9,608.
- Age 58: 10 premium payments of $11,323.
- Age 66: 10 premium payments of $13,785.

Keep in mind, these premium figures assume at each age this individual would still be able to qualify at preferred, non-nicotine rates. Unfortunately, by age 70, the premium cost becomes almost unfeasible and nearly half of all applicants are rejected due to their medical background.

The underwriting process for products varies from carrier to carrier. The largest carrier in today's market has a fairly simple process that does not require a physical examination, but will commonly require a senior questionnaire (this is typically a lengthy phone call where they try to confirm your cognitive stability). Other carriers will require a paramedical examination with medical records, which is not overly cumbersome, but can lead to a lengthier process.

Be Cautious

Never purchase a product that you don't understand. A good risk management consultant will take the time to educate you so that you are comfortable making the right decision for your family. The risk management consultant should also be in lock-step with your comprehensive financial planner to help you down the right path. It's also important that you explore multiple insurance carriers and products. There is no silver bullet product that will be the best option in every situation.

Be sure you fully understand what parts of the contract are "guaranteed" and which parts are "projected." There are several carriers in today's market that have hybrid plans that are based upon the performance of an index, dividend or sub-account return to be successful. These plans are not necessarily inappropriate, but you should fully understand their innerworkings before making any purchases. The concern with these plans is that, if the assumed hypothetical growth rate does not come to fruition, your long-term care benefits could be in jeopardy and your policy could even lapse while you're on claim, if not properly monitored and funded.

Lastly, use extreme caution if a plan does not actually have a true LTC insurance rider. Some agents will propose a cash value-rich permanent life insurance plan with no actual LTC benefit. The concept, in these proposals, is that you can take loans at any point, whether it's for LTC or otherwise. While another book could be written on this concept alone, recognize that these plans offer no leverage on the LTC pool and could lead to catastrophic ordinary income tax consequences if you live too long, withdraw or loan too much, or if the internal costs increase (or all three happen).

Summary

Using a hybrid plan for LTC planning can be an intelligent choice. Discussing options with an independent risk management consultant should expose you to multiple carriers and should not make you feel as though you are obligated to make a purchase. The best practice is to explore options when you are young, healthy, and your insurability is high. Invite your financial planner to attend meetings with you and be a part of the decision-making process.

Despite its importance, we have found that there are many reasons why people fail to plan for long-term care: The natural tendency to avoid thinking about becoming dependent on others for your care; misinformation about the risks of needing care; and lack of knowledge about the cost of care and payment options. In addition, most people just do not like to think about getting older, developing a disability, becoming less independent or needing help with personal care. There's an appropriate adage: "If you do not die, you live. If you live, you get sick. If you get sick, you need care."

The Importance of Long-Term Care: A Monte Carlo Analysis

Using the tool of Monte Carlo analysis, the following case study demonstrates the importance of long-term care.

Mr. and Mrs. Smith are both 65 years old. They have financial assets of $6 million. A Monte Carlo analysis reveals that their portfolio has a high likelihood of providing sufficient assets to maintain their desired lifestyle if neither ever has a need for long-term care. If one or both do need long-term care for an extended period, the portfolio has a significant likelihood of being strained, or even depleted. The Monte Carlo analysis also reveals that the costs of a LTCI policy will not significantly reduce the odds of success.

Long-Term Care Scenarios	Odds the Portfolio Will Have Sufficient Assets (%)
No LTCI, no need for care	94
Have LTCI, no need for care	91
Have LTCI coverage for 20 years, need care for 5 years (age 85–90)	83
No LTCI, need care from age 85–90	74

If no insurance is needed, the additional costs of purchasing a LTC policy increases the odds of running out of money by just 3 percent (94 percent versus 91 percent). If long-term care is needed, and no insurance purchased, the odds of running out of money increase by 20 percent—the odds of success falling from 94 percent to 74 percent. That is almost seven times the 3 percent increase in likelihood of failure caused by the purchase of insurance.

For some affluent investors, the analysis may show they can self-insure and still have sufficiently low odds of failure—outliving sufficient financial assets. Let's take an investor with substantial bequeath objectives, and analyze his likelihood of having at least $1 million, $3 million or $5 million at death. The following assumptions are used in the above analysis:

LTCI Policy Coverages:
- Five years of benefit.
- $200/day in benefit.
- Shared care (ten total years if needed).
- Indemnity (no receipts needed).
- Compound inflation.
- Premium: $10,500 per year total.
- Elimination period: 100 days.
  Care assumptions without LTCI:
- $750/day for five years.
- Both people need some care and are most likely at home for the five-year period age 85–90. This adds $273,750 per year in living needs.
  Care assumptions with LTCI:
- $750/day for five years. Subtract $350 (assumed the coverage was needed, leaving the self-insuring amount at $400). This adds $127,750 per year in living needs.

As you can see, the need for long-term care significantly impacts the odds of success.

Long-Term Care Scenarios	Odds Ending Portfolio Will Have At Least $1mm, $3mm, and $5mm
No LTCI, no need for care	94%, 68%, 48%
Have LTCI, no need for care	91%, 63%, 45%
Have LTCI coverage for 20 years, need care for 5 years (age 85–90)	83%, 55%, 38%
No LTCI, need care from age 85–90	74%, 49%, 32%

We see that while the odds of leaving a large estate decrease somewhat if long-term care insurance is purchased and no care is needed, the odds of success fall by a greater amount if not purchased and care is needed. In this example, both risk averse individuals and those with large bequeath objectives should prefer to purchase such insurance.

Should You Consider LTCI? It Depends

Low Income Families

Unfortunately, LTCI is expensive. Those who have minimal assets and will rely on Social Security as a primary means of retirement income likely are not going to be able to afford the coverage.

The "Big Middle"

A term referenced by Dr. Chernof, President and Chief Executive of The SCAN Foundation, a non-profit focused on improving the quality of health and life for seniors. This group is "on their own: and needs council on how to weigh the cost versus the benefits as it relates to their financial capabilities."

Affluent Families

Affluent families can, and commonly do, self-insure. The concern with this strategy is that affluent households tend to live longer and healthier lives, not taking into account the statistics showing a higher incidence of nursing home need. This need can create significantly higher out-of-pocket costs.

In our experience, many affluent families are turned off by LTCI, because the insurance proposal assumes maximum amounts of coverage to provide for care at elite facilities and they experience "premium shock." Because these families can self-insure, they likely do not need a plan that is going to shoulder 100 percent of the risk. Many affluent families are interested in having a discussion about transferring a portion of the risk to the insurance company and, by doing so, arrive at a more palatable premium.

Disability Income Insurance

According to the Disability Resource Center, Disability Income Insurance (DI) may be the proverbial "canary in the coal mine," as studies show that the possibility of experiencing a long-term disability is several times greater than the possibility of death. For example, from ages 27 through 52 the odds rise from 2.2:1 to 3.5:1.

DI, like term life insurance, is most commonly used to protect against the loss of an income. However, where term life insurance protects against the death of an income earner, DI protects against the disability of an income earner that would preclude them from working. The definition of "disability" can vary and can be defined as the inability to perform the duties of one's own occupation or the inability to perform the duties of any occupation. The purpose of the insurance is to ensure that if the insured individual becomes disabled, the family would be able to maintain a similar standard of living. Most disability income plans provide coverage up to 60 percent of earned income. For those who earn $250,000 or more, the percentage drops significantly, and many carriers have a maximum monthly cap of approximately $17,000. In those scenarios, it is good practice to look at multiple carrier options to provide adequate coverage. DI plans have many riders and other customizable features that can allow for truly personalized coverage and those features can have a major influence on the premium. With these types of plans, the proposed insured can "dial in" to the best options, given their stated goals and objectives. An independent, objective risk management consultant can help guide you to the policies that are most appropriate for your situation.

Do Not Procrastinate

Risk management tends to be one of the most overlooked planning topics. We have seen too many people procrastinate and then be unable to obtain coverage due to a change in their health. We are big proponents of insurance as a part of the financial planning process. As an example, we had a client with whom we had life insurance discussions many times, who "never got around to it." Sadly, that client prematurely passed away and his family's lifestyle was forced to change. It was a terrible thing; he would never have wanted that. However, he also thought it would never happen to him.

We had another client who took the time to explore options, obtained term insurance coverage and passed away in a biking accident six months later. The loss of a loved one is never easy, and the family will always grieve, but the grieving process is much longer and deeper when the death of the loved one causes the family to make major lifestyle changes (like moving homes, switching schools, delaying retirement, etc.). The income-tax-free death benefit provided by an inexpensive term insurance plan made a terrible situation financially bearable.

One individual when purchasing long-term care said, "I hope this is the biggest waste of money in my life". We couldn't agree more. Insurance is something that each of us must address, realizing the morbidity and mortality of the conversation. The importance is not typically for you, the insured. Instead it is for your family, whether for peace of mind or a significant financial impact upon an unplanned for disability, long-term care need, or untimely death.

Personal Lines of Insurance

While going into detail on personal lines of insurance (such as home, auto, and umbrella) is beyond the scope of this book, they each play an important role in the management of risk. As such, an annual review of each of these policies can be invaluable, whether or not circumstances change. The following are a few examples:

Homeowners

It is critical to have proper flood, hurricane or earthquake coverage (as appropriate to your location). It's also important to make sure when renovations have been done that coverage has been updated. And while jewelry and artwork will often be covered by homeowner policies, there are circumstances (and amounts) that would warrant a separate line of coverage.

Auto

Make sure you have coverage for insured and uninsured motorists so that an accident will always be covered.

Umbrella

Providing excess (above the coverage provided by your homeowner's and auto policies) personal liability insurance, this is one of the most underutilized types of coverage. This relatively inexpensive, yet vitally important coverage, provides protection from major claims and lawsuits. A very simple example of where umbrella coverage can come into play is if someone were to slip on your sidewalk during winter and sue you for not properly cleaning and salting. A judgment against you for $500,000 can come from savings—or it can be paid by the insurance company backing your umbrella policy. Many believe that only famous and well-known people need this type of coverage, but that could not be further from the truth.

Summary

As we have noted, because investment plans can fail for reasons that have nothing to do with investing, an important part of the financial planning process is to address each of the types of risk we have discussed. Without considering "the worst-case scenario" the financial plan is built with blinders. It makes sense to hope for the best, but plan for worst.

The next chapter is about the role that reverse mortgages can play in a retirement plan.

CHAPTER 16

Reverse Mortgages

T HERE IS A general consensus that a majority of American households are facing a significant retirement funding gap. Retirees are often house-rich, but cash-poor, with their home being among their largest assets—with the potential to serve as a source of funding spending needs. There used to be just three significant ways to get equity from a home:

- Sell it.
- Rent it.
- Borrow against it using either a cash-out refinance or a home equity loan.

Reverse mortgages present a fourth option, allowing homeowners to receive some of the home's equity without moving or making regular loan repayments. Reverse mortgages provide an alternative financing method (though a relatively expensive one) that can help homeowners maintain their independence as well as an adequate standard of living.

People who take out reverse mortgages often:

- Have a regular need for additional funds.
- Live on a fixed income with their home equity as their most significant asset.
- Desire to pay off their existing mortgage to free up additional cash.
- Do not plan to leave their home to their heirs.

Reverse Mortgage Features

While reverse mortgages resemble conventional mortgages, with homeowners borrowing against the equity in their home, a big difference is that with a reverse mortgage the borrower does not immediately begin paying back the loan. A requirement for a reverse mortgage is that the borrower must pay off any remaining mortgages on the property, including home equity loans (the proceeds from the reverse mortgage will be used to pay off any remaining mortgage debt). Generally, the loans are not due until the home is no longer the homeowner's principal residence. Money received from reverse mortgages is considered a loan and therefore not taxable. Thus, it typically does not affect either the borrower's other assets, or their Medicare and Social Security benefits.

While borrowers can repay reverse mortgages with other assets, they typically repay them by selling the home. Any equity remaining after selling the home belongs to the homeowners or their heirs. Importantly, most reverse mortgages have a non-recourse clause—any debt exceeding 95 percent of the appraised home value cannot be passed along to the estate or heirs.

The amount borrowers receive depends on several factors including:

- Age.
- The current interest rate.
- Loan fees.
- The home's appraised value or the Federal Housing Administration's (FHA's) mortgage limits for the area, whichever is less.

Borrower Requirements and Responsibilities

- **Income requirements:** Income determinations are different for a reverse mortgage and available funds from the reverse mortgage can be included to help the borrower meet the required guidelines. Residual income (RI) is an important part of the financial ability component of the new Home Equity Conversion Mortgage (HECM) financial assessment guidelines. RI is calculated by adding up all monthly qualifying income and deducting debt payments (excluding mortgage payments to be eliminated by the reverse mortgage), monthly property charges (property taxes, homeowner's insurance, HOA dues, etc.), and an estimate of utility and maintenance costs based on the square footage of the home. The leftover residual income must meet a certain threshold based on the region the applicant lives in and the number of people living in the home. If an applicant doesn't meet the residual income standards and will have funds available from the reverse mortgage, the lender may be required to set up a life expectancy set-aside (LESA) unless the applicant can document compensating factors that make up for the income shortfall.
- **Age qualification:** Any borrower must be at least 62. There can be a younger non-borrowing spouse. However, they had to be taken off the title and didn't have any protections. To address this issue the category of eligible non-borrowing spouse was created. For spouses under 62, they can now be included, though they are not a borrower. If the borrower is deceased no additional funds can be withdrawn. However, the non-borrowing spouse is

protected to be able to live in the home as long as they want (while meeting the homeowner obligations) without the loan balance becoming due.

- **Primary lien:** A reverse mortgage must be the primary lien on the home. Any existing mortgage must be paid off using the proceeds from the reverse mortgage.
- **Occupancy requirements:** The property used as collateral for the reverse mortgage must be the primary residence. Vacation homes and investor properties do not qualify.
- **Taxes and insurance:** Borrowers must remain current on real estate taxes, homeowner's insurance, and other mandatory obligations, including condominium fees.
- **Property condition:** Borrowers are responsible for completing mandatory repairs and maintaining the condition of the property.
- **Conveyance of the mortgaged property by will or operation of law to the estate or heir after mortgagor's death:** When a reverse mortgage becomes due and payable upon the death of the last surviving borrower or protected non-borrowing spouse, and the property is conveyed by will or operation of law, the estate or heirs (or parties if multiple heirs) may satisfy the HECM debt by paying the lesser of the mortgage balance or 95 percent of the current appraised value of the property.

Loan Considerations

Reverse mortgages involve not only origination fees, but other up-front closing costs and Department of Housing and Urban Development (HUD) mortgage insurance premiums (MIP).

The amount owed on reverse mortgages generally grows over time. Interest is charged on the outstanding balance and added each month. If the debt exceeds the value of the property, the FHA or lender would take the losses due to the non-recourse nature of most reverse mortgages.

Interest rates on reverse mortgages can be either fixed or variable. However, as of this writing, most are variable. And only the variable version offers the line of credit. Because borrowers retain the titles to their homes, they remain responsible for property taxes and all other homeowner expenses. Failing to pay property taxes or maintain homeowner's insurance puts borrowers at risk of the loan becoming due.

Eligible Property Types

The home must be an owner occupied one-to-four-unit property, which includes townhouses, detached or manufactured homes, PUDs (planned unit development), and units in condominiums. Condominiums must be FHA-approved.

How are Payments Received?

First, there is a limit on the amount of funds a borrower can access during the first 12 months after closing. For example, if a borrower is eligible for a $100,000 loan, no more than $60,000, or 60 percent, can be accessed. In month 13, a borrower can take as much or as little of the remaining proceeds as they wish. There are exceptions to the 60 percent rule. A borrower can withdraw more if there is an existing mortgage, or other liens on the property, that must be paid off. A borrower can withdraw enough to pay off these obligations, plus another 10 percent of the maximum allowable amount. That's an extra $10,000, or 10 percent of $100,000.

In addition to taking a lump-sum payment, borrowers have five options:

1. **Tenure**—Indefinite equal monthly payments.
2. **Term**—Equal monthly payments over a certain time period.
3. **Line of credit**—A set amount borrowers can draw from whenever necessary. This is the most popular choice, with about two-thirds of borrowers choosing this option.
4. **Modified tenure**—Combination of line of credit and tenure.
5. **Modified term**—Combination of line of credit and term.

Types of Reverse Mortgages

There are two types of reverse mortgages:

1. **Home Equity Conversion Mortgages (HECMs)**—Backed by the U.S. Department of Housing and Urban Development (HUD).
2. **Proprietary reverse mortgages**—Loans developed and backed by private companies. Due to their complex nature and infinite variety we will not cover them. Proprietary reverse mortgages are privately insured by the mortgage companies that offer them. They are not subject to all the same regulations as HECMs, but as a standard best practice, most companies that offer proprietary reverse mortgages emulate the same consumer protections that are found in the HECM program, including mandatory counseling. They are sometimes called "jumbo" reverse mortgages, allowing you to borrow more than the current maximum on the HUD-backed loan of $765,600. Thus, if your home is worth several million dollars, you may be able to get more funds from a proprietary reverse mortgage. Since the financial crisis this source had mostly dried up because evicting older homeowners who were not paying taxes and insurance, or keeping up the property, became not only difficult, but harmed the institution's public image. However, in 2018 several companies have introduced new proprietary products that are worth considering.

HECMs

HECMs are the most popular type of reverse mortgage. The size of HECMs depends on the maximum loan limit, which varies by county and changes over time. As of 2020, the federal maximum was $765,600. Before applying for HECMs, borrowers must meet with a counselor from an independent government-approved housing counseling agency. During the meeting, the counselor must explain costs, financial implications, and alternatives.

HECMs tend to be much more expensive than traditional home mortgages (though many of the costs can be included in the loan). First, a lender can charge an origination fee that is the greater of $2,500 or 2 percent of the first $200,000 of your home's value, plus 1 percent of the amount over $200,000. HECM origination fees are capped at $6,000.

Second, there will be a fee for mortgage insurance premiums (MIP)—it is currently a flat 2 percent up-front fee on the home value up to the lending limit, and an annual fee of 0.5 percent on the account balance. MIP fees are paid by the borrower to the Federal Housing Administration to provide certain protections for both the lender and the borrower. For example, if the company servicing the loan can no longer meet its obligations, FHA assumes responsibility for the loan, providing the borrower with uninterrupted access to any remaining reverse mortgage proceeds. And in cases where the sale of the home is not enough to pay back the reverse mortgage, the insurance protects the borrower or estate from owing more than the sale price by covering losses incurred by the lender.

Third, the lender has the option to charge a monthly servicing fee. For loans on which the interest rate is adjusted annually, the fee may not exceed $30 a month. For loans on which the rate is adjusted monthly, the fee cap is $35.

Fourth, there will be an appraisal fee for an appraiser to assign a current market value to your home. Appraisal fees vary by region, type and value of home, but average $450. This is the one fee generally paid in cash or by credit card, sometimes before the loan is made (but often as part of the closing costs), and not with the loan proceeds. In addition to placing a value on the home, an appraiser must also make sure there are no major structural defects. Federal regulations mandate that your home be structurally sound, and comply with all home safety and local building codes, in order for the reverse mortgage to be made. If the appraiser uncovers property defects, you must hire a contractor to complete the repairs. Once the repairs are completed, the same appraiser is paid for a second visit to make sure the repairs have been completed. Appraisers generally charge $125 dollars for the follow-up examination.

If the estimated cost of the repairs is less than 15 percent of the Maximum Claim Amount, the cost of the repairs may be paid for with funds from the reverse mortgage loan and completed after the reverse mortgage is made. A

"Repair Set-Aside" will be established from the reverse mortgage proceeds to pay for the cost of the repairs. The homeowner will be responsible for getting the repairs completed in a timely manner.

Fifth, there are other closing costs that are commonly charged to a reverse mortgage borrower. They include:

- **Credit report fee.** Verifies any federal tax liens, or other judgments, handed down against the borrower. Cost: Generally between $20 to $50.
- **Flood certification fee.** Determines whether the property is located on a federally designated flood plain. Cost: Generally about $20.
- **Escrow, settlement or closing fee.** Generally includes a title search and various other required closing services. Cost: Can range between $150 to $800 depending on your location.
- **Document preparation fee.** Fee charged to prepare the final closing documents, including the mortgage note and other recordable items. Cost: $75 to $150.
- **Recording fee.** Fee charged to record the mortgage lien with the County Recorder's Office. Cost: Can range between $50 to $500 depending on your location.
- **Courier fee.** Covers the cost of any overnight mailing of documents between the lender and the title company or loan investor. Cost: Generally under $50.
- **Title insurance.** Insurance that protects the lender (lender's policy) or the buyer (owner's policy) against any loss arising from disputes over ownership of a property. Varies by size of the loan, though in general, the larger the loan amount, the higher the cost of the title insurance.
- **Pest inspection.** Determines whether the home is infested with any wood-destroying organisms, such as termites. Cost: Generally under $100.
- **Survey.** Determines the official boundaries of the property. It is typically ordered to make sure that any adjoining property has not inadvertently encroached on the reverse mortgage borrower's property. Cost: Generally under $250.

High Costs Make HECMs Expensive for Short-Term Needs

Reverse mortgages carry high up-front costs compared to conventional home loans, though it is important to note that these costs (with the possible exception of an application fee) become part of the loan balance. The initial high costs make reverse mortgages expensive for those with home values below $100,000, those with limited equity in the home, and for the short-term user. The National Center for Home Equity Conversion provided this example:

A 75-year-old single woman gets a $150,000 HECM on her home and finances $6,500 in up-front costs as part of the loan. She receives monthly advances of $562 indefinitely, and her home appreciates at 4 percent per year. If this reverse mortgage is paid off two years later, the loan's effective interest cost is almost 50 percent! She receives only $13,488 for the life of the loan, compared with $6,500 incurred as up-front costs (not counting accrued interest). She would receive $80,928 over the life of the loan if she stayed in the home for 12 years, driving the cost of the loan down to 10.8 percent.

This example demonstrates why reverse mortgages may be riskier for people needing in-home care. If their health condition requires moving into an assisted living or nursing home for more than a year, the reverse mortgage stops making advances and the loan must be repaid. However, borrowers have between six months to a year to sell the home and repay the lender.

Other Points

- HUD provides names of its approved lenders, and these lenders will help with the application and approval process at no cost.
- The lender can begin the foreclosure process if you fail to pay real estate taxes or homeowner's insurance, or allow the house to deteriorate. The lender can also request to have these payments made directly by the servicing company. In addition, as part of their financial assessment, they can also require that an escrow account be established to ensure that there are sufficient funds to cover these payments in the future.
- Although the proceeds are tax-free, depending on the state, reverse mortgages may impact eligibility for certain need-based public benefits such as Medicaid or Supplemental Social Security Income.
- During periods of low interest rates, comfortably sustaining withdrawal rates of 3 percent to 4 percent from conservatively structured portfolios becomes harder to achieve. On the other hand, periods of low interest rates favor reverse mortgages because low initial rates result in larger payouts or monthly payments. Thus, reverse mortgages can supplement portfolio returns when interest rates are low or falling, and may also help individuals (and their advisors) resist the temptation to stretch for yield by extending maturities or lowering credit quality standards.

Before summarizing, there is an interesting strategy that can be used to decrease the risk of outliving your assets.

Strategic Use of HECM

The strategy involves opening a standby HECM line of credit at the earliest possible age (62), but to delay taking down any loan. The key to the strategy is that the principal limit that can be borrowed against will grow automatically at a variable rate equal to the lender's margin, the mortgage insurance premium, and subsequent values of one-month LIBOR rates—the current benchmark rate for the line of credit. (Note that LIBOR as the benchmark will be phased out by 2021, and replaced by the one-month or one-year constant maturity Treasury bill.) Any outstanding loan balance also grows at this rate. The line of credit almost always grows at this rate as well, with rare exceptions when there are set-asides for servicing costs that grow at a different rate. The key feature of the HECM program is that it is a non-recourse loan—no matter how much is borrowed, the amount due cannot exceed 95 percent of the home's appraised value when repayment is due.

When your financial assets are depleted then you switch to funding your needs by drawing on the now larger line of credit. This is a complex issue, beyond the scope of this book, but it works best in a low-interest-rate environment. For those interested, we recommend Wade Pfau's book *Reverse Mortgages: How to Use Reverse Mortgages to Secure Your Retirement* (Second Edition).

Using 50,000 simulations in a Monte Carlo analysis, Pfau studied six different strategies:

1. Using home equity as the last resort.
2. Using home equity first.
3. A combination strategy that opened the HECM line of credit at the start of retirement, and spending was taken from the line of credit, when available, following any years in which the investment portfolio experienced a negative market return. No efforts were made to repay the loan balance until the loan became due at the end of retirement.
4. A modified combination strategy in which spending was taken from the line of credit when possible, whenever the remaining portfolio balance was less than 80 percent of the total amount required in retirement (the retirement glide path). Whenever investment wealth rose above 80 percent of the retirement glide path, any balance on the reverse mortgage was repaid as much as possible without letting wealth fall below the 80 percent threshold, in order to keep a lower loan balance over time and provide more growth potential for the line of credit. The line of credit was opened at the start of retirement.
5. Use home equity last. This strategy differed from the "home equity as last resort" strategy only in that the line of credit was opened at the start of retirement. It was otherwise not used and left to grow until the investment portfolio was depleted.

6. Use tenure payment. This strategy opened the line of credit at the start of retirement and used the tenure payment strategy—indefinite equal monthly payments.

Pfau originally found that the home equity as a last resort, but which opened a line of credit at the start of retirement in order to let the line of credit grow before being tapped, provided the highest increase in success rates. Especially when interest rates were low, the line of credit would almost always be larger by the time it was needed when it was opened early and allowed to grow, than when it was opened later. However, with rule changes that lowered some of the value of line of credit growth, strategies three and four come out on top now. Strategies that spend the home equity more quickly increased the overall risk for the retirement plan—more upside potential was generated by delaying the need to take distributions from investments, but more downside risk was created because the home equity was used quickly without necessarily being compensated by sufficiently high market returns.

One final thought. The fact that Pfau found that the line of credit will almost always be larger at the time needed if it was allowed to grow—versus opening it at a later date—could be helpful if you were to incur large medical expenses, such as the need for long-term care. The costs incurred for the HECM could, therefore, be considered as the premium for an insurance policy.

Summary

Reverse mortgages can be a relatively expensive means of borrowing—at least partly explaining why only about 2 percent of all retired households have used them. However, not all decisions are based solely on financial considerations. Even an expensive reverse mortgage may be appropriate for those individuals who place a greater value on remaining in their home and maintaining their independence. Another possible use, even when there is limited equity—which makes a reverse mortgage expensive—is to pay off an existing mortgage and solve a need for cash flow.

The bottom line is that in the appropriate situation they can be a valuable tool, allowing you to maintain a higher standard of living than you would otherwise be able to do, while also remaining in your home.

CHAPTER 17

Women's Unique Retirement Issues

WOMEN, AS A collective group, face at least 12 unique headwinds from financial and life circumstances relating to long-term retirement planning. Addressing these headwinds can be overwhelming and uncomfortable. However, it is only by first understanding the issues that you can develop strategies that will provide the greatest chance of achieving your goals. Specifically, women:

1. Earn less.
2. Live longer.
3. Have fewer years of earned income.
4. Start investing later.
5. Are less confident about their personal finance and investing skills.
6. Are less aggressive investors.
7. Are less satisfied with the current financial advisory industry.
8. Are more likely to bear the physical, emotional, and financial brunt of the "sandwich generation"—caring for both children and elderly parents.
9. If divorced, face specific challenges and obstacles.
10. Are less likely to remarry after a "gray divorce"—divorce over age 50—or becoming widowed later in life.
11. Are more subject to elder abuse (see Chapter 20).
12. Are statistically likely to die single, divorced, or widowed.

In this chapter we explore the impact of these 12 diverse—and yet often interconnected—dynamics and offer solutions for how to address them in a way that leaves women more financially empowered.

On Women

First, however, we must clarify that "women" are not a collective group. Each woman is unique in her own right and will have her own personal experiences that may or may not deviate from this collective list. Additionally, a woman's individual experience will vary with what stage of life she is in—as defined both by age and life events. For example:

- Young women trying to establish good financial habits.
- Breadwinning women trying to hold it all together with multiple demands on their time.
- Suddenly single women—divorced or widowed, often with limited financial knowledge and/or experience.

Issues Facing Women

1. Women Earn Less

The 2016 Senate Joint Economic Committee 2016 report, "Gender Pay Inequality, Consequences for Women, Families, and the Economy," found that on average, women earn 21 percent less than men. Among African American and Latina women the figures are even lower, shockingly so—40 percent and 45 percent less, respectively. These statistics are so often and widely quoted that many people—including women—have become numb to their implications. With that in mind, we will use some examples to demonstrate the magnitude of the problem.

Joe is 25 years old and earns $50,000 a year. For 45 years, he invests a steady $5,000 a year in a diversified, low-cost portfolio that generates a 6 percent real rate of return. At age 70, Joe's portfolio is worth $1 million.

Jane is also 25 years old. She earns 21 percent less, or $39,500. She also starts out investing 10 percent of her initial income for retirement in the same portfolio with the same returns. At age 70, Jane's portfolio is worth $830,000— $170,000 less than Joe. This assumes Jane never had to take a break from the workforce. As we shall soon see, this is not a realistic assumption. If we re-run the example to reflect a 10-year gap in work history, from age 35 to 45, using the same annual savings rates for years in paid work, Jane's portfolio is worth $435,000—$565,000 less than Joe.

This explains why aggregate retirement data, such as that from Vanguard's 2020 study "How America Saves," shows that the "average Joe" has nearly twice the retirement savings as the "average Jane."

The above scenario is simplistic. It does not incorporate research by Carnegie Mellon professor Linda Babcock and Sara Laschever, authors of *Women Don't Ask*, showing that men are significantly more likely than women to negotiate their salaries. For example, according to their research, women who do negotiate their salaries end up earning $1 million more over the total tenure of their careers than women who do not. Thus, the reality is that if Joe and Jane were both to contribute 10 percent of their annual salaries to their retirement savings, versus the simplistic static annual amount in our example, the gap between Jane and Joe's retirement savings would be even greater.

This fact that women earn less than men is only the first domino in a series that, once pushed, can cause a woman's financial planning for retirement to fall flat much quicker than she may realize.

2. Women Live Longer

The Centers for Disease Control and Prevention puts the average life expectancy for a woman at birth at 81.2 versus 76.2 for a man. According to the Social Security Administration, once both genders reach age 65, the expected lifespan for men is 84.1, and for women it is 86.6. Of course, these are median statistics. One out of four 65-year-old individuals will live past 90 and one out of 10 will live past 95.

At risk of stating the obvious, living longer means women need more resources to cover a longer retirement. The 2016 study "Gender Gap in Financial Wellness" by Financial Finesse indicates that a 25-year-old female who works full-time for 40 years, retiring at age 65, will need to save 1.5 percent more every year than a man in order to reach her target savings goals. The report ties the higher number needed for women to increased longevity and associated health-care costs. In Financial Finesse's updated 2018 report, they found that the retirement preparedness gender gap had widened in recent years, mainly due to the rising market and economy.

Combine earning less than men with a longer lifespan and you see why the research by the Social Security Administration has found that 55 percent of women over the age of 65 rely on Social Security payments for over half of their income, and 27 percent of women over 65 rely on it for over 90 percent of their income.

3. Women Have Fewer Years of Earned Income

According to the 2015 study "Women and Caregiving: Facts and Figures" by the National Center on Caregiving, on average, women spend 12 more years out of the paid workforce than men caring for children and/or elderly parents.

Financial Finesse, a provider of financial wellness programs to corporations as an employee benefit, has done some interesting research on the effect of the aforementioned factors. Women who take career breaks during the 35- to 45-year-old phase of life, often to stay home with children, pay the steepest penalty, having to save at a rate of 25 percent during their working years to come out at the same place as a man who takes no career break. Next up are 45- to 55-year-old individuals, who are often out of the workforce to tend to elderly parents and, thus, need to save 19 percent in their working years to match the no career breaker. And even the 55- to 65-year-old individuals, who have to leave the workforce to tend to elderly parents, need to save at a rate of 16 percent during their working years.

Spending time out of the paid workforce is the final domino that sets women spinning downwards on a path that once started, is hard to stop. The combined impact of earning less than men, fewer years in the paid workforce, earning reduced dollars, and the need (due to longer lifespans) to have more money than men to fund those years, means that women have significantly less margin of error when it comes to planning for their retirement.

Unfortunately, many women are not aware of, or are simply resistant to hearing, these messages. In 2008, award winning journalist Leslie Bennetts wrote the deeply researched, *The Feminine Mistake: Are We Giving Up Too Much?* The book's title was a play-on-words of *The Feminine Mystique*—the 1963 iconic classic questioning what life was like for women without paid work that helped launch the feminist movement. *The Feminine Mistake* enraged large numbers of women when Bennetts highlighted these trio of facts. Bennetts has noted of the response that sadly far too many women are unwilling to place their financial well-being as a priority.

4. Women Start Investing Later

Research from the 19th Annual Transamerica Retirement Survey (2019) shows the average age at which women start saving for retirement is 27, versus 26 for men. While a one-year gap may not seem like much, when combined with lower wages and higher probabilities of career gaps, the math of compounding rears its head in an unfavorable way. The good news is that the gap narrowed from two years in 2018 to just one year in 2020.

Sallie Krawcheck, CEO of Ellevest—an investment firm focused solely on the needs of women—upon reviewing research of a 2017 Ellevest study on the financial habits of women, stated: "Simply put, women do not invest as much as men do. And they do not invest as early as men do." And Sallie should know. As former CFO of Citigroup, CEO of Smith Barney, and CEO of Merrill Lynch Global Asset Management, she has been observing women's financial behaviors for quite some time.

Interestingly, some have noted that perhaps this propensity to start investing later than men is due to the combination of women earning less than men and the fact that many basic products and services for women (such as shampoo, shaving cream, dry cleaning, haircuts, and so on) are more expensive than men's equivalents. In addition, women are often held to tighter appearance standards than men, forcing them to spend even more on clothes and grooming. Given these facts, a case can be made that women's late start is at least partially due to structural issues.

With that said, more often than not it appears that the late start is due to a lack of awareness about the importance of starting early (especially if job disruptions due to child rearing and/or elderly parent care come in to play).

Young men tend to talk to each other more often in casual conversation about topics related to personal finance and investing than do women. Based on a study from Merrill Lynch, "Women and Financial Wellness: Beyond the Bottomline," 61 percent of women reported they would rather talk about their own death than discuss money. Money and investing can be a taboo topic for women.

5. Women are Less Confident About Their Personal Finance and Investing Skills

Another potential reason women may start saving for retirement later than men can be seen in the data on gender and confidence. Studies have shown that women self-identify as being less confident than men self-identify when it comes to their financial knowledge and skill. Ironically, this is happening despite the same studies showing that when actually measured, the knowledge level of both genders is remarkably similar. However, the research shows that women's confidence levels around that same knowledge level is much lower than it should be relative to actual knowledge possessed, while men's is much higher than it should be given what they actually know. Consider the following evidence from the study by Brad Barber and Terrance Odean, "Boys Will Be Boys," which appeared in the February 2001 issue of *The Quarterly Journal of Economics*.

Though the stock selections of women do not outperform those of men, women produce higher net returns because their lower turnover (lower trading activity) leads to lower costs and greater tax efficiency. Also, married men outperform single men. The obvious explanation is that single men do not have the benefit of the spouse's sage counsel to temper their overconfidence, which leads to excessive trading, negatively impacting returns. It appears to be a common characteristic of human behavior that on average men have confidence in skills they do not have, while women simply know better.

According to data from Vanguard's 2020 study "How America Saves," women are actually better savers than men. At all income levels, women are more likely to participate in their employer's retirement plans. In those plans, they typically save at a higher rate. However, they are less likely to put those savings into investments that are likely to outpace inflation.

According to the 2019 study "Women and Financial Wellness Beyond the Bottomline" by the Merrill Lynch Wealth Management Institute, only 52 percent of women report they are confident when it comes to managing their investments, versus 68 percent of men. The July 2017 study "The Gender Gap in Financial Literacy: A Global Perspective," by the Global Center for Excellence in Financial Literacy, shows both that there is a persistent gap in financial literacy between men and women worldwide, and that when women are educated about personal finance and investing they make more appropriate choices relative to their long-term needs.

6. Women are Less Aggressive Investors

Analyses of 401(k)s and IRAs of men and women show there are some distinct gender differences in asset allocation. Women tend at nearly every age range to have more of their portfolio invested in cash and bonds. Some of this may be due to the relentless focus of the broader financial services industry in defining risk simplistically as the "sleep well at night" factor. In other words, if a woman is guided to select her asset allocation based simply on a risk tolerance questionnaire that asks about expected responses to market drops, women may indicate that they prefer a more conservative portfolio.

However, when women are exposed to a broader definition of risk—one which incorporates the willingness, ability, and need to take risk, their viewpoint can change. Unfortunately, in the absence of financial advice that expansively defines risk, women often invest conservatively. To summarize, all the evidence points to women leaving a lot of money on the retirement table.

In a world where even slight increases in the rate of inflation can have dramatic effects on the long-term purchasing power of one's portfolio, it is imperative that those with longer life expectancies have an appropriate allocation to asset classes that have higher odds of outpacing inflation. Yet, due to the combination of lack of confidence and lack of knowledge, many women are investing less aggressively than required. The result is smaller retirement portfolios. Results from the 2018 "Money Census" study by Ellevest show how—depending upon a woman's salary and the market's performance—the real cost of what has come to be known as "the investment gap" over a working lifetime can easily add up to over $1 million dollars over a 35-year career horizon.

7. Women are Less Satisfied with Financial Advisory Services

According to the 2018 "Money Census" study by Ellevest, a mere 17 percent of women feel they are getting competent financial advice and just 47 percent feel they know how to achieve their financial goals. Other studies peg the number of women changing financial advisors upon divorce or widowhood at 70 percent. Clearly, there is a disconnect between what women need (education, advice, guidance) and how they feel about obtaining those things from the financial services industry.

The financial services industry is starting to recognize this, as evidenced by the plethora of "women and wealth" initiatives. However, to date the needle has not moved much in terms of women's satisfaction—perhaps because the upper echelons of the financial services industry remain dominated by men. As a result, many aspects of the financial advisory process, ranging from marketing efforts to client servicing (such as golf outings or investment pitches focused on returns versus life goals), are ones that appeal to men over women.

For many women, interacting with the financial services industry feels like walking into a sports locker room or a men's smoking club. As more women-owned and women-friendly financial advisory firms start up, this dynamic is slowly starting to shift. Our company, Buckingham Strategic Wealth, has acquired several all-female advisory firms.

Key factors that women look for in an advisory relationship include transparency around fees, trust in the advice (see Appendix E), education, and community. These last two items differ from what men tend to seek. The financial firms that are able to provide education and community going forward are the ones that will win the lion's share of women's retirement assets. This is vital as the research shows clearly that when women are financially educated, they make solid financial decisions regarding retirement preparedness.

8. Divorced Women Tend to Face Unique Challenges and Obstacles

Historically, from a financial perspective, divorce has impacted women far more than men. According to the study, "A Re-Evaluation of the Economic Consequences of Divorce," which appeared in the June 1996 issue of the *American Sociological Review*, the average woman's standard of living drops 27 percent after a divorce, while the average man's increases 10 percent. There are a variety of reasons for this. Among them are that women tend to remain the primary caregivers of children, and if they are working outside the home, tend to earn less than men.

There are also some common mistakes that women lacking competent financial advice during a divorce proceeding may make that exacerbate the financial pain of divorce. The following is a list of mistakes that are particularly important for women to be mindful to avoid:

- Insisting on retaining the marital home when she cannot afford it.
- Believing that retirement assets have the same value as an equal dollar amount of non-retirement assets.
- Believing that a 50/50 division of property is always an "equitable" division.
- Not understanding methods or tax implications of dividing stock options.
- Failing to consider the cost basis of property.
- Not understanding the purpose of a Qualified Domestic Relations Order, or the need to get it completed and filed at the time of the divorce, or immediately after the divorce is final.
- Not protecting spousal and child support payments through life insurance.
- Failure to factor in inflation and investment returns when looking at the long-term impact of a settlement or using unrealistic numbers in the evaluation.
- Not understanding how to divide debt.

Just one of these mistakes can have severe long-term consequences for women's financial health. Unfortunately, in the absence of solid financial guidance during the divorce process, mistakes are not limited to just the ones on this list. As a result, there is an increase in the number of financial advisors who are obtaining the Certified Divorce Financial Analyst™ (CDFA®) designation. According to a study by Worthy (an online jewelry broker where divorced women can sell their diamond rings) and the Association of Divorce Financial Planners, 95 percent of women going through a divorce do not seek out the advice of a financial advisor or a CDFA®. These are advisors who have gained the specialized knowledge to help individuals navigate the financial repercussions of divorce.

9. Women are More Likely to Bear the Brunt of the "Sandwich Generation"—Simultaneously Caring for Children and Elderly Parents

According to the 2015 National Center on Caregiving brief, "Women and Caregiving: Facts and Figures," 20 percent of working women are engaged in elder care. The professional consequences of balancing the potentially conflicting demands of elder care and work are substantial. The 1999 paper, "The MetLife Juggling Act Study: Balancing Caregiving with Work and the Costs Involved" by MetLife Mature Market Institute, the National Alliance for Caregiving and the National Center on Women and Aging, found:

- 33 percent of working women decreased work hours.
- 29 percent passed up a job promotion, training, or assignment.
- 22 percent took a leave of absence.
- 20 percent switched from full-time to part-time employment.
- 16 percent quit their jobs.
- 13 percent retired early.

According to the 2014 Kaiser Family Foundation, *New York Times* and CBS News' "Non-Employed Poll," many women who are staying home with children full-time would prefer to be working if only they had the option of flex-time or the ability to work from home. Therefore, it is the lack of societal support and infrastructure for providing this care that forces them to choose caring for loved ones over preparing for their financial futures. The ability to work from home in some industries is becoming more common, particularly with the coronavirus pandemic requiring many employees to operate remotely.

The 2006 Bureau of Labor Statistics study, "The Sandwich Generation: Women Caring for Parents and Children," looked to quantify the costs of being part of the sandwich generation. The authors estimated that 20 million American women are in this state (generally between ages 45 and 54) and that they are responsible for $18 billion of intra-family transfers and 2.4 billion of unpaid hours worked for caregiving. As the population has aged, the problem has intensified and costs increased. In 2011, "The MetLife Study of Caregiving Costs to Working Caregivers" found that 10 million over the age of 50 care for their aging parents, a number that has tripled over the past 15 years. Providing this care has both emotional and financial implications.

10. Women are Less Likely to Remarry After "Gray Divorce" or Becoming Widowed Later in Life

According to the 2017 study, "Led By Baby Boomers, Divorce Rates Climb for America's 50+ Population," by the Pew Research Center, divorce rates for people over the age of 50 have nearly doubled since the 1990s. Their research also indicates a higher percentage of men in this cohort remarry than do women. Roughly twice as many men as women say "they wish to remarry" (29 percent versus 15 percent) and nearly twice as many women as men say "they do not wish to remarry" (54 percent versus 29 percent).

The 2017 study "Who is At Risk for Gray Divorce" from the Institute for Family Studies found that compared to married couples, gray divorced women have relatively low Social Security benefits and relatively high poverty rates. For example, while gray married, remarried, and cohabiting couples have poverty rates of 4 percent or less, 11 percent of men who divorced after the age of 50 were in poverty, while 27 percent of women were in poverty. The implication is that women not only have statistically lower odds of finding themselves in a two-income household after a gray divorce, but they are also less likely to have some of the less quantifiable types of support that come from being part of a coupled household, notably elder care from a spouse as they age.

And it is not just divorced women who must face the challenges of being alone. According to the 2019 study, "Widowhood: Why Women Need to Talk About This Issue," by the Women's Institute for a Secure Retirement (WISER), a third of women who become widowed are younger than age 60, and half of all women who will become widowed become so by age 65. Should gray widows wish to remarry, the odds are against them. According to Deborah Carr at the Institute for Health at Rutgers University, as reported in the October 7, 2016 *New York Times* article, "The Gray Gender Gap: Older Women Are Likelier to Go It Alone": "With 2.55 women for every man among unmarried people over age 65, and 3.27 unmarried women for every unmarried man over 85, a man who wants to remarry has a very large pool."

The implications of this are stark. As per WISER: "Older widows, women who become widowed after age 60, are usually in a more precarious financial situation unless they have substantial savings, pensions, or life insurance due to choices made long before they become widowed. At retirement age, the woman can choose to collect Social Security benefits as the spousal benefit (half of her husband's benefit) or on her own work record. Most often, the woman collects Social Security as the wife of a retired worker because all retirement benefits are based on lifetime earnings, and men generally earn more in a lifetime than women."

The problem is that although a widow receives the greater of her Social Security benefit or her husband's, she does not keep both. After the death of a spouse household income generally declines by about 40 percent. WISER noted that this contrasts with "official income projections that assume that a one-person household needs 80% of their original income to achieve the same standard of living that the couple had. This is the widow's first step into the spiral of poverty."

11. Women are More Subject to Elder Abuse

As elder care specialist and advocate Carolyn Rosenblatt has noted, women are much more subject to elder abuse than men (see Chapter 20). Part of this is due to the fact that women live longer than do men and are thus more likely to live alone when most vulnerable. Other reasons—at least up until now—have included women heading into their golden years without perhaps ever having taken significant responsibility for their household finances (in particular investments). If that is they case, they will be less aware of how to assess financial choices presented to them. Sadly, another factor is that many crooked financial salespeople will actively prey upon older women, viewing them as easy targets.

According to research from New Hope for Women, "Elder Abuse & Women – The Facts":

- Two-thirds of elder abuse and neglect victims are women.
- The median age of elder victims is 78 years.
- One-third of all elder victims are abused by their children.
- Neglect is the most common form of elder abuse in domestic settings, accounting for over 50 percent of all reported incidents.

Elder care advocate Carolyn Rosenblatt highlights these seven steps we can take to protect our elderly parents, which again, will most likely be our mothers:

1. Check in often. If your aging parent lives alone this is crucial.
2. Ask to be a co-signer on the main bank account in case of emergency.
3. Have your parent sign a Durable Power of Attorney appointing a competent and ethical agent, which could be you, a sibling, or trusted other.
4. Suggest having your parent use a licensed fiduciary to handle money if they do not want you to do it.
5. Provide and encourage parents' connection to others.
6. Monitor who comes into your parents' home regularly. Even the most trusted housekeeper, gardener, caregiver, or bookkeeper can be tempted when their own financial circumstances change for the worse.
7. Do background checks on any home care helpers who are hired to work for Mom or Dad.

We would add the creation of a protective "tribe" of people (such as relatives, friends, neighbors, and professionals) who would "swing into action" if needed. Make sure they are introduced to each other and empowered to communicate and establish checks and balances among them. A tribe member may receive duplicate account statements to detect suspicious activity. In addition, a credit freeze could be placed on their credit file.

12. Women are Statistically Likely to Die Single, Divorced, or Widowed

As Sallie Krawcheck, has noted: "Check the gender mix at your local nursing home: 80% of women die single, and they're also 80% more likely to be impoverished in retirement than men." If you want further proof, simply spend a week looking at the obituaries in your local newspaper to see how many men are survived by spouses and how few women are.

The implication is that women have less support, both financial and emotional, as they age. Living longer means they need more funds. Living alone means their households have fewer people contributing income into them. Living alone in one's elder years also means that outside paid help is more often needed and that there might also be less emotional support, which can make a difference in life satisfaction. The last domino to fall, this one may be the saddest of all.

Solutions

The call to action is out and it is loud. With the right knowledge and the right actions, women can mitigate the impact of the above trends on their financial lives. To reiterate an earlier point, when women are educated about personal finance and investing, they make better decisions. The following checklist will increase retirement preparedness:

Financial Empowerment Checklist

- **Basic Numbers:** Be sure to know your household's income, expenses, assets, and liabilities. Have access to all online account information including bank accounts, credit cards, loans, and life insurance policies.
- **Investments:** Know where all your investment accounts are, what investment strategy is being used, and what asset allocation has been implemented.
- **Documents:** Know where all your household's key financial documents are, including wills, durable powers of attorney, health-care directives, home/car titles, and so on. Know the location of the safe deposit box and how to access its contents.
- **Advisors:** Meet all of your family's advisors: financial advisor, estate attorney, accountant, insurance agent or broker. And be sure to understand at a big picture level the game plan each have set for your household.
- **Retirement analysis:** Work with a financial advisor or use online free programs such as the government's "Ball Park Estimator" to understand clearly how much you will need to have saved to maintain your standard of living in retirement. If already retired, work with an advisor to understand how much you can comfortably afford to spend without running out of money.
- **Insurance:** With the expectation of living longer, consider if you have the proper insurance (such as longevity and long-term care, as discussed in Chapter 15) in place to minimize the risk of outliving your assets.

- **Self-educate:** Take financial education classes through local adult continuing education, use free online resources such as The Kahn Academy, or read basic primers on personal finance to start the self-education process.
- **Negotiate:** Take an online course in how to negotiate salary such as those taught by "She Negotiates" or "Take the Lead."

Other more systemic solutions that need to be addressed collectively to support women as a community include:

- Closing the wage gap.
- Providing more systemic support for child care and elder care.
- Increasing the availability of basic financial education in high schools or college.

Women, and those who care about women, can help support these initiatives through their local legislators. There are governmental task forces looking into each of these as well as private non-profits to which you can donate. The more people raise the issue of addressing these systemic issues, the more women will benefit. The goal should be to make it easier for women to overcome the hurdles to achieving their retirement goals.

Sadly, women continue to face financial and life headwinds that make preparing for retirement even more challenging than for men. Consequently, the earlier a woman becomes aware of these factors, the more effective she will be at making the choices that will best position her for retirement success. We hope this chapter and this book will be a helpful resource to smooth the path to retirement.

CHAPTER 18

Estate Planning

A FINANCIAL PLAN is not complete without a well-thought-out design for transitioning assets. Whether that transition occurs during life or at death (or both), it is an inescapable process that every individual will eventually face (voluntarily or not). The design for the transition of wealth and implementing our wishes when we can no longer express them—due to disability or death—is the role estate planning fills. This chapter focuses on the planning of the estate while the next chapter focuses on preparing the heirs.

Estate planning has traditionally focused on passing wealth to future generations and doing so in a tax-advantaged manner. This is an important objective, and the successful implementation of this objective can minimize costs, frustrations, confusion, and disputes upon death. While estate planning is often both motivated and driven by the elimination, or minimization, of estate or other transfer taxes (state and federal), there are other important objectives, such as enhancing creditor protection and divorce protection for beneficiaries, that can also be accomplished. We will address these topics, along with providing advice on how to choose an estate planning attorney in whom you can have confidence.

The Three Important Questions

As anyone who has tried to read a will or a trust agreement knows, estate planning can be complicated. The deluge of tax provisions, transfer formulas, contingencies, and trustee powers can be overwhelming and intimidating. For families with substantial wealth, several different trust agreements, all with an overlapping set of instructions and beneficiaries, can further complicate the situation. While acknowledging that estate planning can be complicated, it helps to boil it down to three simple questions:

1. Where do you want your assets to go?
2. Who do you want to be in charge of your assets?
3. What do you want the rules to be?

For anyone engaging in the estate planning process, their advisor should walk them through these questions, and importantly, at the end of the process, the individual should have a firm understanding of how these questions have been answered and implemented into their estate planning documents.

Overview of the Estate Planning Process

An estate planning advisor should be able to clearly articulate the process from beginning to end. Laying out the process ahead of time not only demystifies it, but also helps provide structure to conversations as well as a framework against which to judge the progress being made. Done well, it is a four-step process as summarized below.

1. Design Phase

As we have discussed, the beginning is the most important of any planning process. And the beginning of the estate planning process is to establish your goals and objectives. Failure to establish them may lead to inefficiencies, unnecessary additional work, and general frustration. Instead, an estate planning advisor should take the time to understand your unique wishes and goals before trying to convert those to words on paper.

A good analogy to the Design Phase is an architect's blueprint for a home. The architect may know the client wants three bathrooms. However, knowing where to put those bathrooms is crucial. The effective design of an estate plan is similar to this process.

2. Implementation Phase

After the estate planning "blueprint" is complete, the next phase is implementation. Continuing with the home building theme, the Implementation Phase is analogous to constructing the home. For an estate planner, this means preparing the documents that will answer in detail the three questions offered earlier:

1. Where do you want your assets to go?
2. Who do you want to be in charge of your assets?
3. What do you want the rules to be?

Typically, these documents will include health care and financial powers of attorney, a will, and a revocable trust (more on these later).

The implementation, or "drafting," phase is often what people dread the most—receiving a 50-plus page trust document full of "legalese" and words no one other than estate planners would use. Although some of this is unavoidable, a helpful advisor should accompany these documents with an outline in plain, easy to understand language, and a summary diagram illustrating the flow of the estate plan. Once the documents have been drafted, reviewed, and approved, signing the documents completes this step.

3. Funding Phase

An estate plan will often consist of one or more revocable and irrevocable trusts. Unfortunately, it is not enough to simply sign the estate planning documents. A necessary next step is to "fund" the trust(s). Using the home building analogy, you are now moving the furniture into the house.

There are an unlimited number of permutations or options to choose between when considering the funding of trusts. These options can impact income, gift, and estate taxes, administrative convenience, costs, access and control of assets, and other issues. As a result, it is necessary that your estate planner work together with your tax professional and investment advisor to provide appropriate counsel, making sure the documents are working together to achieve your goals.

Planners that operate in a vacuum (whether estate planners, financial advisors, bankers, insurance professionals, or accountants) can be dangerous for the overall plan. Communication among advisors should be a basic requirement—especially in the Funding Phase.

4. Monitoring Phase

The last phase is the Monitoring Phase. Just as over time a home needs maintenance to repair structural damage (leaky roof), changing circumstances (the family has expanded and outgrown the home), or to accommodate available improvements (more efficient windows or furnace), when the assumptions upon which the estate plan was built change, the estate plan needs to be reviewed. In addition, a regular review should be scheduled because laws frequently change. This was the case in 2018 when the amount of assets that may be excluded from the estate tax was doubled—providing the opportunity to shield additional assets from estate taxes. It was also the case in 2020 when the Secure Act changed how beneficiaries of retirement plans and IRAs are treated.

In addition to death and taxes being certainties of life, change is also inevitable. Some changes are exciting and desirable (like the birth of children or an increase in net worth), some changes are difficult and undesirable (like health changes, death, or legal problems), and others are beyond our control and may fluctuate periodically (there is no better example than the income, gift and estate tax laws). A good estate planning advisor will help design an estate plan with change in mind.

Flexibility in estate planning documents, and the ability to react to life's changes, is imperative. Even when there are no dramatic changes in health or family changes, it is advisable to have regular meetings with your estate planning advisor to determine if there have been changes in the law that would allow for additional planning opportunities. A good advisor would seek out their clients to discuss these changes—rather than the other way around. Thus, when choosing an estate planning attorney, asking existing clients about this issue should be part of your due diligence process. More on the due diligence process later.

The Specific Four Steps of Estate Planning

After reviewing the four phases of estate planning, let us look at the specific steps in the design of an estate plan. Again, to provide framework, a sequential approach is helpful.

1. Core Estate Planning Documents

All individuals, regardless of net worth, should have "core" estate planning documents—documents governing the distribution of assets and appointment of individuals to make financial and health-care decisions in the event of disability or death. The core estate planning documents commonly consist of the following:

A. HIPAA Release

The Health Insurance Portability and Accountability Act (HIPAA) tightened the rules affecting the privacy of medical records, creating the potential to make it difficult for the designated agents under an individual's health-care power of attorney to obtain the disabled individual's medical records. A HIPAA Release enables the designated agent to obtain information about medical conditions without delay.

B. Durable Power of Attorney for Health Care and Living Will

A Durable Power of Attorney for Health Care and Living Will appoints an agent to make health-care decisions in the event an individual is physically or mentally incapacitated and cannot make these decisions. Additionally, it expresses an individual's intent regarding what actions should, or should not, be taken in the event of an incurable or terminal condition (including end of life decisions).

C. Durable Power of Attorney for Finances

A Durable Power of Attorney for Finances enables an individual to plan for periods of incapacity so that assets may be managed and legal decisions may be made—all without the potentially significant cost, delay, and expense of a guardianship or conservator proceeding.

D. Pourover Will

A pourover will provides that assets not placed in an individual's revocable trust (summarized below) during his or her lifetime are "poured" into the trust upon death. This ensures that all assets pass under the terms of the revocable trust. A pourover also:

- Appoints a personal representative to handle any probate estate administration issues (for example, if any assets are not transferred to the trust during lifetime).
- States an individual's preference regarding burial or cremation.
- Appoints a guardian and conservator for any minor children.

Note that some estate planning advisors may recommend the use of a traditional will in lieu of a pourover will and a revocable trust. This may be advisable if either the individual's assets that will be subject to probate (i.e., assets owned individually without a co-owner or beneficiary designation, such as a payable on death or transfer on death designation) are modest and do not justify the additional expense of creating a revocable trust, or the individual lives in a state where the post-death probate process is less onerous than other states.

E. Revocable Trust

A revocable trust provides for the intended disposition of assets upon death. A revocable trust provides several advantages to planning with a traditional will only.

- **Avoid probate:** Assets transferred to a revocable trust will not pass through probate, which can be a costly and time-consuming process. In addition, probate proceedings are a matter of public record.
- **Retain control:** The individual creating the revocable trust may retain complete control over all of the assets in the revocable trust (as the trustee) during life.
- **Disability protection:** A successor trustee can manage the assets in the trust if the creator of the trust becomes disabled, without the need to rely on a power of attorney or custodianship.
- **Tax planning:** The dispositive provisions of a revocable trust may be tailored to effectively benefit children and future generations by using proper tax planning and lifetime trust provisions (i.e., maximizing the benefit of an individual's estate tax exemption).
- **Creditor and liability protection planning for descendants:** A revocable trust may incorporate lifetime trust provisions to obtain creditor protection for the assets passing to children and more remote descendants, thereby insulating the assets passed to children and succeeding generations from creditors and certain divorce-related claims.

The core documents are the foundational building block of any estate plan. Depending on the individual's net worth and other specific facts and circumstances, the core documents may be the only step that is necessary.

However, for people with significant net worth or unique considerations, the following additional steps should be considered.

2. Beneficiary Designations

In conjunction with the preparation of core estate planning documents, it is critical to review "beneficiary designations." A beneficiary designation, such as a "transfer on death" or "payable on death" designation, can be an effective technique to transfer ownership of an asset upon death while avoiding probate. Many other types of assets also typically have beneficiary designations that should be reviewed. Examples include qualified plan assets, such as 401(k) plans and IRAs, life insurance policies, annuities, pensions, etc. Although the use of beneficiary designations is convenient and may be successfully utilized to avoid probate, they must be accounted for as part of the larger estate plan. This is because a beneficiary designation will likely supersede the provisions of a will or a revocable trust. In other words, the most competently drafted will or revocable trust will have little value if they do not govern the disposition of any assets because the assets are instead governed (intentionally or not) by the use of beneficiary designations.

As discussed in the Monitoring Phase above, as life events occur (birth of a child, death of a loved one, marriage, divorce, illness, incapacity, etc.), or tax laws change, beneficiary designations must be revisited to determine if updates are necessary. For example, with passage of the Secure Act in 2019, trusts named as the beneficiary of a retirement plan or IRA may no longer meet their originally intended goals. In addition, they may result in greater taxes. Estate plans structured like this should be reviewed by an attorney to determine if revisions are necessary. The bottom line is that beneficiary designations must be kept current and coordinated with the overall estate plan, or unintended and inconsistent estate planning results may occur.

3. Discounting

If an individual is likely to be subject to an estate tax upon death (currently the tax rate is 40 percent), he or she may look for opportunities to "discount" the value of assets. Said differently, if an estate tax will be due at a rate of 40 percent, for every $100 that the fair market value of assets is reduced, the estate tax will be reduced by $40.

Common methods to discount are to:

- Fractionalize ownership of assets.
- Contribute assets to closely held business entities (such as family limited partnerships or family limited liability companies) that contain transfer restrictions.
- Recapitalize companies into voting and non-voting interests (with the non-voting interests valued less highly than the voting interests).

These techniques should not be entered into without a complete examination of the benefits and associated risks.

As a simple illustration of one of these techniques, consider a limited partnership. In a limited partnership, there are two types of partners: (i) a general partner who has all of the decision-making control over the partnership and the associated liability; and (ii) a limited partner who is a passive investor with little authority or decision-making capacity.

Assume there is an existing limited partnership with the only asset consisting of $1 million of Home Depot stock. You are offered to purchase a 10 percent limited partnership interest. How much would you be willing to pay for it? The answer is not $100,000 (10 percent of $1 million). Why? First, as a limited partner you will have no control over the investments of the partnership. If you want the partnership to sell its stock in Home Depot and instead buy stock in Lowe's, you cannot cause this result. Only the general partner may make this decision. Next, what if Home Depot pays a dividend? Will you receive your proportionate share from the partnership? The answer is only if the general partner decides to make a distribution. Finally, if you want to sell your 10 percent limited partnership interest to your neighbor, can you? Again, only if the general partner consents to the transfer. As you can see, the 10 percent limited partnership interest has negative features which will likely cause it to trade at a discount.

4. Transferring Assets

As a general rule, under current law beginning January 1, 2020, each individual may transfer assets valued at approximately $11,580,000 during their life (in the form of a gift) or upon death (in the form of an inheritance) without being subject to federal transfer taxes. For married couples, the total value of assets that may be passed free of transfer taxes is approximately $23,160,000. The amount that can be passed tax-free during life is commonly referred to as the "gift tax exemption." The amount that can be passed tax-free upon death is commonly referred to as the "estate tax exemption" (because assets passed that are less than the set value are "exempt" from transfer taxes). Note that we are discussing federal transfer tax laws here—there are several states that impose their own estate taxes and a very small minority that have a state level gift tax.

An individual does not have the ability to gift $11,5800,000 during life and pass another $11,580,000 upon death transfer tax-free, but may use some, or all, of the exemption in the form of lifetime gifts and the remainder in the form of transfers upon death. For example, if an unmarried individual makes a $1 million gift to a friend, no gift tax will be paid by the individual making the gift and no tax will be paid by the recipient of the gift. However, the individual making the gift will have used up $1 million of gift/estate tax exemption and will be left with a total of $10,580,000 of gift/estate tax exemption to be used later.

The value of assets that may be passed free of transfer taxes has changed dramatically over the last few years (and may again). In fact, the value of assets that could be passed transfer tax-free effectively doubled beginning in 2018, pursuant to the Tax Cuts and Jobs Act (prior to the passage of the Act in 2017, the value of assets that could be passed tax-free was $5,490,000 for an individual and $10,980,000 for a married couple). The Tax Cuts and Jobs Act itself provides that starting in the year 2026, the gift/estate tax exemptions will revert back down to 2017 levels, indexed to inflation. The gift and estate tax laws are a political hot button issue, and it is possible the laws may be revised again prior to 2026 if there is a change in the controlling party in the Office of the President and Congress.

We will now discuss how various types of trusts can be used to minimize estate taxes.

Use of Irrevocable Trusts

Given the current high levels of the gift and estate tax exemptions, the potential that these amounts will decrease in the future and the 40 percent estate tax, individuals with significant assets should consider "transferring assets." For individuals that may be subject to an estate tax upon their death, each $1 of appreciation in their assets may actually only represent $0.60 (because of the 40 percent estate tax). Accordingly, individuals may look to transfer assets to others (or to irrevocable trusts created for the benefit of others) so that the appreciation in value avoids estate taxes. Although a detailed discussion of this topic is beyond the scope of this book, the general idea is that an irrevocable trust may be structured so that it is not subject to estate taxes (as opposed to a revocable trust that will be subject to estate taxes).

Besides the estate tax benefits, gifting assets to an irrevocable trust may provide advantages that are unavailable with respect to gifts directly to individuals. An irrevocable trust may provide creditor, divorce and estate tax protection to the beneficiary of the trust. Irrevocable trusts can also facilitate gifts to minors and allow the individual making the gift to put in place rules for the use and investment of the assets.

As a simple example, a husband with a taxable estate may create an irrevocable trust for the benefit of his wife and/or children and gift $1 million to the trust. If the assets in that irrevocable trust appreciate to $3 million over the course of the husband's lifetime, the entire $3 million would avoid estate taxes. In such a situation, the individual would have removed $3 million of assets from his taxable estate, but would only have used up $1 million of his gift/estate tax exemptions (similar to the example above with the gift to a friend)—the $2 million of appreciation would have been transferred free of estate tax.

It is important to note, however, that because the $3 million of assets will not be included in the husband's taxable estate upon his death, these assets will not receive a step-up in income tax basis. Therefore, if the assets in the irrevocable trust are later sold, a capital gains tax may be triggered. This capital gains tax may have been avoided if the assets were not gifted to the irrevocable trust. Ultimately, this potential future capital gains tax must be considered in the gifting analysis. We summarize some of the more common types of irrevocable trusts in Appendix G.

Charitable Planning

Gifting assets to charity can be beneficial in many ways (both to the donor and the charity). Charitable gifting may be accomplished simply by an unrestricted cash gift to a charity. Or, it can be structured in a way that achieves a specific set of goals and continues over many years (i.e., through various types of charitable gift trusts). Individuals can also make gifts currently and retain the right to direct which charities will benefit from the assets in future years (for instance through a donor advised fund or a family controlled private foundation). In addition to benefitting the charitable organization, generally gifts to charity qualify for an income tax deduction and any assets passing to charity upon an individual's death will not be subject to estate taxes.

Choosing an Estate Planning Advisor

Choosing an estate planning attorney can be an intimidating, and even frustrating, experience. It is a relationship in which you will need to place significant faith in the advice you receive, because most individuals do not have a base of estate planning knowledge on which to judge the quality of advice. This is similar to the choice of a physician, or, for some, an auto mechanic. Relying totally on the advice of others can be an uncomfortable feeling.

In addition to the usual methods to find an appropriate advisor (recommendations of trusted friends, appropriate credentials and licenses, and so on), we recommend that your due diligence focus carefully on each of the four areas discussed below. You should be sure to speak with existing clients, as well as your trusted professional advisors, and ask them about their experiences with the attorney in question regarding each of them.

1. Competence

The attorney you choose does not need to be the world's foremost expert. However, he or she needs a mastery of the subject area sufficient to understand, analyze, explain, and creatively find solutions to any problems faced. The attorney should specialize in estate planning and not simply "dabble" in the subject area. You should also seek an attorney who regularly works with clients with similar net worth and goals—you do not want to be your attorney's largest client so that he or she is learning on the job and you are paying for the training. The opposite is true as well. It may be unnecessary and inefficient for an attorney that routinely handles clients with very large estates to work with an individual with simple estate planning needs.

2. Communication

The attorney you choose must be able to communicate complex subjects simply. Attorneys are often guilty of using complex terms rather than simpler ones and using more words rather than fewer words. You will feel more comfortable with an estate plan you understand, and with an advisor who can explain it clearly and concisely.

3. Consistent Accountability

This is no more complicated than an estate planning attorney doing what he or she says they are going to do. Nothing will destroy a relationship quicker than unfulfilled promises, which applies to all areas of contact. For example:

- **Responsiveness:** If the attorney says he or she will get back to you today, the attorney needs to do that.
- **Work Product:** If the attorney says he or she will have documents to you for review by the end of the week, the attorney must do that.
- **Cost:** If the attorney says the project will cost $X, it must cost $X.

It seems like it would be easy to locate an attorney that fulfills these criteria consistently. However, in our experience it is not as common as you might expect.

4. Care

This is a quality that cannot be taught. The attorney either truly cares or does not. An estate planning attorney must be able to put himself or herself in the clients' shoes every time and ask, "If this were me, or my mother, or my best friend, what advice would I give?"

Passing Values Not Just Wealth

Estate planning is about more than preparing to transfer assets. Unfortunately, many plans fail to focus on the important topic of passing on family values, which is a more difficult task.

The next chapter is about passing on those values and preparing your heirs to be able to manage their inheritance.

CHAPTER 19

Preparing Your Heirs

N APOLEON BONAPARTE IS widely regarded as one of the greatest commanders ever to have lived. His campaigns are studied at military academies all over the world. Yet, he developed few military innovations. Perhaps the principal belief underlying his military success can be summed up in this quotation, which is attributed to him: "Most battles are won or lost [in the preparation stage] long before the first shot is fired."

Each year high-net-worth families spend huge sums preparing their assets for transition to their heirs, engaging high-powered estate and tax planners who set up complex vehicles like family limited partnerships, life insurance, charitable remainder, charitable lead, and various other kinds of trusts. Yet, despite the best efforts of top-notch professionals, according to Roy Williams and Vic Preisser in their 2007 book, *Estate Planning for the Post-Transition Period*, it is estimated that "70% of estates lose their assets and family harmony following the transition of the estate." Given the talent engaged, it doesn't seem likely that the failure is due to poor design. So why do the majority of plans fail?

Williams and Preisser state that "the major causes of post-transition failures were discovered to lie within the family." The unsuccessful families failed mainly because the heirs were unprepared, they didn't trust each other and communications broke down. In other words, while high-net-worth families and their advisors pay great attention to preparing assets for transition to the heirs, very little, if any, attention is paid to preparing the heirs for the assets they will inherit.

Note that while this chapter focuses on high-net-worth families, many of the issues are just as relevant to all families. For example, in all families, preparing heirs should involve making them aware of the location of all important documents (such as powers of attorney, wills, trusts, insurance policies, and so on) and financial assets. They should also be aware of all members of the financial services team (CPA, financial advisors, insurance agents) and how to contact them. And they should be aware of how the parents want to deal with end of life and incapacity issues (such as designating a physician who could determine incapacity). A worthwhile exercise is to have a rehearsal of what needs to be done and who is responsible in the event of death or incapacity.

What Do Wealthy Parents Worry About Most?

Consider the following list, compiled by Williams and Preisser, of the five things parents worry about most with respect to wealth and its effect on their children:

1. Too much emphasis on material things.
2. Naïveté about the value of money.
3. Spending beyond their means.
4. Initiative being ruined by affluence.
5. Will not do as well as parents would like.

Now, consider the focus of these concerns. While the typical high-net-worth family worries about these issues, the focus of estate planning professionals tends to be on taxation, preservation of wealth and governance—not on the transfer of family values. Thus, there is an obvious disconnect between the issues that are identified as most important and where the efforts are actually spent. Therefore, it should not come as a surprise when most plans fail. By acting as the "quarterback" on the financial services team, a good advisor can make sure that all the dots are connected between the tactical and emotional elements of wealth transfer.

Are Your Heirs Prepared?

The following are questions that should be asked to help determine if heirs are prepared:

- Do your children (and their spouses, if any) know your estate plan?
- If not, what would make you comfortable sharing this information? With your children? With their spouses?
- What steps should you take to address your concerns?
- Might there be a plan to provide certain information sooner and other information at a later date?
- Have your heirs read your will and other estate planning documents?
- If no, when do you think is an appropriate time for them to see these documents?

- Do your heirs know the family's net worth, both yours and their own (if they have assets in their name)?
- If no, when does providing this information become advantageous to you and your heirs?
- Are your heirs in communication with your team of advisors (your attorney, accountant, insurance advisors and financial/investment advisor)?
- If not, would it be useful for family members to meet those people, even if information-sharing is limited?
- Have the children been involved in the formation of the investment policy statement, and are they familiar with the investment strategy, the goals and how to manage the assets?
- If not, when might this involvement be advantageous?

Taboo Topic

Unfortunately, in the majority of cases, families treat money and the issues surrounding wealth as taboo subjects. And the "lessons" of non-involvement get passed on from one generation to the next. Thus, in most cases the answer to the above questions is "no"—and that explains why the failure rate is so high.

A recent report from BMO Wealth Management, "Estate Planning for Complex Family Dynamics," showed just how poorly heirs are prepared and how that can lead to family discord. For example, they found that 52 percent of all adults surveyed do not even have a will, a figure that rose to 56 percent among adults 35–54. Among other important findings were:

- 40 percent thought the distribution of their parents' estates was unfair, with unmarried adults most likely to feel aggrieved.
- Only 28 percent of all adults said they knew details of their parents' wills or estate distribution plans.
- 40 percent of parents surveyed have never discussed their estate intentions with their children.

Family feuds can easily develop when members do not feel they have been given their fair share and have not been included in the process. Of course, it doesn't have to be that way. The solution to the problem is that, while it is important to treat family wealth as a private matter, it should not be private within the family. Open communication between parents and heirs can prevent many problems.

Williams and Preisser, whose research focused on high-net-worth families, believe that in order for a plan to be successful, heirs (including spouses) should have some influence in how the estate is structured, or at least have input. They recommend that among the issues that should be addressed is whether the estate plan matches the skills and interests of the heirs. And there should be a plan to prepare the heirs for their future responsibilities. Heirs should know the impact of their wealth on their families and the responsibilities of wealth.

The Transition Plan

Achieving an ideal level of knowledge-sharing and family involvement requires its own planning. Each element a family considers "ideal" should be carefully considered and a rollout of an estate transition carefully planned. While each high-net-worth family's situation is unique, in order to maximize the likelihood of success, a transition plan should, at the very least, address the following issues:

1. Have a family mission statement (FMS) that spells out the overall purpose of the family's wealth and a strategy to implement it, with roles well defined. See below for best practices on creating a FMS.
   - A FMS is a superb way to communicate important family values and provide overall direction as future decisions are made. It can be an important standalone activity and serve as a kickoff for the longer transition plan process.
2. The entire family participates in the important decisions.
   - While families are complicated, finding a way to achieve broad-based input is the surest way to achieve a successful outcome.
3. Family members have the option to participate in the management of assets.
   - This is a critical issue for certain families, particularly when a closely held business is involved.
4. Heirs understand and have bought into their roles.
   - This can be a long-term process, and an outside facilitator may play an important role in achieving a desirable and harmonious result.
5. Heirs have reviewed and understand all documents.
   - While this should be the goal, given different interests and aptitudes, a customized approach that addresses each heir's needs should be developed.
6. Asset distributions are based on readiness, not age, of heirs.
   - Too often, distribution provisions are written based on age because of its formulaic simplicity. A more careful, tailored approach is generally better.
7. Mission statement includes incentives and opportunities for heirs.
   - Since it's likely that each family, and each individual member, will have different thoughts about what this might look like, many families have found that the best way to achieve a successful outcome is to use an outside facilitator.

8. Younger children are encouraged to participate in philanthropic grant-making decisions.
   - A good way to pass on philanthropic values early is to begin the process of getting children involved in money issues.
9. Family unity is considered an important asset.
   - Many families have found that this is a critical factor in helping them work through complicated issues.
10. Family communicates well and regularly.

Creating a Family Mission Statement (FMS)

Stephen Covey, author of *The 7 Habits of Highly Effective Families*, defines a family mission statement as follows: "A family mission statement is a combined, unified expression from all family members of what your family is all about—what it is you really want to do and be—and the principles you choose to govern your family life."

A FMS should be a relatively brief statement that encapsulates your family's purpose, goals and standards. Ideally, all members of the family would have a hand in articulating these values and all agree to live by them. Having a shared vision—a shared sense of values and purpose—bonds parents and children together. It can serve as a guide for parenting decisions and provides your heirs with clear ideals to strive for and guidance in making choices. A FMS also articulates the standards by which each member of the family can evaluate each other's behavior, and children and parents will ideally check on and encourage one another as they make their way down this agreed-upon path. Another benefit of a FMS is that it can provide a sense of meaning and identity, giving heirs the feeling of being part of something important and special. Other benefits include:

- The document will articulate why you decided to create a family mission statement, its purpose, and why you are choosing to manage and distribute your estate in this manner. It might include such topics as how the wealth was achieved, the life experiences that have shaped your financial philosophy, what the wealth means to you (how it is important to you) and the values you wish to pass on.
- The process of creating a FMS and its accompanying plan (defining the specific actions to be taken) can help donors' family members identify and examine the people and entities they hold in the highest esteem, leading them, either as first-generation donors or on a deeper generational basis, to make wealth transfer decisions that make the most sense to them. As a clear expression for heirs and others, the FMS can be a tool to help pass

on personal values to future generations. The accompanying plan can identify the charities or organizations you feel passionate about and want to support with your social capital, as well as the individuals for whom you feel responsible and why you feel an obligation to give them a portion of your wealth.

- Both the FMS and the accompanying plan should succinctly inform all advisors of the client's intentions, saving both time and money as they explore appropriate strategies to help their clients implement their wishes. Thus, the plan should specifically identify how much money you need during your lifetime and how much you wish to leave to your heirs. It should also identify why you feel this is an appropriate amount and what you want to achieve by giving them this money.

The FMS document and plan should be signed and dated to demonstrate that it is a valid document and accurately reflects your wishes. And finally, to make sure that it remains relevant and continues to reflect the values of your evolving family, revisiting it annually may play a valuable role in preserving its essence.

See Appendix B for a sample Family Mission Statement.

Summary

Family values, as well as current and future goals, should inform the entire financial planning process. Done well, financial planning is about much more than investment management. And just as most battles are won in the preparatory stage, the success of a family wealth transition plan depends on preparing the family for the transition of not only the family's wealth, but also the family's values.

CHAPTER 20

The Threat of Elder Financial Abuse

T HOUGHTS OF RETIREMENT can be dreams of being free of job responsibilities, and enjoying travel, leisure activity, and having fun. We look forward to having time to do the things we didn't have time to do before. Our thoughts usually do not include fear that someone is going to rip us off. Unfortunately, financial abuse does happen, even to the smartest people. With the help of elder law attorney Carolyn Rosenblatt, in this chapter we will examine what many of us do not want to face: Over time we may lose our sharpness of thinking, creating the potential for financial abuse. We will also discuss the prevention methods you can use to thwart it.

Many of us reach retirement age with physical problems. Typically, these are under some control with doctor visits, medication, and a basic effort to be healthy. We accept that we are getting older and that our bodies are not the same as they were decades ago. Even if we are in decent health, we never want to face the possibility that our mental status could deteriorate along with our bodies. However, declining mental sharpness is inevitable for many. That makes us vulnerable to financial abuse. Even if you do not suffer any decline in mental sharpness, there is no guarantee that you will be untouchable by those seeking to exploit you. There are determined professional thieves who know that many seniors have nest eggs that can be stolen. Educated and powerful people can be taken advantage of and manipulated, right along with those who lack these advantages. No one is immune.

We will examine how elder abuse happens, why it happens, and who are the abusers. Importantly, we explore why every retiree needs to have essential protections in place. And we provide a checklist to help you. In addition, should you suspect financial abuse is happening to a friend or relative, we offer a checklist of the warning signs to watch for.

Is Financial Elder Abuse Really That Big of a Deal?

According to "The True Link Report on Elder Financial Abuse 2015", the amount stolen from elders each year in the U.S. is more than $36 billion. This includes not only outright theft by unscrupulous people in their lives, and online predators who are after them, but also other kinds of more subtle abuse. Research demonstrates that no one is immune from financial manipulation, regardless of their education, sophistication, or experience in financial matters. True Link found that a significant number of victims are younger seniors, college-educated, and not living in isolation—and they lost more to abuse than those who were older, isolated, and less educated.

Who are the Abusers?

Taking advantage of seniors is not limited to shadowy figures on the internet. However, seniors are particularly interesting to them.

Unfortunately, a painful truth is that family members are the most frequent abusers of seniors. Starting from a position of trust, they see opportunity—the older person might not be as astute as they once were and, thus, might not see what is happening. Or, it's a widow who has assets, and her unscrupulous son, daughter, or other relative decides he needs some of that money. He asks for a "loan" to tide him over, start a business, or take advantage of a "wonderful investment opportunity". The loan is never repaid, the business fails, and the investment opportunity is a scam. And the elder often has no recourse.

In some states, the misuse of a position of trust with an older person which harms the elder financially is called "undue influence" and is prohibited by law. In those states, the elder could bring a suit against the abuser for the manipulation and loss. However, most parents do not want to prosecute their own children, or other loved ones. Instead, they endure the abuse, even to the point of impoverishment. The emotional effects are devastating. Relationships are destroyed, depression is virtually inevitable, and after significant abuse suicides have occurred.

Given the risks, should you keep your finances secret from your children and grandchildren? Should you not trust any of them? Secrecy is not the answer.

Your Estate Plan Can Protect You

One important protection against abuse is choosing the most trustworthy person among family members to take over financial management—to be the quarterback on the financial services and caregiving team—in anticipation of the risk we all potentially face for memory loss, or loss of mental clarity. However, trust isn't sufficient. That is why there is the wise adage to trust, but verify.

Therefore, we recommend that each person should appoint and give written permission for communication among a protective team of professionals, friends and relatives that can provide checks and balances. Everyone on the team should have permission to communicate with and report to someone else you have appointed. For example, the person with the power of attorney (POA) should be accountable to others, such as the estate planner, financial advisor, or additional family member on a regular basis to maintain transparency about all spending of your assets. Verbal permission for all on the team to communicate is not sufficient. Letters signed by you should be given to each member of the team, granting permission for each to give and receive information from the others. Such information would otherwise be confidential for any licensed professionals among them, such as estate planning attorneys or financial advisors.

Proper estate planning always anticipates that a backup person is appointed to manage your finances or your family trust, should the trustee (you, and/or your spouse) become disabled, incapacitated, or otherwise unavailable to do that job. Sometimes several successors or persons appointed to be next in line with authority over finances are built into the estate planning documents. Each person's situation is unique, and the availability and suitability of appointees may be limited. To address this issue, we recommend that you work with a highly experienced and sensitive estate planning attorney—someone who is comfortable discussing family relationships extensively with you, so that you make a reasoned decision. Your favorite child, if you have one, might not be the wisest choice for managing your assets or administering your estate. And many lawyers lack training in family dynamics and are not comfortable dealing with emotional subjects. You need to carefully consider your choices for those you name to take over if you become impaired.

For example, the person(s) you choose as POA and successor trustee(s) should have the knowledge and time necessary for the task. Busy children can become overwhelmed and frustrated with these complex and time-consuming responsibilities. A careful estate planning attorney should ask questions about the persons whom you consider appointing, their stability and whether choosing one rather than the other will lead to likely conflicts in the family's management of your assets.

Your choice may also lead to intra-family conflict if you choose one sibling over another without explanation. Naming two or more siblings jointly can be equally problematic, as this can lead to family fights over what should be spent when all in conflict have equal veto power. To avoid family arguments, some choose to appoint corporate trustees to manage finances in the event of an elder's incapacity. A corporate trustee who may never have known you in your healthiest years and is not familiar with your values can also lead to conflicts with family, who may view spending and investing differently from a relative stranger to the family. In addition, corporate trustees can be bureaucratic and may require that you hire them as investment managers.

Unfortunately, for many estate planners their job is about ensuring that the documents involved contain the necessary required language; are in the right order; address all the assets and tax considerations; and that the right phrases are included to protect your estate. They won't typically spend a lot of time focused on what might happen if you become cognitively impaired and someone has to take over decision-making for you. As long as you have a successor trustee named and have a Durable Power of Attorney document signed with an agent identified on it, the lawyer may think the job is done. If we want to anticipate the possibility of abuse, we need to be more thoughtful.

The Value of Making the Right Choice

Choosing the right successor of your family trust can preserve your financial plan, help maintain your dignity, and protect you from abuse. Choosing poorly sets you up to be exploited. Thus, this part of estate planning requires careful consideration. It must be based on logic. For example, choosing your son as the successor because you have a general idea he knows more about money than your daughter, is not logical. On the other hand, if you choose the son because he has been more responsible than another sibling about his own finances, and he has a track record of respecting your wishes, that is a logical decision.

Sometimes there are no children, or none you feel is sufficiently trustworthy. In those situations, choose a non-profit organization that has fiduciaries, or an institutional trustee. An institutional trustee needs to answer to someone if you lose capacity. They need a monitor. Without this protection, even they can do unscrupulous things. In addition, it is difficult and expensive for heirs to challenge them should their actions become questionable. They have greater resources to fight against beneficiaries who raise ethical questions. If institutional trustees never committed financial abuse, we would not mention this. Unfortunately, there are bad institutional apples who can get away with bad conduct if the only one they are responsible to is an incompetent elder.

Protection for your financial safety can be in the form of a "care committee"—a provision that can be built into the trust. With that, a chosen group of trusted others, selected while you, the elder, are competent, is assigned to oversee the institutional trustee, and to receive accountings and monitor transactions. The care committee can ensure that trust assets are spent on long-term or end-of-life care in accordance with your wishes. The institutional trustee should be subject to approval of the care committee for significant financial transactions or changes to your traditional ways of investing and preserving your assets.

You can help assure your future financial security by assigning, in your estate plan documents, a Trust Protector who would be charged with ensuring that you are not manipulated into changing your estate documents if you lose capacity to make reasoned decisions. If we become less than fully competent, losing the ability to understand the consequences of making changes to estate documents, a greedy person whom we trusted can manipulate us without our understanding of what happens next. If you have a trusted adult child, competent and assertive friend, or professional, whom you trust, that person can oversee your estate plan and protect you.

Will You Lose Your Capacity for Managing Your Finances?

At least a third of us who reach age 85 will develop Alzheimer's disease and quickly lose capacity. It is a brain disease for which we currently have no cure. Thus, we have to recognize that we might at some point be unable to manage our finances. Unfortunately, the reality is that many people do not recognize that they are slipping at the onset of the disease process. They feel fine, but are unaware that their thinking is impaired. Others are in denial, fearing that giving up control over their money will cause them to be put in a home.

There's no way to predict the way you will age, which is why you need to consider the worst-case scenario and take action to protect yourself in the event of your own incapacity for financial matters. If you start to lose capacity due to things like memory loss, the best way to stay involved, but with help, is what is called "supported decision making"—the appointed person is there, with you, when important financial decisions are required. You give that trusted other the final word on decisions. That way, even if you are not entirely "with it," your trusted person can act on your behalf. You can weigh in and be heard, though your wishes may not actually be in your best interests. The appointed trusted person will stand up for you, keep you from making mistakes with your assets, and fend off predators.

How Elder Abuse Happens

The following are facts from a case in which Carolyn Rosenblatt was involved as a consultant.

Ron is 87 and lives with his long-time girlfriend. He is wealthy, owning many assets, including some apartment buildings. He has always been cautious with his money. He doesn't trust any single bank. As a result, he has accounts scattered around town. Over the last three years he has begun to have memory problems.

His girlfriend has been with him for 30 years. They share a home. She takes care of him. And he has become dependent on her. He has numerous health problems. She sees opportunity.

Ron has one child, Jake. Their relationship is good and trusting. Jake has wealth in his own right and cares very much for his dad. Ron appointed Jake as his successor trustee and his agent on his durable power of attorney document. In the last year, Ron met with his long-time attorney to update his estate plan to ensure that his girlfriend, Wilma, did not become overly controlling. He gave Jake the power to step in as successor trustee, replacing the bank that formerly was named in that position. He also put consequences into the trust— Wilma's generous gift from him would be reduced if she interfered with his relationship with Jake, or did not cooperate with him. Wilma doesn't like Jake and tries to keep Ron away from him. She won't answer Jake's calls to his dad. She insists on being present anytime Jake wants to visit his father, who lives in a different state.

After the changes to the trust, Wilma got busy. She manipulated Ron into selling apartment buildings he had owned inside his trust. Using Ron's lack of mental sharpness to persuade him, Wilma took the $1 million proceeds and put them into her account. Not only did this create a large tax consequence for Ron, it violated the specific terms of the trust. Yet, Ron was unsure of what to do. He was confused about the sale and needed Wilma to take care of him.

Jake had to hire an elder abuse attorney. Wilma (using Ron's account) hired her own lawyer to fight Jake. The battle went on. It was horribly unpleasant for Jake, and Ron was befuddled by it all. After many months, the case was resolved in Jake's favor. However, large legal expenses were incurred, as well as significant time and effort. Could this have been avoided?

First, it was clear to anyone who knew Ron that he was mentally slipping. At least three years before he became so confused that he agreed to a huge real estate deal that was not in his interests, Jake saw the signs of cognitive decline. However, he was reluctant to get into a fight with Wilma, as his dad seemed comfortable with her and they had been together for many years. *Waiting and not acting on signs of mental decline in his dad was his first mistake.*

Ron had provided in his trust that Jake could take over control when the time came. But, no one had decided when that time was. Wilma would never let Jake talk to his dad alone, so he felt powerless. But he wasn't.

Second, knowing that he had but one adult child, Ron could have appointed Jake sooner than he did to oversee his financial affairs. Leaving this up to a bank to be the successor trustee would not have helped. The bank trustees did not know Ron, did not assess his mental status, and would likely have allowed all that transpired to go on until a court stepped in and informed the bank by court order that Ron was incapacitated. That kind of outcome is generally avoidable. It should not require going to court to be declared incapacitated in order to give up control over financial matters.

There's more to the story. When Wilma took the proceeds from the sale of the apartment building, the bank let her move them into an account in her name. This was improper, particularly in view of the trust itself, a copy of which the bank had. In addition, Jake had, in a letter, warned the bank of potential abuse by Wilma. The bank got the letter and put the funds back into the trust. The next day, Wilma showed up with Ron and likely prompted him to say he wanted the funds back in Wilma's account. He had no idea what he was doing by this point. The bank had put the funds back in the Wilma controlled account, outside the trust.

Jake should have been more assertive once he observed that his father's memory was impaired. He could have seen the red flags and taken Ron to a doctor and asked the doctor to assess Ron's mental status. The doctor who eventually saw Ron did say that he was no longer financially competent. That satisfied the requirements of the trust that would necessitate Ron stepping down as trustee. However, all of those steps did not take place until after Wilma had manipulated Ron into selling the buildings and had moved the proceeds into her account. The legal complications of Wilma's manipulation might have been avoided if a doctor had earlier declared Ron as financially incompetent.

Takeaways

1. Face the possibility of losing capacity for financial decisions

First, we need to recognize that we could decline mentally as we age. Being educated, sophisticated, and familiar with finance is no assurance of mental sharpness in our later years. Be prepared. Do not let anyone who might manipulate you have a chance to do so. Make sure you have carefully chosen the team of family members, friends, relatives, and professionals that will swing into action in the event of cognitive impairment. Teach them your principles of investing, of managing finances, and your values, and put everything in writing. Then be sure your trust, will, and durable power of attorney for finances reflect that the team will be able to assume control promptly when any issues arise over your mental status.

2. Consider what a transition from power would involve

Whether you trust banks and financial institutions or not, they have a lot of power over your accounts. If your trusted other arrives with a Durable Power of Attorney (DPOA) in hand and says, "please do as I say," they may or may not cooperate. If a competing person comes in with a different DPOA in hand and tells them, "no, do what I say," the institutions do not know what to do. They do not want to get sued. They might freeze the account until there is a court order telling them what to do.

You protect yourself from such nightmares by making your estate plan as clear as possible, and by educating your trusted other about what you would want if you ever become impaired and someone else tried to take advantage. Work with your estate planning attorney on this. If he or she doesn't get it, find another lawyer. The most thorough legal documents can usually control the outcome of any scene like this one. Assertive representation of your interests is essential. Many estate planning lawyers do not involve themselves in litigation. Ask, and be sure that the lawyer will either go to bat for you if the need arises, or will know and work with someone who is an assertive litigator, experienced in estate litigation.

3. Know what you want if you become physically dependent on others

The point at which you realize that you need help with day-to-day activities like walking, bathing or getting dressed, you are vulnerable to caregivers. Caregivers are frequent abusers of vulnerable elders. In Ron's case, Wilma was in total control over his well-being. We do not know if she threatened him, or just used his confusion to get him to move money into her name. It is scary to think that we might need physical assistance. However, it is a fact of life. Think about your aging relatives or others who were long-lived. Most of them needed help at some point. To protect yourself, have an honest and open discussion with family and/or friends about the possibility of your needing care. Who would be in a position to give this care? Would help be hired and from whom? The time to explore these issues is when you are still in control of your senses. Careful choice of the right caregiver can also prevent financial abuse.

The Estate Planning Gap

Most estate planning attorneys do a good job drafting documents and addressing most estate planning issues. However, there is one area where Carolyn has seen them consistently failing—the legal documents do not address how to manage the decline of mental capability regarding financial matters, short of becoming completely incompetent. A period of gradual loss of ability can last for years, during which we can make serious financial mistakes. Most trusts do not address this, only stating what to do if we are determined to be incapacitated: we stop being trustee or we resign. This assumes that: a) we know on our own that we need to resign as trustee and we will do so willingly; or b) we will cooperate if someone else tells us it's time to resign and will not resist if asked to do so. These are not safe assumptions.

Unfortunately, the typical trust does not tell us, or the assigned successor, when, or how, to take over during the stage of life when we are well enough to do some things financially, but too impaired for others. A typical trust designates a successor trustee and perhaps a backup or two. It also provides that the trustee (you) can resign or be removed. This is the area of danger. The point at which you might become incapacitated is not clear. It does not necessarily jump out at you, or anyone around you, at a single moment in time. The typical trust does not give anyone enough direction as to how to manage that stage of life when someone is partly competent—"the grey zone."

If you are in the grey zone, it's likely you will think you are capable to handle financial matters. And sometimes you are. But, there will also be times when your judgment is poor, putting you at risk of financial abuse. It's unlikely that you would voluntarily resign as trustee of your own trust as long as you think you are capable. People in the grey zone often do not recognize when they are no longer capable. And even if they have an inkling of their own memory problems, they are often terrified of losing control. Or, they may simply be in denial. Each of these situations creates opportunity for abusers. Carolyn has personally witnessed each of these scenarios in her work at AgingParents.com. Consider the following cases.

A 93-year-old with dementia is still the trustee on her family trust. A 90-year old who is legally blind is still being asked to sign legal documents. A highly impaired 89-year-old is being asked to authorize financial transactions. Do not let any of these cases become you.

The typical trust may say that if you are incapacitated you can be removed as trustee. Being determined incapacitated almost always requires that a doctor (or two) make written statements on your capacity for financial decisions. But if you think you are fine, why would you go to the doctor? In fact, people with dementia, or even those in the grey zone, often refuse to be examined for cognitive decline or incapacity. This creates problems for the successor trustee who is stuck with a lack of the very documentation the trust requires for you to be removed as trustee because of mental incapacity.

Predators love this: There you are with total power to give money away to anyone and you no longer have the judgment to see a scam. Your family, or trusted other, are left with only a few choices or only one choice—try to have a court determine that you need a guardianship (called conservatorship in California). That is a last resort. We suggest that you protect your family and other loved ones from being forced into that choice by having serious discussions with your trusted others about how to spot the warning signs that signal the grey zone and reaching agreements about what they will do when they see them.

Incremental mental declines do not come with loud signals. We may forget to pay an invoice for utilities and the power is cut off. That may or may not be a signal of decline. While everyone makes "normal" mistakes, a pattern of them is a sign of decline and needs someone's attention, someone independent of ourselves. We might do something foolish and fall for a scam. Even if it is not devastating, we will be embarrassed. But, that might not be enough to trigger anyone taking over as successor trustee. This is the danger of the "grey zone." We can be slipping, making us susceptible to manipulation.

Cognitive decline can cause us to lose our antennae for something that doesn't "smell right." For professional thieves, the grey zone is like blood in the water for a shark. They are good at stealing from aging people, knowing exactly how to insinuate themselves into your life without you realizing you're being taken for a ride.

Making Agreements with Trusted Others About Risks of the Grey Zone

It is important that you have open and thoughtful communication with family members, or trusted others. Set up benchmarks for the decision as to when you would resign as trustee. We recommend that you and your successor trustee meet and create a list of warning signs of cognitive impairment. Below is a checklist we recommend you use.

1. Unexplained changes to estate documents.
2. Isolation.
3. Odd changes in investment behavior such as liquidating a portfolio.
4. A new romantic interest under questionable circumstances.
5. Large or unusual withdrawals from an account.
6. Prior instance of financial abuse.
7. Sudden drop in investment income.
8. Unpaid service or tax bills.

The following is a further list of items that members of the financial services team (such as your financial advisor) should be looking for:

- Inability to get access to financial records (no longer coming in the mail, changed password, and so on).
- Unusual activity in bank accounts such as withdrawals from automated banking machines when the elder is homebound, or online transactions if the elder has no computer.
- Signature on documents that does not resemble the elder's signature.
- Changes to investments that have not been used in years (such as annuities).
- Failure to remember reported financial transactions such as IRA distributions, investment sales, and so on.
- Unusual loans against equity in property or life insurance policies.
- New relationships expressing interest in the elder's financial situation.
- Missing documents like a will or stocks, bonds, mutual funds, or certificates of deposit (CDs).
- Change of beneficiary status on investment accounts or life insurance policies.
- Utilities or telephone disconnected.
- Inclusion of additional names on bank and other financial accounts.
- Changes in a power of attorney from a long-time friend or family member to a person new to the situation.
- Refusal or reluctance of family or legal representative to spend money on care.
- Caregiver or provider tries to isolate elder from other relationships.

You can agree with your assigned trusted others that if two or more of these warning signs are present it will be time for you to resign as trustee and manager of your finances. You can build into that agreement that you will see a physician or two, as required by your trust, when they ask you to be examined for cognitive ability.

You can also build into your estate plan that if you refuse a written request from your spouse, or trusted other, to be examined for cognitive ability by a doctor, that you will be automatically replaced as the sole trustee within 30 days.

The following is a checklist you can use as warning signs of cognitive impairment:

1. It appears to trusted others that you are no longer able to process simple concepts.
2. You appear to be forgetful, with short-term memory loss.
3. You appear unable to recognize or appreciate the consequences of financial decisions.
4. You make any decisions that are inconsistent with your long-held goals, investment philosophy, or commitments.
5. You demonstrate erratic behavior.
6. You refuse to follow appropriate investment advice which you have generally accepted in the past.

7. You seem to them to be paranoid about someone taking your money or missing funds that are not missing.
8. You lose the ability to understand recently completed financial transactions.
9. You appear in any way to be disoriented, get lost in usual places, such as finding your way home, or you forget where you are.
10. You forget your grooming, bathing or taking basic care of your physical needs.

Bring the list to a meeting with your loved ones and trusted others. Your message needs to be: If you see me with three of these things (or however many you think is the right number), please get me to a doctor to determine if I'm losing my ability to manage finances. If the doctor says I'm impaired, please take over managing the trust assets. Do not wait until I'm so out of it I do not know what I'm doing at all. The following case, in which Carolyn was involved, shows why this is important.

Bonnie and The Lottery Scam

Bonnie is 92 and lives independently in an apartment in a seniors' community. She is doing well physically, but she has serious memory problems. Her doctor told her son, Michael, that she has dementia. She is a widow and she is the sole trustee on her multimillion-dollar trust. Michael loves his mother and he is hesitant to tell her what to do. He knows she should not be making financial decisions. But, he hasn't gotten around to asking her to resign and let him become the trustee, as the legal documents provide he can do. Things reached a crisis and he was terrified that she could lose everything.

Bonnie liked to play the sweepstakes. Michael found stacks of mailings from various lottery "companies" in her apartment. In chatting with her, he heard that she thought she had won the lotto. All she had to do was pay the "taxes" on her winnings to this nice "Mr. Banks," who called her every day, and he would bring the $1 million check. Bonnie was excited. In fact, Banks and his "lawyer" were coming in person the next day to walk Bonnie across the street to the bank so she could withdraw the money for taxes and deposit her check at the same time. "Wasn't that nice?" she asked Michael.

Michael hired Carolyn. She advised him to notify the bank to cut off her access to the account temporarily and to inform them in writing that she was a victim of attempted elder fraud. He immediately took a letter to them in person. He then stayed at his mother's apartment and when "Mr. Banks" called, Michael demanded to know who he was. The impostor pretended to be a distant relative. Michael thwarted him in that lie and told him to never call his mother again. He went away. That was just the first step.

The next step involved taking his mother to the doctor to obtain a letter verifying that she was no longer financially competent. This was a close call.

Bonnie exhibited items 1, 2, 3, and 8 from the checklist above. And these signs were well known and recognized by Michael. If Bonnie had given him earlier instruction that she was to be removed as trustee when he saw these signs, perhaps it would have been easier for him to be proactive. Bonnie was lucky that she did not lose all her wealth.

Most Elder Financial Abuse is Never Reported to Authorities

It is estimated that only 1 in 44 cases of elder abuse are reported. Even fewer are prosecuted. The reasons are complex. An important one is that the most frequent abusers of elders are unscrupulous family members. According to the National Adult Protective Services Association website, 90 percent of financial abusers are family members or trusted others. Here's an example.

Carolyn worked with a 90-year-old woman who was no longer financially competent. She had always favored her son, though he was probably not the best choice to have as her power of attorney. Nonetheless, she gave him this authority, bypassing her competent daughter. He had taken over $10,000 from her checking account for his personal use and appeared poised to take much more. Carolyn told her that her son, by taking money from her without her permission and against her wishes, had committed a crime. Her response: "I do not want my son prosecuted." She would not have cooperated even if his abuse had been reported. Aggravating matters was that her son was about to get away with stealing her house. There was little that could be done, as the daughter did not have the funds to sue her brother for manipulating their mother, who was what is called a "willing victim."

In your planning, try to imagine a worst-case scenario, anticipating that you may not be in control for the rest of your days. Specify in your estate planning documents what you want, and what authority your trusted others will and will not have. Giving unlimited authority to one person can be dangerous to your financial safety.

How Long Does it Take to Stop Financial Abuse by a Family Member?

Financial advisors are now required by regulators to report financial abuse if they reasonably suspect it. While that sounds fine, regulators have very little real-world experience with stopping abusers.

The regulations give the financial advisors and managers 15 days to hold financial transactions in the face of suspected abuse, with another 10 days that can be added on. Apparently, they never had to carry out the necessary steps to stop abuse when they are permitted to hold transactions. It is likely to be much longer than a maximum of 25 days. Here is another case showing how long it can take to stop a financial abuser.

Charles and The Family Predator

Charles is 94 and lives in a nursing home. He has dementia, though no one ever diagnosed it formally. He has a son, Tommy, who lives in another state, and a daughter, Morgan, who lives in yet a different state. Tommy has never done well financially, and Charles has the co-dependent habit of giving him money over the years. They were never large amounts, but enough to get Tommy out of his frequent jams. At least Charles had the good sense to appoint his daughter to be his successor trustee, as well as his agent, giving her power of attorney.

One day Tommy showed up at his dad's nursing home. He took Charles out to meet with his nearby long-time financial manager who knew Charles' family and knew about his relationship with Tommy. Tommy persuaded Charles to ask the financial manager for a cashier's check for $50,000. The manager balked. He knew that Tommy had been pushing his dad around for years. But, it was never quite like this. And Charles seemed "out of it." The manager said it would take some time to get the check, and he tried to figure out what to do. He knew it would be wrong to just hand over a check that Tommy would immediately cash. Charles didn't leave the nursing home much and surely did not need $50,000. But, Charles had never given the manager permission to talk to Morgan or anyone about his condition or his finances—a big mistake.

Even without the current regulations regarding reporting financial abuse, the manager, "on the Q.T.", called Morgan and told her what was going on. Morgan called Carolyn, who asked to see the family trust. Carolyn found that Charles was still listed as the sole trustee. It specified that if Charles became disabled he had to have two letters from doctors, saying he was no longer able to manage his finances. Carolyn instructed Morgan how to get the letters, what doctors to approach, and what to ask them to say: Language that matched what the trust required.

Morgan jumped into action. She did her research by talking to Charles' primary care doctor who referred her to a neurologist and another doctor. She made the appointments and flew out to take Charles to the appointments. She then flew home and waited for the reports to arrive. That took four weeks. The doctors' letters took another three weeks to get to her. And that was faster than usual. She then made an appointment with Charles' estate planning attorney who had initially drawn up the trust. Fortunately, he knew Morgan, and was cooperative in creating the paperwork she needed to formally establish that Charles was removed as trustee and that she was now the sole trustee. She sent the paperwork, called a Certificate of Trust, to the financial manager. He was required to have it reviewed by his legal department. That took a little over two weeks. Once it was approved, the manager was able to cease allowing Charles to request any financial transactions and was required to go through Morgan who had now taken his place.

The total time it took for Morgan to stop her brother from any further abuse was three months. During that period, the financial manager, feeling pressure from Charles' phone calls, prompted of course by Tommy, gave Charles the $50,000. Tommy got the money. Valuable lessons can be learned from this true case.

- Never appoint a "Tommy" to be your agent, successor trustee, or to have any power over your finances.
- Ask your family member or trusted other to be ready to take over as your DPOA or successor trustee, or both, when you can no longer live independently, if not sooner. Why was a frail 94-year-old with dementia still allowed to be the sole trustee on his trust? Use that discussion in this chapter about the red flags of diminished capacity and get your trusted others' agreement to step up when you start to slide, not on an emergency basis. Just like Bonnie in the previous case study, you should not be left to your own devices when you are cognitively impaired. Plan for the possibility. At 90+, your odds are about 50/50 that you'll be cognitively impaired.
- It takes a lot longer than 25 days to stop an abuser when legal paperwork necessary for getting the impaired elder off the trust is needed. Doctors are involved. At least one lawyer is involved. Institutions where assets are kept will be involved.

Other Ways You Could be Cheated

Elder abuse cons are regularly posted on the Federal Trade Commission website, local law enforcement sites and in community education materials in efforts to stop the scams. Despite the efforts to educate seniors, scammers are stealing huge amounts from seniors every year.

Our suggestion is to take advantage of published information about common scams at the time you retire. By reading about them you might recognize a scam and be better prepared to avoid getting taken. Here are some of the scams described by the Federal Trade Commission:

- "Grandparent scams": You get a call from someone posing as your grandchild convincing you that he has been arrested and needs bail money immediately.

- "Romance scams": Your online sweetheart makes you believe he or she needs funds to come and visit you because you are the one and only.
- "Guardianship schemes": Con artists siphon your financial resources into the bank accounts of deceitful relatives or guardians.

Many other well-known scams are going on daily, targeting elders. If you want to avoid them, you need to not only educate yourself, but your loved ones as well.

Reaching the Last Phase of Life with Your Wishes Honored

Although declines in our health are inevitable if we are long-lived, we do not have to reach the end without some control over how we are treated. Unfortunately, Carolyn has witnessed intrusive, painful, and ultimately useless treatment given to elderly, frail patients who most likely did not want anyone doing these things to prevent them from dying in peace and with dignity.

To ensure that your last days are dignified, make sure you have made your wishes clear to your loved ones. That increases your odds of having things go as you direct them, even if there comes a point when you can no longer speak for yourself. Numerous conditions can cause loss of consciousness. The way to address this issue is to have an advance health-care directive—whether you call it that, or a health-care proxy, a living will, or a health-care power of attorney. Further, it is essential to discuss the matter of how you want things to go with your loved ones in some detail. The document empowers someone else to decide about medical treatment, end of life treatment, and what will be done or not done to you in the event that you can't speak for yourself—a common occurrence.

If you have not created or updated your own advance health-care directive, nor looked at it for some time, now is the time to do so. Here are some suggestions to help you with this task:

- **First, get a clear idea of what you want.** Doctors can do a large number of things most of us do not want—extensive and even painful things to keep us artificially alive. If you want "everything done, no matter what," say so. If you want to allow nature to take its course, put it in writing and make sure family members know.
- **Sign the document.** If you do not have one, you can get one from your doctor, from your hospital, or from the internet. The language varies a bit from state to state, so be sure yours is specific to your state. Keep it in a safe

place. Give a copy to the person whom you appoint to be your agent and be sure your primary care doctor also has a copy.

- **Get guidance from your doctor as to anything you do not understand on the document.** What does it mean to be intubated? What is tube feeding? Most people are unfamiliar with all the terminology. Your doctor, nurse practitioner, or physician's assistant can explain.
- **Have a meeting with your loved ones to be sure everyone knows what you do and do not want done if you are unable to communicate.** Families sometimes disagree, and even fight about this. Some won't want to accept reality when you are going to pass. If you do not want anyone to abuse or neglect your wishes, inform them of your wishes. Tools are available to help you. The American Bar Association offers a free Toolkit for Advance Healthcare Planning on its website.

Wrap Up

We have provided a sobering look at the many ways others might take advantage of you, should you become vulnerable to financial manipulation. All of this may feel uncomfortable. You may have to overcome your own internal resistance to even thinking about these issues. No one wants to consider being helpless or dependent. However, the responsible person you were while working needs to carry forward that sense of responsibility into your retirement years to address your possible decline.

Below is Carolyn's 10-point *smart retirees' checklist* that generally covers many of the bases of how to help your family and yourself be best prepared for things you need to manage in this phase of life and avoid abuse. The bottom line here is transparency and open communication.

1. Decide with whom you want to communicate about your future. Set a date and get together.
2. Have a signed, notarized durable power of attorney.
3. Have a signed advance health-care directive. (Items 2 and 3 are available free of charge on the internet.)
4. Make a list of all bank accounts, passwords, hard drive backup, investment records, and financial planning you have done, and provide contact information. Provide written permission to your loved ones to talk with your lawyer, accountant, and financial planner.
5. Make a list of all insurance policies, including life, disability, health, property, earthquake and anything else you own that will protect your heirs.

6. Make a copy of your mortgage statement, any other loans, financial statements, and bank statements. Keep them in one place. Update when changes are made.
7. List your physicians, care providers, and medications. Give written permission for your loved ones to speak with your doctors.
8. Put in writing your wishes for burial or disposition of your remains.
9. Update your will and/or trust with a local attorney. Laws change and documents need to be up to date in your state.
10. Have a family meeting to give items 2–9 to your loved ones and explain them.

To this list we add one more important item: Assess the protective team of individuals who will swing into action if needed, confirm that they are willing to serve, and set introductions and authorizations for each to talk to the others.

And, finally, because elder abuse and cognitive decline are often related, we offer the following checklist should you have a relative experience diminished mental capacity:

- **To mitigate the risk of elder abuse, establish checks and balances for power of attorney, successor trustee, and key professionals.** Everyone should report to someone else. And when appropriate place a freeze on credit files with the credit bureaus. In addition, have someone monitoring credit card and spending accounts for unusual activity. Controls might be placed on emails and phone to limit vulnerability to scams.
- **Have a plan of care for the primary caregiver.** If a relative becomes the primary caregiver, set up a self-care program to avoid caregiver syndrome (burnout, depression, resentment, guilt, and so on) that might include joining a support group, getting counseling and/or learning to deal with a dementia patient. Compensation for the caregiver should be considered in the form of a contract. We recommend working with an attorney experienced in this area.
- **Put minimum required distributions on autopilot if possible.** Make sure financial firms have durable power of attorney authorizations in place. Brokerage houses do not necessarily accept your signed durable power of attorney. They may require a form signed by the account holder. Make sure this occurs before impairment stops you from being able to sign anything.
- **To pay for care, assess any long-term care (LTC) policies and other benefits (such as military, union, and so on).** If there is the risk of running out of assets, talk to a Medicaid planning attorney. If the person in need is married, consider their joint financial means to avoid leaving a destitute survivor. Legal advice is essential for those who can foresee the possibility of running out of assets.

- **Discuss options for where needed care should be provided.** If the person is still living in their home, what are the situations that may cause that to change, what are the options and how do they feel about them, and how will they approach this decision? What resources are available to better understand the local options? What resources can be used to pay for the best place for caregiving?
- **Understand hospice care for the terminally ill and how to obtain Medicare coverage for it.**
- **Consider the tax effect of medical expenses.** Medical tax deductions might be utilized to harvest gains at low tax rates, make it efficient to do a Roth conversion, cash in an annuity, and so on.

Conclusion

W<small>E HAVE ALMOST</small> reached the end of our journey, a journey which was designed to help you develop a retirement plan that will give you the best chance of not only achieving your financial goals, but of also enjoying a fulfilling life in retirement. We have provided you with all the tools you need to accomplish those objectives. We have shown you:

- How to identify your goals and objectives through the discovery process and provided a sample LifeMap (Appendix A).
- How to build an investment policy statement, and how to choose the right asset allocation mix (using a Monte Carlo simulator) and the right withdrawal strategy.
- How to maintain the portfolio's risk profile in the most effective manner.
- How to manage for tax efficiency by locating your assets to achieve the greatest after-tax returns and harvesting losses.
- How to maximize Social Security and Medicare benefits.
- How to develop a well-thought-out estate plan that allows you to not only effectively pass on assets, but your values as well.
- How to integrate insurance of all types, including longevity insurance, into your planning process.
  But, we are not done yet. In the appendices that follow we:
- Provide samples of both a LifeMap and a Family Mission Statement.
- Demonstrate the math behind our asset location recommendations.
- Provide a list of the investment vehicles we recommend and use in building portfolios for ourselves and the clients of Buckingham Strategic Wealth and Buckingham Strategic Partners.
- Provide a recommended reading list for those who would like to dig deeper into many of the issues we have discussed.
- Address the investment strategy of relying on dividend-paying stocks to provide cash flow, showing why this is an inefficient strategy.
- Provide you with a due diligence process to enable you to choose an advisor you can trust.

Before concluding, we want to remind you that designing a retirement plan is not an end. The plan must be a living document—whenever any of the assumptions underlying the plan change, the plan should be reevaluated.

Finally, we add this: We've greatly enjoyed the thousands of emails and letters we have received over the years from readers of our books. If you have any questions about this book or how to implement the recommended strategies, feel free to contact us at: Buckingham Strategic Wealth, 8182 Maryland Ave., Suite 500, Clayton, MO 63105, or email either of us at lswedroe@buckinghamgroup.com or kgrogan@buckinghamgroup.com. We are always happy to answer questions from our readers.

Appendices

APPENDIX A

LifeMap

Vision & Values
- More quality time with family, close friends, and as a couple
- Less stress from work
- Give back more intentionally

Work & Career
- Work feels like a burden
- Can I really make it another 7 years as planned, or do I need to rethink retirement?

Family & Relationships
- Want to stay close to 2 adult kids, especially with grandkids in the picture.

Health & Wellness
- Stressed at work, and bringing stress home.

Interests & Causes
- We love international travel, especially with family.
- Give more and be more hands-on with giving

Goals & Concerns
- More time at the beach
- Less time at work
- Downsize primary residence or sell beach house?
- Less real estate debt

Sample Family Mission Statement

1. Why We Have a Family Mission Statement

> "You can use your inheritance to maintain what you have, but you can also use it to take a risk, like we did. This is our gift to you."—Mom and Dad

We created our family mission statement to express our family's intentions for future generations. Our mission statement is special because it also provides our family's perspectives on money, finances and living life to the fullest. The fundamental principle of our mission is to have a plan, which allows us to accomplish our chosen goals now and going forward.

Our family is stronger because we work together to make decisions.

The lessons that guide us include understanding the passive investment management philosophy that has guided us for so many years and recognizing the value of working with trusted professional (financial) counsel. This means building a team of experts, including an attorney and accountant, and having them work together to act in our best interest.

The legacy we can leave comes from our shared family values. We have a great opportunity to help others in the community and change the way they view the world.

2. How Our Family Approaches Life

> "In life, you can gain a great deal of satisfaction if you do something yourself rather than having it handed to you. It's alright to start at the bottom and work your way up."—Mom and Dad

Our family is made up of entrepreneurs and risk takers. We have all experienced our share of successes and failures. Because of this, we have each learned in our own way not to take things at face value—to be wary of people passing on inaccurate information and the value of taking the time to research and verify information. We are there to remind each other that, while bad things can happen to good people, often something bad can cause (or is followed by) something good.

Our family is stronger because we persevere. When we have new ideas we follow through, even though we do not expect everyone to believe right away those ideas makes sense.

The lessons that guide us incorporate the knowledge that having something to fall back on is important, because financial security may not always be there. We recognize the danger of spending that last dollar because no one can know exactly what lies ahead.

The legacy we can leave will provide our future generations with the skills to understand people and their motivations in an effort to help those who need it the most.

3. The Origin of Our Family's Wealth

"The world is changing, and it is important to change right along with it."—Mom and Dad

In part, we followed the traditional route (attended college, saved for the future). In part, we chose a creative path and took prudent but calculated risks. While many of our biggest decisions have been made with due diligence and great preparation, we were not afraid to follow our instincts.

Our family is stronger because we are willing to learn from each other.

The lessons that guide us have helped us make changes in our lives and supported us as we took risks. We look to our experiences to teach us more about the world and make smarter decisions as we go forward.

The legacy we can leave is to inspire those around us by proving that hard work and persistence pay off.

4. Our Plan Allows Us to Pursue Individual Goals

"Value happiness above financial standing. Twice as much money doesn't necessarily mean living better."—Mom and Dad

How can we make the greatest contributions to our community? We know from experience that real change happens when the primary reason for getting involved derives from having passion for a particular cause.

Our family is stronger because we value education.

The lessons that guide us have proven that the pursuit of happiness is a worthy one. It should not be subjugated to maintain financial independence. You can sacrifice attempts to achieve financial independence on your own to pursue a career choice or devote your time to society at large.

The legacy we can leave is to change things for the better by pursuing our own interests.

5. Our Motivation for Planning

"Educate yourself about wealth, what to do with it and how to maintain it."—Mom and Dad

We are motivated to preserving our estate by taking advantage of prudent tax-advantaged strategies. We desire that our estate survive through multi-generations.

Our family is stronger because we value informed decisions that help us preserve our estate.

The lessons that guide us have taught us that staying informed will help us make smart decisions on strategies to maximize the opportunity to pass our estate through multiple generations of our family.

The legacy we can leave is to provide for multiple generations of our family.

6. Our Financial Philosophy

"Be thankful for what you have and help other people who do not."—Mom and Dad

Each person should be judged on their personal merits. It is incorrect to prejudge individuals based on their wealth or lack thereof, until we take the time to understand them. It is useful to remember that many charitable organizations conduct their philanthropic efforts in a way that ultimately excludes individuals and conflicts with our family's mission statement.

Our family is stronger because we are grateful for what we have. We invest prudently but believe that risk should be avoided if there is no financial need to take it.

The lessons that guide us have taught us that it is relatively easy for one person to change the course of another person's day—for better or worse. By considering others, we can change people's lives for the better.

The legacy we can leave is one of a great spirit of responsible generosity that reflects our entire family.

7. Family Independence

"Learn how to prudently utilize wealth."—Mom and Dad

We realize that the utility of wealth is a concept that is critically important to understand with respect to how we live our lives.

Our family is stronger because we have achieved a level of financial independence whereby it is more important to preserve our wealth than it is to enhance our wealth.

The lessons that guide us have taught us that it is more important to obtain the wealth necessary to accomplish anything you want, but not necessarily everything that you want.

The legacy we can leave is to educate our children to use our wealth to get them wherever they want to be.

8. Our Family Legacy

"Pursue happiness without worrying about financial constraints."—Mom and Dad

If we truly understand the concept of wealth, we will make prudent life decisions. It is not a matter of how much wealth we can accumulate, but rather a question of determining what is important in our lives and how our wealth can help us accomplish those goals.

Our family is stronger because we accomplish what we set out to do.

The lessons that guide us allow us to see the value of achieving financial independence and simultaneously find equal merit in pursuing goals without financial constraints that would detour us from those goals.

The legacy we can leave is for future generations who seek a role model from whom they can learn.

9. Our Social Legacy

"Be charitable."—Mom and Dad

We can help other people and have a positive effect on our society. To be able to help others in this way gives us a sense of family pride, but also reminds us to remain humble and remember how the course of one's life can change in an instant.

Our family is stronger because we understand how our wealth empowers us to help people in society who were not as lucky as we were.

The lessons that guide us remind us that going through life trying to accumulate the maximum amount possible cannot truly satisfy us; that goes against our financial philosophy.

The legacy we can leave is the image of a family united in the effort to help others. We give to the charities of our choice, but avoid giving to elitist organizations. Instead, we gravitate toward helping broad-based or faith-based organizations.

APPENDIX C

The Mathematics of Asset Location

A S WE DISCUSSED in Chapter 10, "The Asset Location Decision," our recommendation on asset location is to have a preference for locating tax-inefficient assets in tax-advantaged accounts. This approach to asset location is based on the peer-reviewed academic and practitioner literature on the topic. Specifically:

- Dammon, Spatt and Zhang (2004): "Optimal Asset Location and Allocation with Taxable and Tax-Deferred Investing." Published in *The Journal of Finance*.
- Reichenstein (2006): "After-Tax Asset Allocation." Published in the *Financial Analysts Journal*.
- Horan (2007): "An Alternative Approach to After-Tax Valuation." Published in the *Financial Services Review*.
- Horan and Al Zaman (2008): "Tax-Adjusted Portfolio Optimization and Asset Location." Published in *The Journal of Wealth Management*.
- Reichenstein, Horan and Jennings (2012): "Two Key Concepts for Wealth Management and Beyond." Published in the *Financial Analysts Journal*.
- Reichenstein and Meyer (2013): "The Asset Location Decision Revisited." Published in the *Journal of Financial Planning*.

This appendix is broken into two sections. First, we will discuss how a security's expected return and risk characteristics can change based on where the assets are located. Second, we will walk through a Roth versus taxable asset location decision using after-tax asset allocation.

Section One: Asset Location's Effect on Expected Return and Risk

The table below indicates the principal effectively owned by, return received by, and risk borne by, individual investors in each savings vehicle. As shown, in contrast to bonds and stocks held in a Roth IRA, for bonds and stocks held in a tax-deferred account, the investor effectively owns (1 − tax rate) of the principal but receives 100 percent of the returns and bears 100 percent of the risk.

Savings Vehicle	Principal	Return	Risk
Roth IRA	100%	100%	100%
Tax-deferred account	1 − tax rate	100%	100%
Taxable account			
Bonds	100%	1 − tax rate	1 − tax rate
Stocks	100%	1 − tax drag	1 − tax drag

To illustrate the risk and return sharing of bonds held in taxable accounts, we assume bonds have a 3 percent expected return and a 4 percent standard deviation and that the investor is in the 25 percent tax bracket. We also assume bonds earn returns of −1 percent, 3 percent, and 7 percent in three years; that is, they earn the mean return and 1 standard deviation below and above the mean. The standard deviation of these returns is 4 percent. Assuming the 1 percent loss is used to offset that year's taxable income, the investor's after-tax returns are −0.75 percent, 2.25 percent and 5.25 percent, for a standard deviation of 3 percent. In this case, the investor receives (1 − tax rate) of pre-tax returns and bears (1 − tax rate) of pre-tax risk.

When stocks are held in taxable accounts (with cost bases equal to market values), the investor owns 100 percent of the principal, but the after-tax return and risk of stocks is reduced by a tax drag on returns, specifically the taxes due on dividends and realized capital gains. The tax drag number depends upon how actively the stocks are managed, but for the purposes of this example we will assume that 15 percent of the return on stocks is lost to taxes each year. (This effectively assumes that all capital gains are realized 366 days after the stocks are purchased.)

To illustrate risk and return sharing, we assume stocks have a 7 percent expected return and a 19 percent standard deviation. Stocks earn pre-tax returns of −12 percent, 7 percent and 26 percent in three years; that is, they earn the mean return and 1 standard deviation above and below the mean. The standard deviation of these returns is 19 percent. If the losses are used that year to offset long-term capital gains, the after-tax returns are –10.2 percent, 5.95 percent and 22.1 percent for a standard deviation of 16.15 percent (or 85 percent of the pre-tax standard deviation).

The key message from these examples is that the same underlying asset can have different expected return and risk characteristics depending upon where the asset is located.

Section Two: Asset Location and Roth IRAs

Using the framework in section one, we can evaluate asset location decisions when it comes to Roth IRAs versus taxable accounts. This section assumes that all assets will be used in the investor's lifetime, and that they are not designating Roth accounts for future heirs. If the investor is designating the Roth for heirs, then this account is effectively being managed for a different purpose and should have its own Investment Policy Statement.

The following are our capital market and tax assumptions:

Expected Return on Stocks	7.0%
Expected Return on Bonds	3.0%
Standard Deviation on Stocks	19.0%
Standard Deviation on Bonds	4.0%
Tax Rate on Stocks	15.0%
Tax Rate on Bonds	35.0%

Assume that our hypothetical investor has $200 split evenly between a taxable account and a Roth account. Let us also express the investor's risk tolerance in terms of acceptable volatility, and in this case the individual is comfortable with a portfolio after-tax standard deviation around 9.7 percent.

One way to accomplish this would be to locate $100 of bonds in the taxable account and $100 of stocks in the Roth account. The table below has the results:

Scenario 1: Incorrect Location

		After-Tax Expected Return	After-Tax Expected SD	Start $	End $ Pre Tax	End $ After Tax
Taxable Account	Stock	6.0%	16.2%	0.00	0.00	0.00
	Bond	2.0%	2.6%	100.00	103.00	101.95
Roth IRA	Stock	7.0%	19.0%	100.00	107.00	107.00
	Bond	3.0%	4.0%	0.00	0.00	0.00
TOTAL		**4.5%**	**9.6%**	**200.00**	**210.00**	**208.95**

The portfolio has an after-tax expected return of 4.5 percent and an after-tax standard deviation of 9.6 percent. At the end of the one-year period, the investor wound up with $208.95.

An alternative way to get to virtually the same after-tax standard deviation would be to locate the assets in the optimal manner, with $100 of stocks in the taxable account, and a 15/85 mix in the Roth account.

Scenario 2: Correct Location

		After-Tax Expected Return	After-Tax Expected SD	Start $	End $ Pre Tax	End $ After Tax
Taxable Account	Stock	6.0%	16.2%	100.00	107.00	105.95
	Bond	2.0%	2.6%	0.00	0.00	0.00
Roth IRA	Stock	7.0%	19.0%	15.00	16.05	16.05
	Bond	3.0%	4.0%	85.00	87.55	87.55
TOTAL		**4.8%**	**9.7%**	**200.00**	**210.60**	**209.55**

The after-tax standard deviation of Scenario 2 is virtually the same as Scenario 1 (9.6% versus 9.7%), even though the portfolio contains a higher allocation to stocks. The reason for this is that the government shares in the volatility of the stocks held in the taxable account. The after-tax return is higher in Scenario 2 than in Scenario 1, and the investor winds up with $209.55 at the end of the period.

Let's look at one more scenario where the investor's risk tolerance is expressed in terms of actual dollars allocated to stocks and bonds. In this scenario, we will say our investor wants a 50/50 asset allocation.

Scenario 1 still applies, but Scenario 2 is too aggressive because it has a higher allocation to equities than the investor desires. Scenario 3 locates $100 of stocks in the taxable account and $100 of bonds in the Roth.

Scenario 3: Correct Location

		After-Tax Expected Return	After-Tax Expected SD	Start $	End $ Pre Tax	End $ After Tax
Taxable Account	Stock	6.0%	16.2%	100.00	107.00	105.95
	Bond	2.0%	2.6%	0.00	0.00	0.00
Roth IRA	Stock	7.0%	19.0%	0.00	0.00	0.00
	Bond	3.0%	4.0%	100.00	103.00	103.00
TOTAL		**4.5%**	**8.3%**	**200.00**	**210.00**	**208.95**

Scenario 3 provides the exact same after-tax return as Scenario 1, but with less volatility. The reason for this is that the government is sharing in the volatility of stocks.

It is important to recognize that the government shares in the risk and returns on assets held in taxable accounts. Therefore, a bond or bond fund held inside a Roth is effectively a different asset than the same bond or bond fund held in a taxable account. Using the example above, the return and risk for a bond held in a Roth are 3 percent and 4 percent, but only 2 percent and 2.6 percent for the same bonds held in a taxable account. Using this framework, we learn that the best assets to hold in the taxable account are those that make the best use of the preferential long-term capital gains treatment. This will typically be stocks as long as the investor is willing to avoid intentionally realizing short-term capital gains.

APPENDIX D

Should Investors Prefer Dividend-Paying Stocks?

I T HAS LONG been known that many investors, especially those using a cash flow approach to spending, have a preference for cash dividends. From the perspective of classical financial theory, this behavior is an anomaly. We hope by providing you with a better understanding of the relationship between dividends and price changes, you will be able to characterize the gains from each appropriately and avoid some of the negative consequences that can result from this anomaly.

In their 1961 paper, "Dividend Policy, Growth, and the Valuation of Shares," Merton Miller and Franco Modigliani famously established that dividend policy should be irrelevant to stock returns. As they explained it, at least before frictions like trading costs and taxes, investors should be indifferent to $1 in the form of a dividend (causing the stock price to drop by $1) and $1 received by selling shares. This must be true, unless you believe that $1 isn't worth $1. This theorem has not been challenged since.

Moreover, the historical evidence supports this theory—stocks with the same exposure to common factors (such as size, value, momentum and profitability/quality) have the same returns whether they pay a dividend or not. Warren Buffett made this point in September 2011. After announcing a share buyback program for Berkshire, some people went after Buffett for not offering a cash dividend. In his 2012 shareholder letter he explained why he believed the share buyback was in the best interests of shareholders. He also explained that any shareholder who preferred cash can effectively create dividends by selling shares.

Despite theory, evidence, and Warren Buffett's response, many investors express a preference for dividend-paying stocks. One frequently expressed explanation for the preference is that dividends offer a safe hedge against the large fluctuations in price that stocks experience. But, this ignores that the dividend is offset by the fall in the stock price. It is what can be called the fallacy of the free dividend.

The Math of Cash Dividends versus Home-made Dividends

To demonstrate the point that cash dividends and home-made dividends are equivalent, we will consider two companies that are identical in all respects but one: Company A pays a dividend and Company B does not. To simplify the math, we assume that the stocks of both companies trade at their book value (while stocks do not always do that, the findings would be the same regardless).

The two companies have a beginning book value of $10. They both earn $2 a share. Company A pays a $1 dividend, while Company B pays none. An investor in A owns 10,000 shares and takes the $10,000 dividend to meet his spending requirements. At the end of year one the book value of Company A will be $11 (beginning value of $10 + $2 earnings – $1 dividend). The investor will have an asset allocation of $110,000 in stock ($11 × 10,000 shares) and $10,000 in cash for a total of $120,000.

Now let's look at the investor in B. Since the book value of B is now $12 ($10 beginning book value + $2 earnings), his asset allocation is $120,000 in stock and $0 in cash. He must sell shares to generate the $10,000 he needs to meet his spending needs. So, he sells 833 shares and generates $9,996. With the sale, he now has just 9,167 shares. However, those shares are $12, so his asset allocation is $110,004 in stock and $9,996 in cash, virtually identical to that of the investor in Company A.

Another way to show that the two are equivalent is to consider the investor in A who, instead of spending the dividend, reinvests it. With the stock now at $11, his $10,000 dividend allows him to purchase 909.09 shares. Thus, he now has 10,909.09 shares. With the stock at $11 his asset allocation is the same as the asset allocation of the investor in B: $120,000 in stock.

It is important to understand that Company B now has a somewhat higher expected growth in earnings because it has more capital to invest. The higher expected earnings offset the lesser number of shares owned, with the assumption being that the company will earn its cost of capital.

There is one more issue that should help to understand why dividend-based strategies are not optimal.

The Explanatory Power of Dividends

For most of the past 20 years, the workhorse model in finance was what is generally referred to as the Fama-French four model—with the four factors being beta, size, value, and momentum. The model explains the vast majority (well over 90 percent) of the differences in returns of diversified portfolios. If dividends played an important role in determining returns, the four-factor model would not work as well as it does, since dividends are not one of the factors. If, in fact, dividends added explanatory power beyond these factors, we would have a factor model that included dividends as one of the factors. But we do not.

The reason is that stocks with the same "loading," or exposure, to the four factors have the same expected return regardless of their dividend policy. This has important implications because about 60 percent of U.S. stocks and about 40 percent of international stocks do not pay dividends. Thus, any screen that includes dividends results in portfolios that are far less diversified than they could be if dividends were not included in the portfolio design. Less-diversified portfolios are less efficient because they have a higher potential dispersion of returns without any compensation in the form of higher expected returns (assuming the exposures to the factors are the same).

Taxes Matter

What is particularly puzzling about the preference for dividends is that taxable investors should favor the self-dividend (by selling shares) if cash flow is required. Unlike with dividends, where taxes are paid on the distribution amount, when shares are sold, taxes are due only on the portion of the sale representing a gain. And if there are losses on the sale, the investor gains the benefit of a tax deduction. Even in tax-advantaged accounts, investors who diversify globally (which is the prudent strategy) should prefer capital gains because in tax-advantaged accounts the foreign tax credits associated with dividends have no value. And finally, if dividends were throwing off more cash than needed to meet spending requirements, the total return approach we discussed in Chapter 6 would benefit from not only the time value of not having to pay taxes on the "excess" amount of dividends, but also dividends could push investors into a higher tax bracket.

We will now take a review of the historical evidence, beginning with a look at the returns from three of the largest ETFs that employ a high-dividend strategy for U.S. stocks.

The Evidence

The U.S. ETFs we will review are:

- Schwab U.S. Dividend Equity ETF (SCHD). The fund has an expense ratio of just 0.06 percent and its assets under management are about $12.1 billion. It holds 99 stocks.

- Vanguard High Dividend ETF (VYM). The fund has an expense ratio of just 0.06 percent and its assets under management are about $30.0 billion. It holds 399 stocks.
- iShares Core High Dividend ETF (HDV). The fund has an expense ratio of just 0.08 percent and its assets under management are about $7.5 billion. It holds 75 stocks.

With almost $50 billion collectively in AUM in just these three funds, clearly a high-dividend strategy is a very popular one. Have investors been rewarded for their belief in the strategy? To answer that question, we will compare the returns of the high-dividend ETFs, which Morningstar classifies as large value funds, to the similar large value funds from two prominent providers of passively managed funds, Dimensional and Vanguard.

Before we begin with the analysis, we will review the historical evidence on the performance of high-dividend strategies compared to that of other value strategies. From 1952 through 2019, the value premium was significantly larger when the metric used to determine value was price-to-book (4.3 percent), price-to-earnings (4.9 percent), or price-to-cash-flow (4.3 percent) instead of price-to-dividend (0.7 percent). In other words, historically, a high-dividend strategy was an inefficient way to access the value premium—and investors engaging in high-dividend strategies were either unaware of the evidence or chose to ignore it.

In order to review the performance of all three domestic ETFs, the period covered is from 2012 through 2019 (2012 was the first full year for both VYM and HDV).

Fund	Annualized Return (%)
Schwab U.S. Dividend Equity ETF (SCHD)	13.7
Vanguard High Dividend ETF (VYM)	13.0
iShares Core High Dividend ETF (HDV)	11.2
Dimensional U.S. Large Value III Fund (DFUVX)	14.2
Vanguard Value ETF (VTV)	13.7

The three high-dividend ETFs underperformed Dimensional's Large Value Fund (DFUVX) from 0.7 percent per year to as much as 3.0 percent per year— despite DFUVX's slightly higher expense ratio of 0.13 percent. The average underperformance was 1.5 percent per year. DFUVX held 328 stocks and is thus far more diversified than either SCHD (99 stocks) or HDV (75 stocks), though it does hold fewer stocks than VYM (399 stocks). Greater diversification reduces idiosyncratic risks which are uncompensated. Thus, all else equal, we should prefer the more diversified fund. The three high-dividend ETFs also underperformed Vanguard's (Large) Value ETF (VTV) by from 0.1 percent per year to 2.6 percent per year. The average underperformance was 1.1 percent. VTV does have a slight advantage with an expense ratio of just 0.04 percent. And VTV held 329 stocks.

Given the evidence, why do investors prefer high-dividend strategies?

The Dividend Disconnect

Samuel Hartzmark and David Solomon contribute to the literature on the dividend anomaly with their May 2017 study, "The Dividend Disconnect." They examined whether investor behavior was disconnected from financial theory and reality by examining the trading and pricing of securities. In other words, do investors behave as if dividends are a free lunch? They found that by creating a separate mental account for dividends, the dividend disconnect did in fact have considerable impact on investor trading related to gains and losses, the prices of dividend stocks, and dividend reinvestment.

First, the authors found that investor trading behavior is driven by past *price changes* rather than past *returns*. In other words, they treat two stocks whose prices rose from $5 to $6 the same, even though one first went to $7 and then paid a $1 dividend, which lowered the price to $6.

Second, when they examined the disposition effect (the tendency to sell winners more often than losers), they found that there was considerably less selling response to the dividend component (investors focused on the price instead of the total return).

Third, they found that investors are less likely to sell stocks that pay dividends, holding them for longer periods. Dividends also made investors less sensitive to past price changes when selling.

A fourth important finding was that investors' demand for dividends is higher when interest rates are low and recent equity returns have been poor. They also found that investors' demand for dividends is higher when dividends are more stable. Once again, this demonstrates that investors have separate mental accounts for the two components of return, treating dividends more like interest payments while ignoring the source of the dividend and its impact on the stock price. Additionally, the authors found that the demand for dividends is lower when recent stock returns have been higher—the dividend component appears less attractive than capital gains despite both contributing to the total return.

Fifth, they found that dividends tend not to be reinvested in the same company. This was true of both retail investors, who may find it difficult to reinvest dividends unless the company has a DRIP program, and more sophisticated institutional investors, who do not have the same consumption motivation that retail investors have. Specifically, they found that, for individual investors, dividend reinvestment is only about 2 percent as common as no change in the number of shares held. For institutional investors, it was only about 10 percent as common. In other words, investors seem to be expressing that they have a desire to reduce their holdings by the exact amount of the dividend paid! It seems far more likely that there is separate mental accounting and that investors ignore the equivalency theory behind the actions.

These results provide direct evidence that investors do, in fact, treat dividends in a more naïve way than predicted by financial theory, creating separate mental accounts for them. The findings are also consistent with prior research, which has shown that investors prefer to consume out of their dividends.

Hartzmark and Solomon concluded that "the free dividends fallacy not only explains psychologically why dividends may be desirable, but also why the shifting attractiveness of dividends and capital gains can generate time-varying demand for dividends which firms respond to." For example, it has been well-documented that some mutual funds "juice" their dividends by buying stocks just before the ex-dividend date. In addition, the research has shown that firms tend to increase their dividends when dividends are more overvalued. The authors added that the mental accounting of dividends as an income stream can also explain the documented preference among older investors for dividends.

Another important finding involved the investor preference for dividends during periods of high demand (low interest rates and bear markets), causing them to be relatively overpriced (which shows up in higher price-to-book value). This negatively impacted returns by 2 percent to 4 percent, resulting in a significant loss of the equity risk premium. Unfortunately, this is not the only negative impact of the preference for dividends.

Implications

As mentioned previously, taxable investors should have a preference for capital gains over dividends. And there are negative implications in terms of diversification. Because about 60 percent of U.S. stocks and about 40 percent of international stocks do not pay dividends, any screen that includes dividends results in portfolios that are far less diversified than they could be if dividends were not included in the portfolio design. Less-diversified portfolios are less efficient because they have a higher potential dispersion of returns without any compensation in the form of higher expected returns (assuming the exposure to investment factors are the same).

These negative implications are why the preference for dividends is considered an anomaly. The field of behavioral finance has attempted to provide us with explanations for the anomalous behavior.

Attempting to Explain the Preference for Dividends

Hersh Shefrin and Meir Statman, two leaders in the field of behavioral finance, attempted to explain the behavioral anomaly of a preference for cash dividends in their 1983 paper, "Explaining Investor Preference for Cash Dividends." They offered the following explanations.

The first explanation is that in terms of their ability to control spending, investors may recognize that they have problems with the inability to delay gratification. To address this problem, they adapt a cash flow approach to spending—they limit their spending to only the interest and dividends from their investment portfolio. A total return approach that would use self-created dividends would not address the conflict created by the individual who wishes to deny himself a present indulgence, yet is unable to resist the temptation. While the preference for dividends might not be optimal (for tax reasons), by addressing the behavioral issue it could be said to be rational. In other words, the investor has a desire to defer spending, but knows he doesn't have the will, so he creates a situation that limits his opportunities and, thus, reduces the temptations.

The second explanation is based on what is called "prospect theory." Prospect theory (otherwise referred to as loss aversion) states that people value gains and losses differently. As such, they will base decisions on perceived gains rather than perceived losses. Thus, if a person were given two equal choices, one expressed in terms of possible gains and the other in possible losses, he or she would choose the former. Because taking dividends doesn't involve the sale of stock, it's preferred to a total return approach, which may require self-created dividends through sales. The reason is that sales might involve the realization of losses, which are too painful for people to accept (they exhibit loss aversion).

What they fail to realize is that a cash dividend is the perfect substitute for the sale of an equal amount of stock whether the market is up or down, or whether the stock is sold at a gain or a loss. It makes absolutely no difference. It's just a matter of how the problem is framed. It's form over substance. Whether you take the cash dividend or sell the equivalent dollar amount of the company's stock, at the end of the day you will have the same amount invested in the stock. It's just that with the dividend you own more shares but at a lower price (by the amount of the dividend), while with the self-dividend you own fewer shares but at a higher price (because no dividend was paid).

As the authors point out: "By purchasing shares that pay good dividends, most investors persuade themselves of their prudence, based on the expected income. They feel the gain potential is a super added benefit. Should the stock fall in value from their purchase level, they console themselves that the dividend provides a return on their cost."

They also point out that if the sale involves a gain, the investor frames it as "super added benefit." However, if a loss is incurred, he frames the dividend as a silver lining with which he can "console himself." Given that losses loom much larger in investors' minds, and they wish to avoid them, investors prefer to take the cash dividend, avoiding the realization of a loss.

Shefrin and Statman offer yet a third explanation: regret avoidance. They ask you to consider two cases:

1. You take $600 received as dividends and use it to buy a television set.
2. You sell $600 worth of stock and use it to buy a television set.

After the purchase, the price of the stock increases significantly. Would you feel more regret in the first or second case? Because cash dividends and self-dividends are substitutes for each other, you should feel no more regret in the second case than in the first. However, evidence from studies on investor behavior demonstrates that for many people the sale of stock causes more regret. Thus, investors who exhibit aversion to regret have a preference for cash dividends.

Shefrin and Statman go on to explain that people suffer more regret when behaviors are taken than when behaviors are avoided. In the case of selling stock to create the home-made dividend, a decision must be made to raise the cash. When spending comes from the dividend, no action is taken, thus less regret is felt. Again, this helps explain the preference for cash dividends.

The authors also explain how a preference for dividends might change over the investor's lifecycle. As was mentioned earlier, the theory of self-control is used to justify the idea of spending only from the cash flow of a portfolio, never touching the principal. Younger investors, generating income from their labor capital, might prefer a portfolio with low dividends, as a high dividend strategy might encourage dissavings (spending from capital). On the other hand, retired investors, with no labor income, might prefer a high dividend strategy for the same reasons, to discourage dissavings. A study of brokerage accounts found that there was in fact a strong and positive relationship between age and the preference for dividends.

While the preference for cash dividends is an anomaly that cannot be explained by classical economic theory, which is based on investors making "rational" decisions, investors who face issues of self-control (such as being subject to impulse buying) may find that while there are some costs involved, the benefits provided by avoiding the behavioral problems may make a cash dividend strategy a rational one.

Conclusion

The bottom line is that both theory and historical evidence demonstrate that dividends are just another source of profit, along with capital gains, and that dividends mechanically reduce the price of stock. Yet, many investors treat the two sources of profit very differently, with negative consequences both in terms of lower returns and greater risk. Shefrin and Statman provide us with explanations demonstrating that, at least for some investors who are otherwise unable to control their spending, the negative consequences may be outweighed by the benefits in terms of controlling behavior that would have had even greater negative consequences.

APPENDIX E

Should You Hire a Financial Advisor?

W HETHER WE ARE talking about home repairs or investing, individuals can be categorized into two broad groups: those who hire professionals and the do-it-yourselfers—those who do not want to pay professionals for something they believe they can do just as well. Of course, there are some who belong to the do-it-yourself group who would be better off hiring professionals. One reason is that if something is not done right the first time, the cost of correcting errors can far exceed the cost of a professional to do it right in the first place. Another is that while you can recover from making a mistake while trying to fix a leaky faucet, the damage done by financial errors can take years to recover from—and can even be irreversible.

If you are considering being a do-it-yourself investor, ask yourself the following five questions:

1. Do I have all the knowledge needed to develop an investment plan, integrate it into an overall estate, tax and risk management (insurance of all types) plan, and then provide the ongoing care and maintenance that is required?
2. Do I have the mathematical skills needed? Investing requires a knowledge that goes well beyond simple arithmetic. You need advanced knowledge of probability theory and statistics, such as correlations and the various moments of distribution (such as skewness and kurtosis).
3. Do I have the ability to determine the appropriate asset allocation, one that provides the greatest odds of achieving my financial goals while not taking more risk than I have the ability and willingness to take? An important part of the planning process includes the use of a Monte Carlo simulator (see Chapter 5) to estimate the odds of achieving your financial goals under various asset allocations, saving and spending assumptions. Required assumptions include expected returns of asset classes, expected standard deviations of asset classes, and expected correlations among asset classes.

There are many of these programs available, many of which have serious flaws. And because of their complexity, it is easy to make mistakes.

4. Do I have a strong knowledge of financial history? You should be aware of how often stocks have provided negative returns, how long bear markets have lasted, and how deep bear markets have been. Those who do not know their history are likely to repeat past mistakes.

5. Do I have the temperament and the emotional discipline needed to adhere to a plan in the face of the many crises I will almost certainly face? Are you confident that you have the fortitude to withstand a severe drop in the value of your portfolio without panicking? Will you be able to rebalance back to your target allocations (keeping your head while most others are losing theirs), buying more stocks when the light at the end of the tunnel seems to be a truck coming the other way? Think back to how you felt and acted after the events of September 11, 2001 and during the financial crisis that began in 2007. Experience demonstrates that fear often leads to paralysis, or even worse, panicked selling and the abandonment of well-developed plans. When subjected to the pain of a bear market, even knowledgeable investors, who know what to do, fail to do the right thing because they allow emotions to take over, overriding what the brain knows is the right thing to do. This results in what Carl Richards calls "the behavior gap." The term is used to describe the failure of investors to earn the same return as that earned by the very funds in which they invest. Ask yourself: Have I always done the right thing? Have my returns matched those of my investments?

If you have passed this test, you are part of a small minority. This book not only provides you with the winning strategy of broad global diversification and passive investing, but it provides you with guidance on how to construct a portfolio to address your unique circumstances. Alternatively, you may recognize you do not have the knowledge, temperament or the discipline to succeed on your own. And even if you decide that you meet these requirements, you may recognize that a good financial advisory firm can add value in many ways, including freeing you to focus your attention on the most important things in your life, such as time spent with family, friends, or meaningful endeavors. Thus, you may place a greater value on that time than the cost spent on advice. It is a choice about finding the right balance in your life.

Hiring an Advisor

If you decide to hire a financial advisory firm, because of the impact it can have, that choice will be one of the most important decisions you will ever make. Thus, it is critical that you get it right. With that in mind, the following advice is offered.

There are four criteria which should be absolutes when searching for the right advisor:

1. A fiduciary standard of care.
2. The advisor invests their own capital in the same vehicles being recommended.
3. Advice based on science (evidence from peer-reviewed journals), not opinions.
4. The firm integrates investment planning into an overall financial plan.

1. Require a Fiduciary Standard of Care

There are two standards of care that financial professionals operate under: fiduciary and suitability. Under a fiduciary standard, the finance professional must always act in your best interests. Under a suitability standard, the finance professional only has to buy products that are suitable. They do not necessarily have to be in your best interest. There is no reason why you should settle for anything less than a fiduciary standard. And there is no reason you should ever work with an advisor or firm not prepared to meet this standard. The bottom line is this: You must be convinced that the guiding principle of the advisor or firm is that advice offered is solely in your best interest.

There are actions you can take in your due diligence to give you the best chance to receive unbiased advice. First, require that the advisory firm serve as a fee-only advisor, which avoids the conflicts that commission-based compensation can create. With commission-based compensation, it can be difficult to know if the investment or product recommended by the advisor is the one that is best for you, or the one that generates greater compensation for the advisor. Avoiding commissioned-based compensation helps to ensure that the advice you receive is client centric: The only thing being "sold" is advice and solutions to problems, not products.

Second, you need to make sure that all potential conflicts of interest are fully disclosed. Along with asking questions, you should review the firm's Form ADV—a disclosure document setting forth information about the firm's advisors, its investment strategy, fee schedules, conflicts of interest, regulatory incidents and more. Careful due diligence helps minimize the risk of an expensive mistake.

2. Eat Their Own Cooking

You should require that the firm's advisors invest their personal assets (including the firm's profit sharing and/or retirement plan) based on the same set of investment principles and in the same or comparable securities that they recommend to their clients. While you should expect to see different asset allocations than are being recommended to you (as each investor has their own unique circumstances), the investment vehicles should be the same. There is simply no reason to ever hire an advisor who isn't willing to demonstrate to you that they are investing in the same vehicles they are recommending.

3. Evidence-Based Advice

You should only consider working with a firm whose investment strategy and advice is based on the science of investing, not on opinions. To demonstrate the wisdom of this advice, consider the following situation.

You are not feeling well. You make an appointment to visit a doctor your friend has recommended. The doctor's job is to diagnose the problem and recommend treatment. After a thorough exam, he turns around to his bookshelf and reaches for the latest copies of *Prevention* magazine. Before hearing his advice, you are probably thinking it is time to get a second opinion. Therefore, you make an appointment with another doctor. After her exam, she reaches for a copy of the *New England Journal of Medicine*. At this point, you are feeling much better about the advice you are about to receive.

The financial equivalents of the *New England Journal of Medicine* are such publications as *The Journal of Finance*. The advisory firm should be able to cite evidence from peer-reviewed journals supporting their recommendations. You should not be getting your advice from the equivalents of *Prevention*—such as *Investor's Business Daily* or *Barron's*. Again, there is no reason to hire an advisor who cannot demonstrate that their advice is based on evidence, not personal opinions.

4. Integrated Financial Planning

Because plans can fail for reasons that have nothing to do with an investment plan, it is critical that the advisory firm you choose will integrate an investment plan into an overall estate, tax and risk management (insurance of all kinds) plan, acting as the quarterback on the financial services team, coordinating the efforts of each of the advisors.

It is important to understand that plans can even fail when estate planning is done well. For example, far too often individuals pay for high-powered attorneys to develop well-thought-out estate plans only to have the trusts created go either totally unfunded, or be funded with the wrong type of assets. Some trusts are designed to generate stable cash flows and should be funded with safe bonds. Others are designed with a growth objective in mind and should be funded primarily with stocks.

Estate plans can also derail because the beneficiaries have not been properly named (resulting from a failure to update documents to address life events such as divorce or death), or because the type or method of asset distribution is inappropriate (for instance, directing assets to be distributed directly to a beneficiary with demonstrated creditor, bankruptcy or financial management issues). This is another example of why a financial plan must be a living document, one that is reviewed on a regular basis.

It is also critical to understand that estate plans can fail despite the best efforts of top-notch professional advisors. Unfortunately, it is not uncommon for estates to lose their assets and family harmony following the transition of the estate. This occurs because beneficiaries are unprepared, they do not trust each other, and communications break down. While great attention is typically paid to preparing the *assets* for transition to the beneficiaries, very little, if any, attention is being paid to preparing the *beneficiaries* for the assets they will inherit. A good advisory firm can add great value by helping to prepare and educate beneficiaries for the wealth they will inherit.

We have already described many other ways a good financial advisory firm can and should add value. The following is a partial list of other ways:

- Regular, ongoing communications, especially during times of crisis. Education protects you from emotions taking control over your portfolio.
- Ongoing education about innovations in finance. The knowledge of how markets work advances on a persistent basis. You should be sure that the firm has the depth of resources to stay on top of the latest research.
- The ability to analyze complex financial products, helping you avoid purchasing costly products that are meant to be sold, not bought.
- College funding.
- Selecting investments for 529 plans, 401(k), 403(b) and other employer plans, ensuring that they are integrated into the overall plan.
- Gifting to heirs and charities in the most effective manner.
- Home purchase and mortgage financing decisions.
- The management and ultimate disposition of large concentrated positions with low-cost basis (typically the stock of your employer or stock that has been inherited).
- Separate account management of bond portfolios, eliminating the expense of a mutual fund, while maximizing tax efficiency and after-tax returns.
- Ongoing performance tracking, measuring the progress versus your plan and recommending adjustments that are necessary to prevent failure.
- Act as an "insurance policy" in the event of a death of a family member who is responsible for managing financial matters.

Clearly, no one advisor can be an expert in all of these areas. Therefore, when choosing a firm be sure that it has a team of experts that can help address each of these areas. You should also make sure that the firm's comprehensive wealth management services are provided by individuals that have the PFS (personal financial specialist), CFP (certified financial planner), or other comparable designations. Note that the PFS credential is granted to CPAs who have demonstrated their knowledge and expertise in personal financial planning. And once these designations are granted, they must be maintained through required professional development to keep them current.

It is also important to be clear that the firm will deliver a high level of personal attention and develop strong personal relationships. This should be part of your due diligence process as you check the firm's reputation with other local professionals (such as CPAs and attorneys) and client references.

Another part of your investigation should be asking the advisor how he or she spends time at work. You might ask: Can you please tell me about your average day? What you are looking for is an advisor who spends the majority of their time solving their clients' concerns about such issues as:

- Making smart decisions about money.
- Minimizing income, gift and estate taxes.
- Transferring assets to the next generation.
- Protection from third parties unjustifiably taking their assets.
- Interest in making significant charitable gifts.

Your investigation should include sharing all of your concerns with the advisor. The objective is to develop a deep understanding of how the advisor can help you address these concerns and ensure that you are confident you have a high level of trust in the advisor, his/her support team, and the advisory firm as a whole.

There is one last point we need to cover. As is the case with the choice of investment vehicles, costs matter. But what really matters is the value added relative to the cost. The lowest-cost investment vehicle may not be the best choice. Remember, while good advice doesn't have to be expensive, bad advice almost always will cost you dearly, no matter how little you pay for it.

The choice of a financial advisor is one of the most important decisions you will ever make. That is why it is so important to perform a thorough due diligence. The bottom line is that you want to be sure that the firm you choose is one where the science of investing meets true wealth management, and that the services are delivered in a highly personal manner.

Implementation: Recommended Mutual Funds and ETFs

T HE FOLLOWING LIST of funds has been approved by the investment policy committee at Buckingham Strategic Wealth.[1] Thus, these are the products we believe you should consider first when constructing your portfolio. Where more than one share class for a mutual fund is available, the lowest-cost version is shown. That fund version may not be available to all investors because minimums may be required. AQR, Bridgeway and Dimensional funds are available through approved financial advisors and in retirement and 529 plans. (Note that for some AQR funds, lower-cost R Share versions may be available to some investors.)

Considerations for selecting a fund should include how much exposure it provides to each desired/targeted factor, its expense ratio, and the amount of diversification it offers (that is, the number of securities held and their weightings). For ETFs, the liquidity of the fund is an added consideration. Our recommendation is that the ETFs you consider have more than $100 million in assets and an average daily trading volume in excess of $5 million.

---

[1] Provided for informational purposes only and is not intended to serve as specific investment or financial advice. This list of funds does not constitute a recommendation to purchase a single specific security and it should not be assumed that the securities referenced herein were or will prove to be profitable. Prior to making any investment, an investor should carefully consider the fund's risks and investment objectives and evaluate all offering materials and other documents associated with the investment.

Single-Style Funds

Market Beta

Domestic

- Fidelity Spartan Total Market Index (FSTVX)
- Schwab U.S. Broad Market (SCHB)
- Vanguard Total Stock Market Index (VTI/VTSAX)
- iShares Core S&P Total US Market (ITOT)

International Developed Markets

- Fidelity Spartan International Index (FSIIX)
- Vanguard FTSE All-World ex-US (VEU/VFWAX)
- Vanguard Total International Stock (VXUS/VTIAX)
- Schwab International Equity (SCHF)
- iShares Core MSCI EAFE (IEFA)

Emerging Markets

- Dimensional Emerging Markets (DFEMX)
- Schwab Emerging Markets (SCHE)
- Vanguard FTSE Emerging Markets (VWO/VEMAX)

Small

Domestic

- Bridgeway Ultra-Small Company Market (BRSIX)
- Dimensional US Micro Cap (DFSCX)
- Dimensional US Small Cap (DFSTX)
- iShares Russell Microcap (IWC)
- Vanguard Small Cap Index Fund (VB/VSMAX)
- Schwab U.S. Small Cap (SCHA)
- iShares Core S&P Small-Cap (IJR)

International Developed Markets

- Dimensional International Small Company (DFISX)
- SPDR S&P International Small Cap ETF (GWX)
- Vanguard FTSE All-World ex-US SmallCap (VSS/VFSVX)

- Schwab International Small-Cap Equity (SCHC)

Emerging Markets

- Dimensional Emerging Markets Small (DEMSX)
- SPDR S&P Emerging Markets Small Cap (EWX)

Large and Value

Domestic

- Dimensional US Large Cap Value III (DFUVX)
- Dimensional Tax-Managed US Marketwide Value II (DFMVX)
- Schwab U.S. Large-Cap Value (SCHV)
- Vanguard Value Index (VTV/VVIAX)

International Developed Markets

- Dimensional International Value III (DFVIX)
- Dimensional Tax-Managed International Value (DTMIX)
- iShares MSCI EAFE Value (EFV)

Emerging Markets

- Dimensional Emerging Markets Value (DFEVX)

Small and Value

Domestic

- Bridgeway Omni Small Cap Value (BOSVX)
- Bridgeway Omni Tax-Managed Small-Cap Value (BOTSX)
- Dimensional US Small Cap Value (DFSVX)
- Dimensional Tax-Managed US Targeted Value (DTMVX)
- iShares S&P Small-Cap 600 Value (IJS)
- SPDR S&P 600 Small Cap Value ETF (SLYV)
- Vanguard Small Cap Value (VBR/VSIAX)

International Developed Markets

- Dimensional International Small Cap Value (DISVX)
- Dimensional World ex US Targeted Value (DWUSX)

Momentum

Domestic

- AQR Momentum (AMOMX)
- iShares MSCI USA Momentum Factor (MTUM)

International Developed Markets

- AQR International Momentum (AIMOX)

Profitability/Quality

Domestic

- iShares MSCI USA Quality Factor ETF (QUAL)

International Developed Markets

- iShares MSCI International Developed Quality Factor ETF (IQLT)

Term

- Dimensional Five-Year Global Fixed Income (DFGBX)
- iShares Barclays 7–10 Year Treasury (IEF)
- iShares US Treasury Bond ETF (GOVT)
- Vanguard Intermediate-Term Treasury (VGIT/VFIUX)

Carry

- PowerShares DB G10 Currency Harvest ETF (DBV)

Multi-Style Funds

Small and Value and Profitability/Quality

Domestic

- Dimensional US Core Equity 2 (DFQTX)
- Dimensional TA US Core Equity 2 (DFTCX)

International

- Dimensional International Core Equity (DFIEX)
- Dimensional TA World ex US Core Equity (DFTWX)

Value and Momentum and Profitability/Quality

Domestic

- AQR Large Cap Multi-Style (QCELX)
- iShares Edge MSCI Multifactor USA ETF (LRGF)

International

- AQR International Multi-Style (QICLX)

Small + Value + Momentum + Profitability/Quality

- AQR Small Cap Multi-Style (QSMLX)

Value + Momentum + Quality + Defensive (Stocks, Bonds, Currencies and Commodities)

- AQR Style Premia (QSPIX)

Trend-Following (Stocks, Bonds, Currencies and Commodities)

- AQR Managed Futures (AQMIX)

Alternative Funds

Value + Momentum + Quality + Defensive (Stocks, Bonds, Currencies and Commodities)

- AQR Style Premia Alternative (QSPRX)

Value + Momentum + Quality + Defensive + Trend + Variance Risk Premium (Stocks, Bonds, and Currencies)

- AQR Alternative Risk Premia Alternative (QRPRX)

Alternative Lending

- Stone Ridge Alternative Lending Risk Premium Interval Fund (LENDX)
- Cliffwater Corporate Lending Fund (CCLFX)

Reinsurance

- Stone Ridge Reinsurance Risk Premium Interval Fund (SRRIX)
- Pioneer ILS Interval Fund (XILSX)

Variance Risk Premium

- Stone Ridge All Asset Variance Risk Premium Interval Fund (AVRPX)

APPENDIX G

Types of Irrevocable Trusts

T HERE ARE DOZENS of types of irrevocable trusts designed to meet specific goals (most of which include at some level transferring assets outside of an individual's taxable estate). Below is a summary of a few of the most common types of irrevocable trusts with a brief description.

- **Irrevocable Life Insurance Trust (ILIT):** Typically designed to own life insurance on the life of the creator of the trust with the goal of avoiding estate taxes on the life insurance death benefit. While life insurance benefits are generally paid free of income tax, without an ILIT, they are still subject to estate taxes.
- **Intentionally Defective Irrevocable Trust (IDIT):** This type of irrevocable trust goes by many different names including a "defective trust" or "defective grantor trust." The core goal of this type of irrevocable trust is to transfer assets that will not be subject to estate tax, but which will continue to be taxable, to the creator of the trust for income tax purposes. The trust is "intentionally defective" because the transferor of the assets will continue to be liable for the income tax generated by the assets of the irrevocable trust. Although the concept sounds strange, it is a desirable tax-planning structure. By paying the trust's taxes with money outside the trust, the trust assets will grow faster and will not be subject to estate taxes. Paying the income taxes on behalf of the trust is in essence making additional gifts to the trust, but it is not treated as a gift for income tax purposes. Note that some of the other irrevocable trusts summarized here may also be structured as "defective grantor trusts" for income tax purposes.
- **Grantor Retained Annuity Trust (GRAT):** A GRAT is a trust an individual creates for his or her own benefit. It provides the individual with an annual annuity payment for a specified number of years (the "retained annuity"), after which any remaining assets in the trust will be continued for the other trust beneficiaries (the transferor's children for instance). If the assets transferred to the GRAT appreciate faster than the interest rate on

the annuity required to be paid back to the creator of the trust, assets will remain in the trust after the term of the annuity for the benefit of the trust beneficiaries.

- **Qualified Personal Residence Trust (QPRT):** A QPRT is a type of irrevocable trust that owns a personal residence (or a fractional ownership interest in a personal residence) for a specified term of years. The creator of the QPRT retains the right to rent-free use of the residence during the term. Title to the property owned by the QPRT passes at the end of the term to the remainder beneficiaries of the trust. If the creator of the trust survives the term, the residence should be excluded from his or her taxable estate for estate tax purposes. Note that by gifting a residence to the trust while retaining the right to live in the residence for a number of years, the value of the gift is "discounted." This is another form of the discounting technique discussed above.

- **Charitable Trusts:** Charitable planning is discussed briefly below and it is important to know that irrevocable trusts may be utilized in this planning area as well. Two commonly used variations of charitable trusts are a Charitable Remainder Trust (CRT) and a Charitable Lead Trust (CLT). Like the name suggests, a CRT typically provides for an annual income payment to the creator of the trust for his or her lifetime, with the "remainder" of the trust assets passing to charity upon the creator's death. Alternatively, a CLT provides for periodic distributions to charity for a certain number of years, with the remaining trust assets at the end of the term being distributed (or continued in trust) for the beneficiaries of the creator (family members for instance). In addition to passing assets to charity, charitable irrevocable trusts may provide for certain income tax benefits for the creator of the trust.

As we discussed in Chapter 6, not all passively managed funds are created equal. As you will see, there can be very significant differences in the average market capitalization (exposure to the size factor) and the average prices to such metrics as price-to-earnings and price-to-book market (exposure to the value factor). Such differences can lead to dramatic differences in both expected and realized returns.

The following table shows the market capitalization (to indicate the relative exposure to the size premium) and price-to-book (P/B) ratio (to indicate the relative exposure to the value premium) for three small value funds from three different fund families—the index fund of Vanguard, and the structured funds of Dimensional and Bridgeway. Data is from Morningstar as of January 2020.

Fund	Weighted Average Market Cap	P/B
Vanguard Small Value (VISVX)	$3.9bn	1.5
Dimensional Small Value (DFSVX)	$1.9bn	1.0
Bridgeway Omni Small Value (BOSVX)	$0.9bn	1.0

What you should be noting is that the Vanguard fund holds stocks that are much larger (more than twice as large) than the stocks held by Dimensional, and Bridgeway's holdings are much smaller than Dimensional's (less than half as large). Those differences are created by the structure of the funds—the definitions they use to determine buy, hold, and sell ranges. The smaller the market cap, the greater the expected return over the long term. In addition, what we should expect to generally see is that when small stocks outperform large stocks, Bridgeway's fund will have the highest return and Vanguard's the lowest, with Dimensional in the middle. We should expect the reverse when large stocks outperform small stocks. This won't always be true because Dimensional and Bridgeway both incur lots of random tracking errors in order to achieve their goal of having the highest long-term returns. And these are not small-cap funds, but small value funds.

With the data and concepts in mind, let's now take a look at how the funds have performed—did we get what we expected? We will examine the returns for each of the full years since 2012, the first full year for BOSVX. To see if we got what we expected we will also look at the returns of Vanguard's 500 Index Fund (VFINX). Note that Vanguard's value funds include REITs, while Dimensional's and Bridgeway's funds do not—this is because REITs are treated by those firms as separate asset classes. That can create/explain some of the differences in performance. The differences in expense ratios can also explain some of the performance differences: VISVX 0.19 (the admiral's share version, VSIAX, has an expense ratio of just 0.07 percent); DFSVX 0.52 percent; BOSVX 0.47 percent.

In 2012, VFINX returned 15.8% and VISVX returned 18.6%. Since small value outperformed, we should again expect to see DFSVX outperform VISVX—and that's what happened, as DFSVX returned 21.7%. Bridgeway's BOSVX returned 17.7%. Given its greater exposure to the size and value factors, we should have expected BOSVX to outperform. The likely explanation is that with a new fund, the risk of tracking error is greater as the fund builds its positions.

In 2013, VFINX returned 32.2% and VISVX returned 36.4%. Since small value outperformed, we should again expect to see DFSVX outperform VISVX—and that is what happened, as DFSVX returned 42.4%. And BOSVX outperformed both, returning 44.6%, just what we should have expected. Vanguard's performance was hurt by the performance of REITs—Vanguard's Real Estate Index Fund Admiral Shares (VGSLX) returned just 2.4%.

In 2014, VFINX returned 13.5% and VISVX returned 10.4%. Since small value underperformed, we should expect to see DFSVX underperform VISVX—and that is what happened, as DFSVX returned 3.5%. And BOSVX underperformed both, returning 0.8%, just what we should have expected. VISVX also benefited from the strong performance of REITs—VGSLX returned 30.3%.

In 2015, VFINX returned 1.3% and VISVX lost 4.8%. Since small value underperformed, we should expect to see DFSVX underperform VISVX—and that is what happened, as DFSVX lost 7.8%. BOSVX also underperformed VISVX, losing 6.6%, though it unexpectedly slightly outperformed DFSVX. VISVX again benefited from the relative performance of REITs, as VGSLX returned 2.4%.

In 2016, VFINX returned 11.8% and VISVX returned 24.7%. Since small value outperformed, we should expect to see DFSVX outperform VISVX—and that is what happened, as DFSVX returned 28.3%. And as we should have expected, BOSVX outperformed both, returning 34.5%. The performance of VISVX was negatively impacted by the performance of REITs, as VGSLX returned just 8.5%.

In 2017, VFINX returned 21.8% and VISVX returned 11.7%. Since small value underperformed, we should expect to see DFSVX underperform VISVX—and that is what happened, as DFSVX returned 7.2%. And BOSVX underperformed both, returning 6.0%, just what we should have expected. REITs hurt VISVX, as VGSLX returned 4.9%.

In 2018, VFINX returned –4.58% and VISVX returned –12.3%. Since small value underperformed, we should expect to see DFSVX underperform VISVX—and that is what happened, as DFSVX returned –15.1%. And BOSVX underperformed both, returning –17.2%, just what we should have expected. VISVX benefited from the relative performance of REITs, as VGSLX lost just 6.0%.

In 2019, VFINX returned 31.3% and VISVX returned 22.6%. Since small value underperformed, we should expect to see DFSVX underperform VISVX—and that is what happened, as DFSVX returned 18.1%. And BOSVX underperformed both, returning 13.9%, just what we should have expected. VISVX benefited from the relative performance of REITs, as VGSLX returned 28.9%.

Note that the exposure to the factors of size and value explain the relative performance of the three funds—there were just two outliers in the data, the underperformance of BOSVX in 2012 and its outperformance of DFSVX in 2015 (in both cases the likely explanation is random tracking error).

There are a couple of important takeaways. The first is that all three passively managed funds were doing their jobs well. The differences in performance weren't explained by good or bad management. Instead, they're explained by the fund's structure—how they're designed, and the "laws of style purity." When an asset class does well (poorly), you should expect the fund with the most (least) exposure to the factors explaining its outperformance (underperformance) to have the highest (lowest) return.

The choice of the fund you use should be based on how much exposure you want to the factors, and also a fund's expense ratio. When making the decision you want to be sure you weigh both factors. It might be that the fund with a higher expense ratio is the better choice as it might have more exposure to the factors that determine returns and carry premiums. In other words, it is not just cost, but cost per unit of expected return (and risk), that matters.

APPENDIX H

Recommended Reading

For those interested in learning more about evidenced-based investing and the academic research on investing, we recommend:

- *Asset Management* by Andrew Ang
- *The Hour Between Dog and Wolf* by John Coates
- *Quantitative Value* by Wes Gray and Tobias Carlisle
- *Deep Value* by Wes Gray and Tobias Carlisle
- *Quantitative Momentum* by Wes Gray and Jack Vogel
- *Expected Returns* by Antti Ilmanen
- *Thinking, Fast and Slow* by Daniel Kahneman
- *Adaptive Markets* by Andrew Lo
- *Successful Investing is a Process* by Jacques Lussier
- *The Success Equation* by Michael Maubossin
- *Behavioral Finance* by James Montier
- *Efficiently Inefficient* by Lasse Pedersen
- *Behavioral Finance and Wealth Management* by Michael M. Pompian
- *What Investors Really Want* by Meir Statman
- *Finance for Normal People* by Meir Statman
- *Market Sense and Nonsense* by Jack Schwager
- *The Physics of Wall Street* by James Weatherall

For those interested in learning more about retirement planning we recommend:

- *Strategic Financial Planning over the Lifecycle* by Narat Charupat and Huaxiong Huang
- *Retire Secure* by James Lange
- *The $214,000 Mistake: How to Double Your Social Security and Maximize Your IRAs* by James Lange
- *The Ultimate Retirement and Estate Plan for Your Million-Dollar IRA* by James Lange

- *Someday Rich* by Timothy Noonan and Matt Smith
- *How to Make Your Money Last* by Jane Bryant Quinn
- *Social Security Strategies: How to Optimize Retirement Benefits* by William Reichenstein and William Meyer
- *Hidden Truths About Retirement & Long Term Care* by Carolyn Rosenblatt and Mikol Davis
- *The Family Guide to Aging Parents: Answers to Your Legal, Financial, and Healthcare Questions* by Carolyn Rosenblatt
- *Money for Life* by Steve Vernon

For those interested in living a more meaningful life after retirement we recommend:

- *The New Retirementality* by Mitch Anthony
- *The Retirement Detox Programme* by Ann Harrison
- *Simple Money* by Tim Maurer
- *Your Retirement Quest* by Alan Spector and Keith Lawrence

For those interested in learning about how to prepare the next generation (your heirs) we recommend:

- *Preparing Heirs: Five Steps to a Successful Transition of Family Wealth and Values* by Roy Williams and Vic Preisser
- *Philanthropy, Heirs & Values: How Successful Families Are Using Philanthropy to Prepare Their Heirs for Post-transition Responsibilities* by Roy Williams and Vic Preisser
- *Strangers in Paradise: How Families Adapt to Wealth Across Generations* by James Grubman

Index

Data Sources

CRSP Data: Calculated (or Derived) based on data from The Center for Research in Security Prices at the University of Chicago for CRSP Indices.

Five-Year Treasury & Treasury Bills: © 2019 Morningstar, Inc. All Rights Reserved. Reproduced with permission.

The MSCI data contained herein is the property of MSCI Inc. (MSCI). MSCI, its affiliates and its information providers make no warranties with respect to any such data. The MSCI data contained herein is used under license and may not be further used, distributed or disseminated without the express written consent of MSCI.

S&P® and S&P 500® are registered trademarks of Standard & Poor's Financial Services LLC, and Dow Jones® is a registered trademark of Dow Jones Trademark Holdings LLC. © 2018 S&P Dow Jones Indices LLC, its affiliates and/or its licensors. All rights reserved.